Tempo
A Rowman & Littlefield Music Series on Rock, Pop, and Culture
Series Editor: Scott Calhoun

Tempo: A Rowman & Littlefield Music Series on Rock Pop, and Culture offers titles that explore rock and popular music through the lens of social and cultural history, revealing the dynamic relationship between musicians, music, and their milieu. Like other major art forms, rock and pop music comment on their cultural, political, and even economic situation, reflecting the technological advances, psychological concerns, religious feelings, and artistic trends of their times. Contributions to the **Tempo** series are the ideal introduction to major pop and rock artists and genres.

Bob Dylan: American Troubadour, by Donald Brown
Bon Jovi: America's Ultimate Band, by Margaret Olson
British Invasion: The Crosscurrents of Musical Influence, by Simon Philo
Bruce Springsteen: American Poet and Prophet, by Donald L. Deardorff II
The Clash: The Only Band That Mattered, by Sean Egan
Patti Smith: America's Punk Rock Rhapsodist, by Eric Wendell
Paul Simon: An American Tune, by Cornel Bonca
Ska: The Rhythm of Liberation, by Heather Augustyn

BRITISH INVASION

The Crosscurrents of Musical Influence

Simon Philo

ROWMAN & LITTLEFIELD
Lanham • Boulder • New York • London

Published by Rowman & Littlefield
A wholly owned subsidiary of
The Rowman & Littlefield Publishing Group, Inc.
4501 Forbes Boulevard, Suite 200, Lanham, Maryland 20706
www.rowman.com

Unit A, Whitacre Mews, 26-34 Stannary Street, London SE11 4AB

British Library Cataloguing in Publication Information Available

Library of Congress Cataloging-in-Publication Data

Philo, Simon, 1966–
British invasion : the crosscurrents of musical influence / Simon Philo.
pages cm. — (Tempo : a Rowman & Littlefield music series on rock, pop, and culture)
Includes bibliographical references and index.
ISBN 978-0-8108-8626-1 (cloth : alk. paper) — ISBN 978-0-8108-8627-8 (ebook)
1. Rock music—United States—1961–1970—History and criticism. 2. Rock music—Great Britain—1961–1970—History and criticism. I. Title.
ML3534.3.P55 2014
781.660941'0973—dc23
2014023380

Printed in the United States of America

To Linda and Amélie, for melting the ice.

CONTENTS

FOREWORD

A dribble. A ripple. A skiffle. A flood. It's the little things that often make big differences between the merely incidental and the momentously influential. American roots, blues, and jazz music traveled to England's shores between the two world wars of the twentieth century, but the revival of skiffle in 1950s England proved the tipping point. A primitive, DIY music of some of America's poorest peoples and regions, skiffle was all but dead to the American mainstream by the 1930s, but in it young British musicians found its skip-and-step rhythm to be just what they needed to lift their postwar spirits. They were searching for something new, something fun, and something that might upset their parents a little or a lot. The whole blend of American rhythm and blues was refreshingly foreign and satisfyingly invasive. It caught the ear of John Lennon and Paul McCartney. When the Beatles arrived on American soil in 1964, what they brought with them, or rather brought back with them, was just as fresh to American youth. The sounds and fashions of the newly modern rock 'n' roll were simultaneously a continuation of America's reinvention story and the most artistically significant and prosperous culture exchange Great Britain and the United States have enjoyed to date.

Invasions, welcomed or not, often have an element of surprise and unpredictability. It's hard to imagine, now, the Beatles ever running the risk of failure, especially in America. Equally hard to conceive are no other British bands following the Beatles through the 1960s, giving back to America an interpretation of its already diverse musical heritage. But the revolutions of the '60s, as inevitable as they seem now, rode in on stronger cultural currents stirring in America and England. By 1970, nearly nothing in Anglo-American popular culture was the same as a decade before, largely because of the flood of popular music coming through radio, television, and film. Following the Beatles were, as the most tremendous examples of the groups who carried out the full-on British Invasion, the Rolling Stones, the Who, the Animals, the Dave Clark Five, the Kinks, Herman's Hermits, the Hollies, and the Yardbirds, all of whom make it impossible to imagine the sound of rock 'n' roll now had they not each made their distinct contributions. In addition to their music, their attitudes and opinions constructed an entire social ethos many of that generation watched and emulated in the interest of staying "contemporary." Many of these artists willingly fed a growing cultural desire to have a celebrity artist's point of view instead of a politician's or a priest's, as many of us still do to this day.

But it all might have gone differently. A day in your life is composed of minor incidents, as is the next day and the next. Drip. Drip. Drop. Then, a flood. You meet someone or do, see, or hear something, and everything changes profoundly. All those days add up to *this* day, and now nothing is the same. Someone once pointed out to me that the entire catalog of the Beatles' studio albums is less than eight hours of music. Seven years of work runs to about eight hours. You could listen to their artistic oeuvre in one workday, a morning and an afternoon. It's true. (You can, as well, "see" the Mona Lisa in the time between two blinks of the eye.) But for millions of listeners, that "one day" of Beatles music is like a thousand years of evolutionary change in their personal lives, their career paths, their culture, their politics, and even, for some, their faith. The British Invasion was that influential. It was that momentous.

Scott Calhoun
Series Editor

TIMELINE

World and Cultural Events

September 1939: Britain declares war on Germany.

December 1941: Japan attacks U.S. naval base at Pearl Harbor, Hawaii; U.S. declares war on Japan; Germany declares war on U.S.

1942–1945: Thousands of U.S. personnel stationed in the UK for the duration of the war.

May 8, 1945: VE Day.

August 14, 1945: Japan surrenders.

April 1948: Marshall Plan provides financial aid for postwar reconstruction; UK receives billions of dollars in loans and grants.

British Invasion Events

November 1952: World's first singles chart compiled in the UK by *New Music Express*; Top 12 features American singer Al Martino at no. 1.

Fall 1955: Commercial TV arrives in the UK to challenge the British Broadcasting Corporation's (BBC) monopoly.

December 1955: Rosa Parks's momentous act of civil disobedience gives impetus to the civil rights movement.

December 1955: Bill Haley's "Rock Around the Clock" at no. 1 in the UK; rock 'n' roll arrives!

Early 1956: Lonnie Donegan's "Rock Island Line" sparks the skiffle craze in the UK; it is also a sizable hit in America.

September 1956: Elvis Presley appears on *The Ed Sullivan Show*.

Fall 1956: Suez crisis ends in humiliation for the British government.

September 1957: National Guard oversees desegregation in Little Rock, Arkansas.

1958: British teenager Laurie London enjoys rare American success with his single "He's Got the Whole World in His Hands"; it reaches no. 2 on Billboard.

February 1959: Buddy Holly dies in a plane crash.

August–October 1960: The Beatles play a series of gigs in Hamburg, Germany.

November 1960: John F. Kennedy elected. He is the

youngest ever president and the first Roman Catholic.

December 1960: End of compulsory military service for all British males.

May 1961: Attack on "Freedom Riders" in Birmingham, Alabama.

November 1961: U.S. increases "Special Advisors" in South Vietnam.

May 1962: Acker Bilk's "Strangers on the Shore" at no. 1 in America.

July 1962: Telstar satellite allows live transatlantic TV links.

July 1962: Rolling Stones' live debut at London's Marquee Club.

October–November 1962: Cuban missile crisis.

October 1962: The Beatles' first UK single, "Love Me Do," is released and peaks at no. 17 on the British chart.

December 1962: Tornados' instrumental "Telstar" at no. 1 in America.

Spring 1963: Profumo spy scandal rocks British establishment.

March 1963: The Beatles release *Please Please Me*, which spends 30 weeks at no. 1.

August 1963: Martin Luther King delivers "I Have a Dream" speech at March on Washington; Bob Dylan performs.

August 1963: Launch of TV music show *Ready Steady Go!*

September 1963: Racists bomb Birmingham church.

September 1963: "She Loves You" at no. 1 in UK, sparks Beatlemania.

November 22, 1963: Kennedy assassinated.

November 22, 1963: Beatles' second LP, *With the Beatles*, released.

January 1964: Military coup in South Vietnam.

January 1964: Capitol Records releases and promotes *Meet the Beatles* in U.S.

February 1, 1964: "I Want to Hold Your Hand" is Billboard's no. 1 single. It will occupy the top spot for seven weeks.

February 9, 1964: Over 70 million Americans watch the Beatles perform on *The Ed Sullivan Show*.

March 1964: Offshore "pirate" radio station Caroline begins broadcasting to UK.

April 1964: Beatles' singles at nos. 1–5 on Billboard, with 11 more in Top 100; between February and May, only Beatles' singles are at no. 1.

June 1964: Peter and Gordon have the first non-Beatles' American no. 1 of the Invasion era; "A World without Love" is, though, written by Paul McCartney.

July 1964: Civil Rights Act ends legalized segregation; race riots in Rochester, New York.

August 1964: President Lyndon B. Johnson orders retaliatory strikes against North Vietnam.

August–September 1964: Beatles' first major U.S. tour; *A Hard Day's Night* movie released.

Fall 1964: No. 1 singles for the Animals ("House of the Rising Sun") and Manfred Mann ("Do Wah Diddy").

October 1964: After 13 years out of office the Labour Party wins UK election; it will align itself with the Invasion and youth/pop culture.

November 1964: Johnson elected.

December 1964: Martin Luther King wins Nobel Peace Prize.

January 1965: U.S. Labor Department denies UK acts touring visas.

February 1965: U.S. planes bomb North Vietnam; Malcolm X assassinated; Dr. King arrested in Selma, Alabama.

October 1964: Rolling Stones appear on *The Ed Sullivan Show*. The band's physical appearance sparks controversy—and sales.

January 1965: British actress-singer Petula Clark has U.S. no. 1 with "Downtown."

March 1965: Beatles' "Eight Days a Week" at no. 1.

April 1965: Billboard number ones for Freddie and the Dreamers ("I'm Telling You Now") and Wayne Fontana and the Mindbenders ("Game of Love").

May 1965: Beatles' "Ticket to Ride" at no. 1 for one week only; Dylan tours the UK; Herman's Hermits have American no. 1 with "Mrs. Brown, You've Got a Lovely Daughter."

June 1965: U.S. troops launch major ground offensive in South Vietnam against the Vietcong.

July 1965: Dr. King calls for end to Vietnam War; President

June 1965: Beatles each awarded Member of British Empire (MBE).

July 1965: Rolling Stones' "Satisfaction" is U.S. no. 1 for four

Johnson sends 50,000 more troops weeks.
into Vietnam.

August 1965: Race riots in Watts, California.

August 1965: Beatles play Shea Stadium gig on U.S. tour, breaking attendance and revenue records; Hermits at no. 1 with "I'm Henry VIII, I Am."

September 1965: Beatles' *Help!* LP at no. 1.

October 1965: Beatles' "Yesterday" is no. 1 for four weeks.

November 1965: Rolling Stones' "Get Off My Cloud" is no. 1 for two weeks.

January 1966: "Psychedelic Shop" opens in San Francisco's Haight-Ashbury district; "Trips Festival" signals birth of the hippie movement.

January 1966: Beatles' "We Can Work It Out" at no. 1.

February 1966: Petula Clark's "My Love" spends two weeks at no. 1 on Billboard.

April 1966: *Time* magazine cover story on "Swinging London," declares UK capital "city of decade."

May 1966: 8,000 protest the Vietnam War outside the Pentagon.

June 1966: U.S. bombs Hanoi and Haiphong.

June 1966: Rolling Stones' "Paint It Black" is at no. 1 for two weeks; Beatles' "Paperback Writer" also spends two weeks at Billboard's summit.

July 1966: 31 arrested at antiwar demo in London; race riots in New York, Chicago, and Cleveland; England wins the soccer World Cup in London final.

July 1966: John Lennon's "bigger than Jesus" comment is widely reported in the U.S., sparking protest in the southern states; Troggs' "Wild Thing" at no. 1.

August 1966: "Yellow Submarine" / "Eleanor Rigby" double A-sided single fails to reach no. 1 in the U.S.; last live Beatles' performance at Candlestick Park, San Francisco.

September 1966: Beatles release *Revolver*; Donovan's "Sunshine Superman" at no. 1 for a single week.

October 1966: LSD criminalized.

October 1966: London launch of countercultural paper *International Times*.

November 1966: Ronald Reagan elected governor of California.

December 1966: UFO Club opens in London.

January 1967: Inaugural hippie happening "Human Be-In" at Golden Gate Park, San Francisco.

March 1967: Rolling Stones' "Ruby Tuesday" at no. 1 for one week; the Beatles receive three Grammys for "Michelle," "Eleanor Rigby," and *Revolver*; "Penny Lane" at no. 1 for a week.

April 1967: 400,000 protest the Vietnam War outside the United Nations headquarters in New York.

April 1967: 14-hour "Technicolor Dream," a happening in London; Pink Floyd perform, Lennon in attendance.

May 1967: Peace rally in London against the war.

May 1967: BBC bans the Beatles' "A Day in the Life" for encouraging drug use.

June 1, 1967: Beatles' *Sgt. Pepper* LP released.

June 1967: Monterey Festival.

July 1967: Mick Jagger and Keith Richards, having been initially jailed for drugs offenses, are released on appeal; the Beatles perform "All You Need Is Love" to a global TV audience of 400 million.

July 1967: Race riots in Detroit and Newark, New Jersey; homosexuality decriminalized in the UK.

August 1967: Beatles' manager Brian Epstein dies of overdose.

October 1967: UK reports worst-ever monthly trade deficit; "death of hippie" ceremony held in Haight-Ashbury.

October–November 1967: Scottish singer Lulu's "To Sir with Love" at no. 1 for five weeks; it will become Billboard's Single of the Year.

November 1967: Antidraft demos in New York.

December 1967: Beatles' "Hello Goodbye" is last U.S. no. 1 of the year.

January–February 1968: Tet Offensive marks a significant turning point in the Vietnam War; U.S. public opinion starts to turn against support for the war effort.

March 1968: My Lai massacre—an American-committed atrocity that only comes to light in 1970, in which hundreds of Vietnamese civilians are murdered; antiwar demo ends in casualties and arrests outside the U.S. embassy in London.

April 4, 1968: Dr. King assassinated.

May 1968: Beatles launch own record label, Apple.

June 1968: Robert Kennedy assassinated.

August 1968: Violent scenes outside the Democratic Convention in Chicago; race riots in Watts.

September 1968: Beatles' "Hey Jude" at no. 1 for nine weeks. It is the year's biggest-selling single; Rolling Stones release "Street Fighting Man."

October 1968: Led Zeppelin formed.

November 1968: Richard Nixon elected.

November 1968: Cream disband; *The Beatles* double LP released.

December 1968: Graham Nash leaves the Hollies.

January 1969: U.S. premiere of *Yellow Submarine* movie.

March 1969: John Lennon and Yoko Ono's "bed-in" peace protest in Amsterdam.

April 1969: Major antiwar protests in New York.

May 1969: New York campuses closed after student riots.

May 1969: Blind Faith form; the Beatles' "Get Back" is an American no. 1 for five weeks.

July 1969: Moon landing; Manson Family murders.

July 1969: Rolling Stones play a free gig at London's Hyde Park— and dedicate it to guitarist Brian Jones, who has died just days before.

August 1969: Woodstock Festival.

August 1969: Stones' "Honky Tonk Women" at no. 1 for four weeks.

September 1969: Release of Beatles' *Abbey Road* LP.

October 1969: Trail of "Chicago Eight"; "Days of Rage" protests; Vietnam Moratorium.

November 1969: Beatles' "Come Together" / "Something" double A-side at no. 1 for a week.

December 1969: Murder of a fan at Rolling Stones' free concert at Altamont Speedway, Northern California; the Stones release *Let It Bleed* LP.

April 1970: U.S. "invades" Cambodia to attack Vietcong bases.

April 1970: Beatles' post-breakup "Let It Be" at no. 1 in the U.S.

May 1970: National Guard opens fire on student protestors at Kent State, Ohio, killing four.

June 1970: In the UK the Conservative Party regains power after six years of Labour Party rule.

June 1970: "The Long and Winding Road" becomes the Beatles' second post-breakup no. 1 American single.

August 1970: 600,000 attend the Isle of Wight festival to see Jimi Hendrix, the Doors, the Who, Joni Mitchell, Emerson, Lake & Palmer, and Sly Stone.

September 1970: Jimi Hendrix dies.

January 1973: Cease-fire in Vietnam.

April 1973: Pink Floyd's LP *Dark Side of the Moon* at no. 1 in the U.S.; in this year British acts—Floyd, George Harrison, Wings, Led Zeppelin, the Rolling Stones, Jethro Tull, the Moody Blues, and Elton John—hold the no. 1 position on the Billboard album chart for a total of 27 weeks.

May–August 1973: Televised hearings into Watergate break-ins.

October 1973: OPEC quadruples the price of oil, effectively ending the affluence that has marked the preceding 10 years.

August 1974: President Nixon resigns.

April 1975: Fall of Saigon ends Vietnam War.

May 1979: Margaret Thatcher elected—UK's first woman prime minister.

November 1980: Ronald Reagan elected—will firm up the "special relationship" with the UK through the 1980s.

November 1980: Release of Lennon's "comeback" *Double Fantasy.*

December 1980: John Lennon murdered outside his New York apartment by psychotic "fan," Mark Chapman.

June 1981: Starsound's "Stars on 45," a Beatles medley, is no. 1 for a week.

August 1, 1981: MTV is launched in America.

November 1995: Release of the Beatles' panmedia *Anthology* project—incorporating a TV documentary broadcast on ABC, a book, and three albums/CDs of career-spanning outtakes, versions, live tracks, and two "new" songs.

ACKNOWLEDGMENTS

At Rowman & Littlefield, I would like to thank Bennett and Monica. And for his eternal vigilance and constructive, always timely support and feedback, I am sincerely grateful to Scott. At Derby, for their support and encouragement, I would like to thank, in particular, Doug, Stuart, Ruth, and Alasdair. Never underestimate the value of a simple "How's it going?" Thanks also to Neil for his insider knowledge and expertise—a proper mentor since way back when. On a more formal tip, I would like to thank the ICR Research Centre for inviting me to try out some ideas. For financial help to secure some release from teaching and enable the production of some of this book, I am grateful to the Faculty of Arts, Design and Technology. I would also like to express my gratitude to Blends and especially The Loaf—for coffee, toast, light, and heat. Finally, and most importantly, a great big heartfelt thank-you to Linda and Amélie, without whose patience, faith, love, and selflessness this book would have never happened. For losing me for nearly two years of weekends, and for making you listen to *Sgt. Pepper* over and over when I was around, this one's for you!

INTRODUCTION

"Atlantic Crossing"

July 29, 1981—a momentous day for Britain. The wedding of Prince Charles to Lady Diana Spencer had effectively brought the country to a standstill. A public holiday had ensured that the roads were empty. This was convenient as my parents drove me down a deserted M1 to London. For I was heading west, to America, unaccompanied, on the trip of a lifetime. Like many young Britons, I was most definitely not transfixed by the national celebration in my own backyard. I had nothing against Charles or Diana. It was just that their union failed to excite me. In fact, I was supremely indifferent to every aspect, every little detail relating to the royal wedding. When the day arrived, I did have particular cause to be distracted from my patriotic duty to take an interest. I was fifteen years old when I visited the United States for the first time. Crossing the Hudson into Manhattan, the cityscape set before me was thrillingly "modern," thrown into sharp relief on that of all days in its pointed contrast to the feudal celebration I had left behind just seven hours earlier. It was all simultaneously alien and familiar—as it would have been for any Briton raised on a full-fat diet of Americana, as it would have been for the Beatles themselves when they made an identical, though more momentous, journey from JFK to the city center seventeen or so years earlier. When, "despite the fervor of the American welcome, and the avid attention of the media, the people who were the most excited on that first day in New York City were the Beatles themselves" (Millard 33). "It was like a dream," Paul McCartney observed. "The greatest fantasy ever" (qtd. in Millard 33).

Just like McCartney and hundreds of thousands, maybe even millions, of Britons before and since, I had "been" to America in my mind way before I actually visited. And chief among the rocket fuels that fired this journey to an imaginary America was its popular music. It was this music that had enabled me to build my altar, supplying an array of texts for worship. From the classic rock 'n' roll of the 1950s to the heavier stuff of the '60s and '70s, from the sounds of Motor City and Memphis to Philly soul and disco, from the art rock of the Velvet Underground to the new wave of Talking Heads, the Cars, and Blondie. Here were hymns to America, which, from "Route 66" to "Union City Blue," provided the images, textures, and "messages" that resonated. This music was propulsive, physical, progressive, romantic, modern, and optimistic—an intoxicating set of tendencies, particularly when set in opposition to the bloodless provincialism and parochialism of young English lives that, as the royal wedding had proven, had not really budged all that much, if at all, in the years between my first trip and McCartney's. "I wanted to find America, in all its different colors and horizons, that's been my trip," explained former Led Zeppelin front man Robert Plant in a recent interview. "I never inhaled a chemical after 1977, but I'm still inhaling America" (qtd. in *Daily Telegraph* 34).

"Musically," writes Andrew Blake, "the twentieth was the American century," characterized by an overwhelming "sonic Americanisation" ("Americanisation" 149). Generations of British youth would have absolutely no argument with this, presumably finding themselves in fervent agreement with John Lennon's proud declaration that "I've been half-American ever since I first heard Elvis on the radio and me head turned" (qtd. in Gould). But of course the story of how this came to be is deeply rooted in the past, when those lines of communication and trade between Britain and America were first established, facilitating a flow of people, goods, and ideas that seemed to head in only one direction. Music has always been central to this transatlantic flow—key to the interaction between U.S. popular culture and British society and to a relationship that goes back to the late 1800s, when American popular music was first heard and performed in Britain. British audiences had received an early taste of U.S. popular music when thousands flocked to see and hear touring gospel choirs and minstrel shows. It is reported that the minstrel show, for example, was the most high-profile form of American entertainment in cities like nineteenth-century Liverpool, where traveling shows including the well-known Christy and Virginia Minstrels toured with increasing regularity through the 1850s and 1860s. Between 1890 and 1920, a craze for ragtime had swept the country, just as it had done in the United States. The interwar years also witnessed the arrival of jazz in Britain. Celebrated jazz clarinetist Sidney Bechet visited London several times, performing at the prestigious Royal Philharmonic Hall in 1919, while Louis Armstrong toured in 1932 and Duke Ellington in 1933. During this period both the white Original Dixieland Band and the black Southern Syncopated Orchestra also played to appreciative British jazz fans. The 1920s also saw major American performers of classic blues, such as Alberta Hunter and Ethel Waters, spending time in the UK on lucrative swings through Europe. It was also during these years that British audiences developed a taste for Tin Pan Alley music. In the twenties, Fisher's "Chicago" (1922) and Rodgers and Hart's "Manhattan" (1925) were among the decade's most popular songs. However, after 1917, it was the widespread availability of comparatively inexpensive records that was to ultimately have far greater significance than live performance by touring artists in the dissemination of American popular music. As Andre Millard confirms, "American ragtime, minstrelsy and syncopated dance music started in music halls and tent shows," but as the twentieth century progressed these styles "travelled the world in mass-produced records and films" bringing "American music to England and [making] American entertainers household names there" (54).

Writing of his growing up with jazz in the 1930s, the English poet Philip Larkin identifies what was to be a familiar function for a variety of U.S. popular music genres down the years—its acting as "a fugitive minority interest" for young Brits (2). Whether or not the political establishment was conscious of such identification at this time, the British Broadcasting Corporation's (BBC) ban on so-called hot music instituted in 1935 clearly indicated a fear of the music's power to disrupt and disturb. It was in this same year that the Musicians' Union introduced a blanket refusal of work permits for American bands, permitting individual artists to appear as "variety" guests only, as Duke Ellington did in 1948. This act of semisuccessful protectionism, which lasted for twenty-one years and arguably succeeded in its primary intent (where, incidentally, similar action taken in relation to Hollywood movies failed miserably), was designed to boost the homegrown industry by encouraging British musicians to form their own bands and by safeguarding work for them. However, while the expense of touring and the Musicians' Union ban made it very difficult for American artists to visit the UK, and there were limited outlets for their recordings on the BBC, Hollywood movies and newsreels effectively allowed such restriction to be bypassed, and exposed British audiences to sounds and styles that were both enjoyed en masse and often slavishly copied by homegrown performers. In this way, the ban unwittingly contributed to an indigenous—albeit, for the time being at least, limited—musical practice based on American styles.

As expected, the Second World War brought Britain and America even closer together, and strengthened still further the financial, technological, and cultural bonds between the two nations. In Liverpool, for example, as a result of the city's strategic wartime importance, this process of Americanization was notably accelerated. American troops stationed in the UK during World War II bequeathed a legacy of jazz and blues records that were obsessed over by many young British musicians. The mass influx of U.S. servicemen brought with it American Forces Network (AFN) radio, which began broadcasting in Europe in 1943 and continued long after the war was over. By 1960 an estimated fifty million Europeans were listening to the AFN. Around this time, the commercial station Radio Luxembourg began broadcasting in English from continental Europe—and, of crucial importance for British audiences, neither Luxembourg's nightly six hours of airtime nor the AFN's round-the-clock broadcasts was subject to restriction. The UK had no home-based Top 40 or commercial stations, so the American popular music playlisted on both Luxembourg and AFN found an audience hungry for country, swing, and pop.

The widespread popularity of American music in the 1940s and 1950s was a cause for persistent concern. The Songwriters Guild of Great Britain, together with the Music Publishers Association, tried to persuade the BBC to create a "specifically British contemporary culture in the realm of the popular song" in order to combat what they saw as the undue influence of American popular music. What they wanted were radio programs made up of "modern ballads by British composers." In 1947, when the guild was founded, its key members wrote to the BBC complaining about the Americanization of public taste in light entertainment that they believed had become disturbingly evident toward the end of the war and during its immediate aftermath. There might have been reasons for this American bias because of the large numbers of Americans in the country as the war ended, but now, they argued, the time was ripe for change. It was absurd to continue singing American words and expressing American sentiments, when Britain had lyricists capable of conveying British sentiment and humor. In evidence that the guild gave to the Broadcasting Committee in 1949, it claimed that 77 percent of the airtime allotted by the BBC to current popular songs was filled with foreign compositions, most of them from the United States. It argued that the BBC, as the "sole radio organisation of Britain," had a duty to "encourage and propagate British music." In the wake of the inquiry, the pianist Winifred Atwell's jaunty instrumental hits, "Britannia Rag" (1952) and "Coronation Rag" (1953), were perhaps typical of the officially sanctioned, homegrown pop products that emerged during this period: musically derivative of American styles but clearly British in theme and sentiment. However, while the war had ended and the bulk of America's troops had returned home, Britain's reliance on Marshall Plan dollars to support its reconstruction had undoubtedly helped speed the process of Americanization. The UK was easily the biggest single beneficiary of U.S. financial aid, receiving nearly a quarter of the billions of dollars in loans and grants that kicked in from 1948. Much of this money was used to purchase American goods, while its distribution was directly overseen by an envoy—usually a prominent American businessman—resident in London.

The late 1940s witnessed the beginnings of the British traditional ("trad") jazz movement, spearheaded by the likes of the Ken Colyer Band and the Humphrey Lyttelton Band. In a clear echo of Larkin's active consumption of prewar forms, jazz—as a product of black Americans forged "in the face of racial and economic oppression"— became for British youth "a symbol of revolt" against, among other things, U.S. commercialism (Oliver 81–82). Trad jazz's young fans would thus come to champion it as a direct counterweight to what many of them viewed as postwar Britain's narrow cultural restrictions. Here, in its conscious mobilization, American popular music somewhat ironically contributed to what in some quarters was perceived as an explicitly *anti*-American protest movement. Trad jazz in Britain has indeed been long understood as anti-American, and so arguably demonstrated the contradiction of embracing American culture while critiquing American power. Kenny Ball, Chris Barber—who continued the practice of inviting key U.S. blues performers such as Muddy Waters and Sister Rosetta to Britain—and Acker Bilk all traded on the British public's thirst for U.S. musical forms in producing their trad jazz music. Ball and Bilk even scored sizeable transatlantic hits in the early 1960s with pieces such as "Stranger on the Shore"—a Billboard number one in 1961—and "Midnight in Moscow" (1961). However, by this time, trad jazz had been eclipsed by another American import. Rock 'n' roll comprehensively rearranged Britain's popular musical landscape. So much so that, in less than ten years after its arrival, the transatlantic flow would be reversed as America's cultural dominance was challenged.

July 29, 1981. Leaving the airport in a courtesy minivan, the first music I heard on American soil in crystal-clear FM—noteworthy, because back then the UK's only national pop station, Radio 1, was broadcast in tinny, ebbing and flowing AM—was the Beatles' 1968 single version of "Revolution." An entirely fitting soundtrack to my arrival. Growing up in a household full of Beatles' music, I knew of course that the band was British. But Beatles' music was woven so seamlessly and prominently into the fabric of popular music history that it didn't strike me as strange that theirs should be the first music I heard. In fact, the excitement I felt at finally being in New York was effectively bottled but barely contained by the distorted fuzz-tone rush of the song's thrilling opening salvo.

Before 1964, only two UK acts had topped the Billboard singles chart. British-made Billboard best sellers were such a rarity in the pre-Invasion era that Laurie London's 1958 American hit "He's Got the Whole World in His Hands" was front-page news on both sides of the Atlantic at a time when pop music simply did not warrant such coverage. In 1963 there had been just one UK act in the Billboard Top 10 all year—an all-time low, and a low ebb that only served to make the high tides that followed all the more noteworthy. In the first quarter of 1964, the Beatles accounted for a jaw-dropping 60 percent of all recorded music sold in America, thirty-two British-made singles would reach the Billboard Top 10 in that year, and UK acts would be at number one for a total of fifty-two weeks through 1964 and 1965. At the Invasion's peak, from 1964 to 1970, British acts were the source of 28 percent of Billboard number-one singles, and between them—perhaps helping to prove that it was not all about one band—the Rolling Stones, Herman's Hermits, Dave Clark Five, the Animals, the Kinks, the Hollies, the Yardbirds, and the Who placed more than 130 songs in the American Top 40.

While this book will, of course, focus on this substantial body of Invasion work, acknowledging the dramatic turnabout in the commercial fortunes of British pop music in America that it represents is also merely the "count-off" that propels us into a full assessment of its meanings. What this study will demonstrate, then, is just how much this unprecedented commercial success has elided deeper significances. *British Invasion* will track the journey of '60s British pop from peripheral irrelevance through exotic novelty to the very heart of the rock mainstream, examining how and why British artists came to achieve commercial and artistic dominance. In doing so, it will document a distinctive chapter in the story of Anglo-American relations, in that so-called special relationship. The Invasion is, for example, commonly credited with bringing the curtain down on surf rock, pre-Motown female vocal groups, teen idol pop, and even the folk music revival. It has also been charged with denting the careers of many, from Elvis Presley down, while simultaneously reinvigorating others, from Bob Dylan down. In the process, the Invasion played a major part in cementing the primacy of the rock band, and of the self-generated material this unit would now typically produce. In Andrew Blake's memorable phrase, it helped transform the very "political economy" of popular music making, leading to a seismic shift in the musician's "status and subjectivity" that, in turn, had a considerable impact on the listener-consumer (*Land* 91–92).

Shaped and defined by the "British Invasion," it is often claimed that '60s rock did not simply supply a soundtrack for social change, but offered young people new ways to interpret their surroundings and to construct their identities, marking a defining moment at which "mere" pop comes of age as a potent cultural force. Rock music proved on numerous occasions in the 1960s that it could move quicker than other forms of popular culture, and that it also possessed the reach to simply outstrip those that just might be more responsive: "here, there and everywhere." The Invasion gave rock music its mojo back, allowing it to "regain its disruptive power with a joyful vengeance, until by [the end of the 1960s] it would be seen as a genuine force of cultural and political consequence" (Gilmore 23). It has thus shaped an understanding of what popular music can be and should do that has endured for half a century. In 2009, an American Public Broadcasting opinion poll voted the Beatles "the world's most influential artists" (qtd. in Millard 184); and, as if confirmation of this preeminence was necessary, a few years later over one million Beatles tracks were downloaded in the first week of their availability on iTunes. Led by the Beatles, the Invasion "revolutionized the way records were made, the way records were listened to, the nature of popular song-writing, the role popular music played in people's lives" (Gould 8); and, while there can be no doubting their centrality in any attempt to explain the multidimensional significance of the British Invasion—since it could be argued that the band "wrought the kind of changes that made the Sixties the Sixties" (Millard vii)— what will also become clear is that the Beatles could not have done it alone.

The British Invasion marked a reversal of, and significant disruption in, the normal flow of pop cultural influence, goods, and ideas, as British music was successfully exported to the United States in significant volume for the very first time. Yet it also represented something more than, as many commentators have rather glibly suggested, British acts simply conquering America with its own music. However, it cannot be denied that American records formed the basis of the Invasion bands' musical education and development. "We were all very interested in American music," Paul McCartney told anyone who would listen, "and all had the same records" (qtd. in Millard 2–3). It is, though, in the way these influences were mixed and modified that elevated Invasion music above and beyond mere pale copy.

This book examines how and why the music of the British Invasion reflected, commented upon, and even helped shape transatlantic culture in the 1960s and beyond. In doing so, it investigates its origins, development, impact, and ironies. Set against a backdrop of key contexts—artistic, political, psychoemotional, sexual, demographic, and commercial—it offers a nuanced examination of a meaningful chapter in that long-standing Anglo-American relationship.

I

"SHAKIN' ALL OVER"

1956–1963

The British Invasion has its roots in the mid-1950s, when an aggregation of key circumstances and influences—some homegrown, others imported—shaped the context out of which its music and musicians would emerge. Performing on stage in Dublin in 2001, the Scottish comedian and movie actor Billy Connolly told his audience that he "remember[ed] the 1940s and the 1950s. The world," he said, "was beige and the music was crap." Connolly's typically droll assessment of the postwar state of the nation is confirmed by a host of more sober firsthand accounts. In common with most of these, Shawn Levy selects a different if no less incriminating color to help define those times: "*Gray*. The air, the buildings, the clothing, the faces, the mood. Britain in the mid-fifties was everything it had been for decades, even centuries. . . . England . . . was dowdy, rigid and, above all, unrelentingly gray, gray to its core" (Levy 3–4, my emphasis).

Celebrating Queen Elizabeth II's golden jubilee, *Times* journalist Richard Morrison emphasizes how much better off the kingdom was in the fiftieth year of her reign by comparing it to the "exhausted, inert and skint country" (3) she inherited. This was a time when, notwithstanding the best efforts of the Marshall Plan, one in three homes had still no bath; one in twenty did not even have running water; food was subject to strict rationing; television sets could be found in just 4 percent of UK households; very few families could afford a fridge, car, or washing machine; and the urban landscape was still badly scarred by bomb craters. Yet if Britain was a dull, drab, pinched place yet to emerge into full postscarcity—making it seem materially and psychologically "a lot like the 1930s" for most of its residents (Levy 5)—there were some, principally but not exclusively among the young, who actively sought to transform their immediate environment, to inject some color, to counter the beige and gray, by embracing the exciting cultural alternatives offered in particular by the United States and its popular culture. Deploying a familiar simile, applied by numerous historians and commentators to this moment, Morrison goes on to note that "a dam was about to burst" (3).

Growing up in the fifties, as Pete Frame recalls in his memoir, *The Restless Generation*, "worship of America and all things American was an established religion among the young and progressive" (154). To young Britons "who had spent their childhood in a battered bruised world of Woodbines, war widows, ration books, bus queues, bomb sites, outside toilets, Butlins, smog, fish and chips in newspapers, utility furniture, downcast faces, them and us," America represented some kind of Promised Land: *"But the United States!* The United States had the best music, cars, girls, clothes, gangsters, Negroes, cowboys, songwriters, singers, jazz musicians, films, film stars, records, trains, planes, jukeboxes, flag, weather, beaches, history, geographical features, place names, rivers, hair styles, money, television programmes, sport, street names, food, skyscrapers, athletes, boxers, confectionary, sunshine, comics, the best of everything, so we believed" (Frame 154, my emphasis).

The political significance in British youth's enthusiastic embrace of American popular culture elevated these preferences and enthusiasms way beyond the level of any simple pleasures to be had from consumption. For it was becoming increasingly—and, for some, disturbingly—obvious that young Brits like Pete Frame wore their "T-shirts and blue jeans, chewed gum and drank Coca-Cola, as a gesture of rebellion against both the older generation and all forms of authority" (Pells 240). As the story of rock 'n' roll and its subsequent development into native variants will demonstrate, American popular culture often appealed to teenage Britons precisely because it was openly frowned upon by the nation's cultural gatekeepers. So, just as in other forms of readily available and easily enjoyed American popular culture, rock 'n' roll was enticingly and brazenly vulgar and classless. This "provocative Americautopia" (Wicke 69) that could be readily and so satisfyingly extracted from rock 'n' roll then had a precedent that could be measured in the thrill and promise British youth drew from other forms of American culture that predated rock 'n' roll. Young audiences in the interwar years, for example, often found that openhearted Hollywood movies offered them pleasurable alternatives to the confines and restrictions of British cultural life that were so evidently projected in buttoned-down homegrown films. In the same period, the poet Philip Larkin wrote of the "provocative" significance of another, less mainstream, American cultural import. "For the generations that came to adolescence between the wars," he writes, "jazz was that unique private excitement that youth seems to demand": "Sitting with a friend in his bedroom that over- looked the tennis court, I watched leaves drift down through long Sun- day afternoons as we took it in turn to wind the portable HMV [record player], and those white and coloured Americans, Bubber Miley, Frank Teschmacher, J. C. Higginbotham, spoke immediately to our under- standing. Their rips, slurs and distortions were something we under- stood perfectly. This was something we had found ourselves, that wasn't taught at school (what a prerequisite that is of everything worthwhile!), and having found it, we made it bear all the enthusiasm usually directed at more established arts" (1–3).

For Larkin and his school friends, an appreciation of and obsession with jazz was evidently bound up with both pleasure *and* resistance— resistance that was to be found in the pleasures to be had from listening to and collecting this music in often difficult circumstances. Much like rock 'n' roll twenty years later, jazz in 1930s Britain possessed an oppo- sitional potential that its young fans found they could satisfyingly mobi- lize against cultural convention and suffocating "good taste." That its pleasures were bound up with resistance did not go unnoticed among its opponents. Jazz musician and critic George Melly recalls how in the 1930s his headmaster would scream "filthy jazz" and quickly turn off the radio whenever it caught his ear—a reaction that meant young George would "mentally add jazz to Bolshevism and the lower classes" to the things he was in favor of (qtd. in Wynn 12).

As George Melly's headmaster demonstrated, there was always open hostility to "things American" within the British establishment, among social elites right across the political dial. If anything, this antipathy was even stronger and more openly expressed in the 1950s, when fears of

Americanization fueled by Marshall Plan dollars reached fever pitch as a range of popular cultural imports flooded in—Hollywood movies, commercial TV, magazines and comic books, white goods, and of course rock 'n' roll.

The noisy and hence high-profile arrival of rock 'n' roll in late 1955 also meant that these fears over Americanization would become increasingly conflated with those relating to the apparent rise of British youth, prompting the sort of woe-is-me headlines that featured in a 1957 edition of *Everybody's Weekly* when it asked, "Are we turning our children into little Americans?" Echoing George Orwell's memorable description of Cold War UK as "airstrip one"—functioning as no more than a glorified aircraft carrier permanently moored in the Atlantic at the United States' convenience—the sociologist Raymond Williams declared it to be "culturally an American colony," and like many viewed American popular culture as particularly destructive and detrimental to the nation's good health. This was a diagnosis shared by Richard Hoggart, and memorably expressed in his late fifties study *The Uses of Literacy* (1957) in which he contrasted what he saw as the "full, rich" working-class life and culture of the interwar years with the "thin," "pallid," "insipid," and evidently Americanized life being—increasingly, enthusiastically, and for him so disturbingly—led by fifties teens in particular. In this extract, there is a barely concealed hysteria that does more than hint at the rising sense of moral panic gripping the nation:

> There is [a milk bar] in almost every northern town with more than, say, fifteen thousand inhabitants. . . . Girls go to some, but most of the customers are boys aged between fifteen and twenty, with drape suits, picture ties, *and an American slouch.* . . . The young men waggle one shoulder or stare, as desperately as Humphrey Bogart, across the tubular chairs. . . . Compared even with the pub around the corner, this is all a peculiarly thin and pallid form of dissipation, a sort of spiritual dry-rot amid the odour of boiled milk. *Many of the customers—their clothes, their hairstyles, their facial expressions all indicate—are living to a large extent in a myth-world compounded of a few simple elements which they take to be those of American life.* (Hoggart 189–90, my emphasis)

In an alliance with an overwhelming majority of British politicians and parents, educators like Hoggart typically figured American popular culture as the spectacularly destructive vanguard of an invasion, and after 1955 would come to conflate rock 'n' roll with other imports like comics and movies as evidence of the decay wrought by American cultural imperialism. On "a trail of signs, storms and sensations" (Booker 32), rock 'n' roll was perhaps the most visible and audible marker of a cultural revolt that flowered between the Suez crisis of late 1956—commonly viewed as the first substantial fissure in the British establishment's facade—and the Profumo spy scandal of 1963. These two national traumas dealt hammer blows to the conservative order, and so helped create the right conditions to allow rock 'n' roll in Britain to transcend the relatively narrow parameters of pop music style. As historian Arthur Marwick has pointed out, "The challenges to established authority were particularly striking in Britain, partly because Britain had long been such a conservative and homogeneous society, but partly also because Britain had generally been such a sensible society" (68). One of rock 'n' roll's defining characteristics was its assault on sense, both common and good—one that young British fans gleefully embraced. *Awopbopaloobopawopbamboom!* It also heralded change, and during this period Britain was changing fast. In 1959 there were more than four million single people between thirteen and twenty-five years old, making for a younger nation. Of equal—and clearly not unrelated—significance, the late 1950s and early 1960s were economic boom years, which witnessed rising wages, virtually full employment, and the country awash with consumer goods now available via the expansion of credit.

The so-called long boom had in fact begun in the late 1940s, but its beneficial effects were only really experienced by the majority from the mid-1950s onward—during a period that witnessed solid economic advances. Motored by Marshall, Britain's youth, in particular, harvested the benefits, having more disposable income and the leisure time to make use of it. This, in turn, served to significantly raise their profile. The late 1950s and early 1960s witnessed a sharp rise in spending on music and fashion. In 1960, for example, Britain's estimated five million teens commanded around 10 percent of the nation's total personal income but accounted for an estimated £850 million or 59 percent of all consumer expenditure. Predictably, this was concentrated in certain areas. British teens purchased 40 percent of all record players, 30 percent of all cosmetics and toiletries, and 28 percent of movie tickets.

Teen affluence made a significant contribution to the perfect storm of circumstances that ultimately birthed the music of the British Invasion, since imported rock 'n' roll would simply not have been so impactful if young Brits could not have afforded to purchase it or enjoy it live. And, while it has been pointed out that the British class structure remained largely unaltered during this time, it has also been noted that the working class—and especially its younger members—undoubtedly gained a new visibility and self-confidence as a result of this rising affluence. So, change was palpably in the air—making the propulsive, kinetic beat of rock 'n' roll at once a highly apposite soundtrack, symptom, and harbinger. However, it is important to stress that, in contrast to the United States where rising prosperity seemed to lead to conformity, in Britain, particularly among the young, the reaction was markedly different. For it left them "all shook up"—invigorated and agitated, whereas in the States affluence appeared to have an almost tranquilizing effect.

Teenage jazz aficionado Philip Larkin had demonstrated back in the 1930s that American popular culture could be used as a means to diagnose English culture's failings. In this way, an enthusiastic preference for and embrace of all things American could well constitute some kind of revolutionary gesture, as Pete Frame's litany had confirmed; and, what is more, it was clear to those on all sides—to supporters and opponents alike—that rock 'n' roll "proposed an imaginative and alternative idea of 'culture' to that officially on offer" (Chambers 27). In its British context, the cornerstones of rock 'n' roll's manifesto—particularly its celebration of disruption and total commitment to instant rather than deferred gratification—meant that it carried plenty of force. Possibly even more force and meaning that it possessed in its native land. For British teens, rock 'n' roll served as a vessel for emotional investment, enabling them to define themselves in ways that differed from the official models provided, and, in so doing, offered many fans a different way to live altogether. John Lennon first heard Elvis Presley's "Heartbreak Hotel" on Radio Luxembourg's *Jack Johnson Show* in May 1956. For Lennon and thousands of young Brits like him, rock 'n' roll meant more than the headline promise of "good times," more than Saturday night kicks. It spoke of freedom, sex, and rebellion—of an escape into an alternative psychoemotional space. "I could hardly make out what was being said"—the future Beatle recalled—"It was just the experience of hearing it and having my hair stand on end. We'd never heard American voices singing like that" (qtd. in Courrier xxx). The music's powerful pull did not go unnoticed by other members of the Lennon household, either: "It was nothing but Elvis Presley, Elvis Presley, Elvis Presley. In the end I said 'Elvis Presley's all very well, John, but I don't want him for breakfast, dinner and tea'" (Lennon's guardian Aunt Mimi qtd. in Kynaston 641).

Although mildly annoying for John Lennon's exasperated guardian, it was evident that some in authority found the immersive nature of British youth's relationship with American rock 'n' roll to be a more serious irritant. Here, though, official culture's objections and disapproval only served to heighten and deepen rock 'n' roll's appeal to British youth, as did the related difficulty experienced in actually getting to hear it. As might be expected, rock 'n' roll was marginalized by the BBC—a highly conservative cultural institution that at the time exercised near-total control over Britain's musical diet. In July 1956 Jim Davidson, head of the corporation's Light Music division, dismissed Elvis Presley and Bill Haley as "freaks" at "the bottom of the gimmick noise barrel" (qtd. in Frame 179). Compounded by the restrictive impact of a Musicians' Union–driven limit on "needle-time" to just twenty-two hours per week, this meant that rock 'n' roll could only be heard with any regularity on Radio Luxembourg or the American Forces Network (AFN)—a situation that only added to its romantic cache and fugitive appeal. Clearly, the nation's lack of innovative, youth-friendly radio programming and, in particular, the BBC's unwavering commitment to classical and dance band music helped reinforce a yearning in the young for this new and exciting music coming out of the States. The perception that British youth was not being served by national radio in the rock 'n' roll era was proven by ratings that showed that they were going elsewhere en masse for their music. It should therefore come as little surprise to discover that, even as late as 1964, the "pirate" radio station Caroline had more young listeners than the BBC. Named for John F. Kennedy's daughter, Radio Caroline had announced its arrival by playing the Beatles' "Can't Buy Me Love," and its shamelessly Americanized Top 40 format had soon won it more than seven million listeners. By the end of 1964 there were half a dozen pop pirate radio stations operating offshore, outside the jurisdiction of Britain's highly restrictive broadcasting laws.

Bill Haley had first charted in the UK in December 1954 with "Shake, Rattle and Roll." However, modest sales and minimal airplay meant that this track had gone largely unnoticed to all but the hard core and the curious. "Rock Around the Clock," though, undoubtedly left its mark. This is the track that noisily announced the arrival of rock 'n' roll in Britain. A total of seven Haley singles had been released in Britain through 1955, but it was "Rock Around the Clock" that had inarguably the biggest impact of these. According to David Pichaske, "Rock 'n' roll presents a fairly succinct and radical critique of fifties life, along with an equally coherent alternative," and he notes that Haley's "Rock Around the Clock"

> was a potent song in 1955, although it seems innocuous now. It is saying that we're gonna rock 'n' roll. And we're gonna do it all night long. And we're gonna drive this thing right out front of us because we're in charge now and we're gonna have fun (the one thing money can't buy). So what if dancing is a cheap revolution; so what if all the standard rhythm and blues sexual overtones of rock are underplayed if not submerged entirely? To a . . . teenager stuck inside the fifties, "Rock Around the Clock" was a *declaration of independence.* In words as well as music. (44, my emphasis)

While Pichaske's valiant attempt at defining its meaning relates to a specifically American context, "Rock Around the Clock" played out similarly in Britain. In fact, there is a strong argument for the song having an even greater potency for British youth—like the teenage John Lennon, for example—"stuck" much deeper "inside the fifties." Although musically and lyrically alien to most, the song still managed to forge a powerful bond with its many young fans.

"Rock Around the Clock" had first entered the UK singles chart in the fall of 1955, eventually enjoying a seven-week run at number one extending from late November into the new year. Its success blazed a trail for other high-charting rock 'n' roll records through 1956. In May, Elvis Presley charted for the first time with "Heartbreak Hotel," which reached a high of number two. Presley's "Hound Dog" and "Blue Moon" also quickly followed "Heartbreak Hotel" into the UK Top 10, and other successful rock 'n' roll imports in 1956 included Carl Perkins's "Blue Suede Shoes" (no. 10), Little Richard's "Rip It Up" (no.

30), Frankie Lymon and the Teenagers' "Why Do Fools Fall in Love?" (no. 1 for three weeks), and the Platters' "The Great Pretender" (no. 5).

Cliff Richard—who, two years later would be marketed as Britain's answer to Elvis—has described the life-changing moment when he first heard "Heartbreak Hotel" leaking out of the open window of a parked car. Suitably inspired, Richard's next step was to "tune into American Forces Network and Radio Luxembourg trying to find out more about him" (qtd. in Odell 35). Presley then first came to the attention of British youth in the spring of 1956, although he did not top the singles chart until July 1957. Between the spring of 1956 and the summer of 1957, his UK popularity is roughly on a par with Haley's—both had six hit records in this period and occupied the charts for a similar number of weeks. However, in the early months of 1956, it was still very much Haley's show so far as Britain was concerned. During this time, "Rock Around the Clock" achieved its greatest and widest impact via its top-and-tail appearance in the movie *Blackboard Jungle*. On general release from late 1955 onward, *Blackboard Jungle* not only widened the song's potential reach, it also enabled "Rock Around the Clock" to be experienced as never before by those who were already familiar with the track. In movie theaters up and down the land "Rock Around the Clock" was channeled through large and powerful speakers, making it—as one contemporary observer noted—the "loudest and clearest that anyone had ever heard rock 'n' roll played" (Frame 186). At this time only one other form of public entertainment could match the movie theater in its capacity to deliver rock 'n' roll at such exhilarating volume. Liverpool teenager Ian James remembers how he and his young friend, Paul McCartney, would enjoy the music at fairgrounds: "We would stand around the Waltzer as they would play rock 'n' roll hits. . . . The first time I heard 'Heartbreak Hotel' was at a fairground in Southport—I was transfixed" (qtd. in Leigh 73).

When *Blackboard Jungle* premiered in London in the winter of 1955, future Rolling Stone Keith Richards recalls that "people were saying 'Did ya hear that music, man?' Because in England we had never heard anything: the BBC controls it and won't play that sort of music. But everybody our age stood up for that music, and the hell with the BBC" (qtd. in Szatmary 116).

Viewed at the time, even by rock 'n' roll's most fervent advocates, as B-movie trash, *Rock Around the Clock* (1956) nevertheless offered British audiences another opportunity to experience rock 'n' roll at high decibels. In the late summer of 1956, screenings of *Rock Around the Clock* were often accompanied by what a hysterical British press described as "riots" but were really no more than high spirits—jiving in the aisles, a few ripped seats, and copycat rumbles that occasionally spilled out into the streets. Inevitably, the movie was banned in a number of cities—in Bristol, Bradford, Ipswich, and England's second city, Birmingham—while its supposed ill effects on impressionable youth were hotly debated in Parliament, church, and the media. In an interview with the BBC, member of Parliament Jeremy Thorpe expressed his concern that "a fourth-rate film with fifth-rate music" could "pierce the thin shell of civilisation and turn people into wild dervishes" (qtd. in Kynaston 655). Clearly, both the "riots" and, arguably even more so, the establishment's disproportionate and hysterical response to them illustrate the impact of Haley's music on British life.

It was chiefly via movies, newsreels, and photographs that rock 'n' roll first worked its way into the British consciousness. However, from late 1956 onward, television entered the fray; in marked contrast to radio, it was noticeably more responsive (even if not quite welcoming) to rock 'n' roll. In particular, the advent of independent television (ITV) in the mid-1950s helped ensure that British youth culture and its preferences had a much greater on-screen presence. ITV's arrival witnessed a significant restructuring of British television, as it quickly established itself as a genuine rival to the BBC and as an organization apparently committed unashamedly to turning the latter's Reithian ethos on its head. Putting entertainment ahead of education, ITV evidently appealed. In December 1955, just months after it commenced broadcasting, a Gallup poll revealed that 57 percent of respondents preferred ITV to the BBC, with a paltry 16 percent expressing a positive preference for the corporation.

By the late 1950s, it was apparent that television had superseded radio as Britain's principal engine of mass communication; and television, and in particular ITV, was open to new trends. The slew of pop shows that appeared at this time demonstrated that UK TV was more tolerant of rock 'n' roll, as the networks traded blows in the battle to win over younger viewers. The first dedicated pop music show on British television was *Cool for Cats*, which debuted in late 1956. In February 1957 the BBC responded with *6.5 Special*, a show which consistently drew ten million viewers. ITV then premiered *Oh Boy!* in June 1958, and a year later the BBC show *Juke Box Jury* launched. This televisual tit for tat would eventually lead to the appearance of ITV's beat music flagship *Ready Steady Go!* in August 1963.

Whether delivered on record, via movies, or TV, rock 'n' roll undoubtedly played a crucial role in simultaneously encapsulating and ratcheting up the nation's excitement levels. As future Brit-pop impresario Simon Napier-Bell confirms, by 1956: "The pop scene in London was now fascinating. Rock 'n' roll groups appeared on bills along with traditional groups and pop singers—even some modern jazz made it into the [sales] charts. And on top of all this, Elvis burst onto the scene" ("First Teenage Dream").

However, while change might well have been palpable for many young Britons, no one appeared to have told those who controlled the UK music business. Even after the arrival of rock 'n' roll, it was evident to the likes of the teenaged Napier-Bell that "pop wasn't aimed at people who were under twenty [but] at young marrieds" ("First Teenage Dream"). So it was that, alongside breakthrough rock 'n' roll hits, other best sellers in 1956 included Winifred Atwell's ragtime piano instrumental "Poor People of Paris," Doris Day's saccharine "Whatever Will Be Will Be," Johnny Ray's histrionic crooner "Just Walkin' in the Rain," and Pat Boone's anodyne "I'll Be Home"—which occupied the top spot for five weeks, went on to become the year's best-selling 45 rpm disc, and perhaps best indicated the industry's current understanding of what constituted "pop." Both indigenous pop music and industry-endorsed American imports were then indelibly marked by conservatism.

Throughout the 1950s, British pop was indistinguishable from variety and light entertainment—and so, for many teens, it simply failed to excite. A major reason for this was that it was tightly policed by four major record companies—EMI, Decca, Pye, and Philips—the BBC, and two music weeklies, *Melody Maker* and *New Music Express*. The fact that its UK distributor Decca had classified Bill Haley's "Rock Around the Clock" as a "foxtrot" was indicative of the industry's willful obtuseness and intransigence. Alma Cogan's "Dreamboat" (EMI/HMV), which had topped the British singles chart in the summer of 1955, is representative of the kind of officially sanctioned popular music that held sway in Britain at this time—smooth, crafted, inoffensive to the point of soporific, it skips along politely with its most noteworthy feature being a plinky-plonky, casually xenophobic music-hall piano figure that appears at the briefest mention of "the China Sea." Hits like Cogan's confirmed that popular music was all about entertainment, and that "entertainment" was all about bland escape.

When rock 'n' roll hit, the popular music scene in Britain was dominated by homegrown big bands playing American-sourced or American-influenced dance music familiar to people from the war years. Featuring Alma Cogan as a lead singer, Cogan's career had been effectively launched and then profitably sustained by one of these dance bands, singing ballads aimed squarely at adults. That "Dreamboat" should have sounded as it did should have come as no great surprise. It was typical of material either sourced from reliable professionals based in Britain's answer to Tin Pan Alley, located in and around London's Denmark Street, or simply reworked well-known American songs as slavish covers. So, whether cover or pseudo-original, British pop on the eve of rock 'n' roll's arrival was effectively a version of popular U.S. hits. However, this pop musical dominant was increasingly not to the liking of many young Britons who had been introduced to a headier brew. "It was all big bands and Frank Sinatra, Bing Crosby and Perry Como. It was OK but it didn't grab me," explains Cliff Richard. "And then suddenly . . . you had Bill Haley coming out with this incredible sound—slapping bass and big beat—and it blew our minds. The sense of 'us' and 'them' was extraordinary and exhilarating" (qtd. in Odell 36).

Change, though, was imminent. Unsurprisingly, this was driven by economic consideration, rather than any genuine desire to satisfy the musical tastes and preferences of young Britons. Still, however it came about, those young Brits would surely take it. Fueled by rising teen affluence—as sales of 45 rpm singles rocketed from around four million in 1955 to fifty-two million by 1960 and so killed off the market for the 78 rpm format favored by the pop acts of the pre–rock 'n' roll era—the deep reservations about rock 'n' roll harbored by Britain's popular music establishment were cynically set aside in the interest of fast, fat profit. The widespread belief shared by those in the business that this was no more than a potentially lucrative fad must also have made embracing rock 'n' roll a little easier. With the British music industry now on board, this predictably prompted lackluster homegrown attempts. Just as predictably, most of these were woeful.

A principal reason for this abject failure to convincingly re-create rock 'n' roll was the sharp contrast between this essentially alien musical form and what was familiar and understood. Whereas the thirty-two-bar format was the cornerstone of the Tin Pan Alley tradition, the African American tradition from which rock 'n' roll emerged is founded on the twelve-bar blues, with three chords alternating in a fixed pattern. The fact that the blues scale is comparatively sparse, comprising five notes and not the seven of the European scale, compounded this contrast—a sensation of foreignness further reinforced by the rhythm, which was perhaps where the sharpest difference between European and American music lay, as European classical and white pop music were both notably undercooked here. All of this meant that to the British, fan or critic alike, the music of Bill Haley and all those other American rock 'n' rollers sounded very unusual—a strangeness compounded by the typically loud guitar and drum-led sound delivered with unfamiliar speed, which at live shows and via movie theater speakers was experienced as something thrillingly and/or threateningly new.

In 1956 the Deep River Boys' buttoned-down cover of Haley's "Rock Around the Clock" demonstrated perfectly how and why British attempts at performing rock 'n' roll were doomed to embarrassing failure. Listening to this track alongside, say, Little Richard's "Rip It Up" or even the original merely served to highlight the extent to which British pop was operating on an entirely different musical wavelength, unable to converse in the language of rock 'n' roll. Although the Deep River Boys were in fact expat Americans, the track was recorded for EMI's HMV imprint in London and easily betrayed the time and place of its production. It is rock 'n' roll consciously reinterpreted as trad jazz—the Boys' barbershop quartet-style vocal, all crisp enunciation and polite delivery, interspersed with a clarinet and trombone solo. Quite simply, these are the wrong instruments for rock 'n' roll. The Boys did not make the charts with their effort. Youthful British consumers were not convinced. The Boys' only chart appearance resulted from an easy listening union with the Sid Phillips Orchestra, which tells us all we need to know about their rock 'n' roll credentials and suggests that British rock 'n' roll fans were right to be dismissive of their efforts.

Even after the rock 'n' roll invasion was under way, mainstream British pop continued to draw from a familiar American well—as Pat Boone's aforementioned British best seller of 1956 "I'll Be Home" had proved. It was not surprising that Britain struggled to produce credible rock 'n' rollers right up to the beat boom of 1963. Compounded by industry resistance, this was because rock 'n' roll was simply not in the bloodstream of British music makers. At this time, the British pop impresario Larry Parnes was principal among a number of manipulating entrepreneurs, grooming a stable of British teens for rock 'n' roll stardom. As Simon Napier-Bell describes: "First they were sanitised—had their skin problems dealt with and were taught to wash and clean their teeth—then they were given a thin veneer of anarchy by being renamed with tough-sounding words—Duffy Power, Marty Wilde, Billy Fury. But there was nothing truly anti-establishment about them; they weren't true rock 'n' rollers, they were just pop stars—Larry's pretty boys, all living together in one big house" ("First Teenage Dream").

For a variety of reasons, then, when it was attempted by Brits in the 1950s, rock 'n' roll usually amounted to little more than pale imitation. This was faux rock 'n' roll. Who, for example, would be able to supply the credible musical chops for Parnes's "pretty boys"? Early exponents of British rock 'n' roll, Tony Crombie and His Rockets, best encapsulate these shortcomings. Their brief career and limited recorded output highlighted early Brit-rock's lack of authenticity and credibility. Having been persuaded by his manager to form a British version of the Comets, jazz drummer Tony Crombie premiered his rock 'n' roll band on September 11, 1956, in the south coast town of Portsmouth. With the by-now-familiar barely concealed disdain it reserved for all things rock 'n' roll, the British music weekly *Melody Maker* reported rather sniffily that the "younger element were contented, perhaps even sated" by the performance. The Rockets' absurdly presumptuous debut "Teach You to Rock"—widely regarded as Britain's first homegrown rock 'n' roll single—reached number twenty-five in the fall of 1956. Like the Deep River Boys' cover of "Rock Around the Clock," it lacked rock 'n' roll's stomp and stamp of authority. Yet, if "Teach You to Rock" lacked credibility, then its follow-up 45 confirmed that the Rockets definitely did not have rock 'n' roll in their DNA. "Sham Rock" is an innocuous shuffle—a novelty record with its fiddle-dee-dee references to "the streets of Dublin city" and "sweet Molly Malone." Most unfortunate but appropriate of all, however, is the fact that its (presumably unintention-al) title draws attention—if this were needed—to the "sham" being perpetrated in the name of rock. Crombie disbanded his Rockets in August 1957 and returned to jazz.

In retrospect, the short-lived and unsuccessful existence of the Rockets should come as little surprise, given Crombie's reported reasons for starting up the band—"I've been a martyr long enough. Now I want to eat." To make matters worse, Crombie could barely disguise his contempt for the music he was playing. It was not surprising then that British rock 'n' roll fans had little difficulty spotting an opportunist and fake. As Paul McCartney notes, "The people we copied were all American, of course, because there was no one good British" (qtd. in Gould 58).

Although Tommy Steele did not share Crombie's open disdain for rock 'n' roll, the end product still emerged as inauthentic. Peaking at number thirteen in the fall of 1956, Steele's "Rock with the Caveman" was at least up front about its novelty status. With lyrics by Lionel Bart—who would go on to write the musical *Oliver*—"Rock with the Caveman" was a conscious spoof: "The British Museum have got my head / Most unfortunate, 'cos I ain't dead!" Possessed of the best British approximation thus far of rock 'n' roll's rhythm, swing, and drive—there are no clarinets and trombones here, just some competent sax and piano work—it nevertheless had the lyrics of a revue, which ultimately made it as much an empty pastiche as Crombie's "Sham Rock." The song alluded to the bones of a skeleton christened the Piltdown Man that had recently been discovered in an English quarry. The Piltdown Man was heralded as evidence of the missing link but was then quickly exposed as a hoax, sparking a tabloid scandal that fueled "Rock with the Caveman." Although it was an irony lost at the time, here then was a cash-in that took as its subject a hoax. Yet more British sham rock.

Closely choreographed by his managers, John Kennedy and the ubiquitous Larry Parnes, Tommy Steele's career was indicative of so much that combined to characterize early British rock 'n' roll. Signing up for West End shows, pantomimes, and movies, Steele was speedi-ly—and it should be stressed, willingly—absorbed into "the grooves of show-business," demonstrating that even rock 'n' roll could not prevent a "rapid return to . . . musical and cultural conformity" (Chambers 38). The apparent iron grip of this "conformity" and the depth of its "grooves" is best illustrated by the career of Steele's successor to the British rock 'n' roll crown, Cliff Richard, as he journeyed rapidly from the promise of credibility with his first hit "Move It" (1958)—commonly acknowledged as a decent stab of propulsive Brit-rock—to soft-soap hits like the Lionel Bart–penned "Living Doll" (1959), "The Young Ones" (1962), and "Summer Holiday" (1963), which seemed to confirm his status as a light entertainer.

Given the way it worked, it is not surprising that the British music business did not see skiffle coming. Yet it is clear that skiffle happened precisely *because* of the way the British music business worked. Skiffle was sourced from a musical style that was not drawn directly from the American pop mainstream. In this respect, it could be said to have been generated from *without* rather than within. Quite simply, there was nothing comparable in the States at the time. Born in 1953, baptized in 1954, booming in 1957, and pretty much bust by the end of 1958, skiffle is absolutely key to an understanding of the British Invasion, as its thousands of amateur and teenage practitioners functioned as forerunners of the beat groups of just a few years later. In his memoir, young skiffler Ian Whitcomb has claimed that "skiffle was the most influential event in British pop history," since "for better or worse, the long-term result was The Beatles, The Rolling Stones and punk" ("Chas McDevitt"). Frequently derided because it rarely ventured beyond a very rudimentary three-chord progression (i.e., C, F, and G7), its many critics have surely missed the point. Skiffle's musicality or otherwise is not really the issue here, since it was more about the ethos that lay behind the music making. Above all, skiffle's significance is rooted in its accessibility.

Skiffle predated the arrival of rock 'n' roll in Britain. It emerged as early as 1953 in London's Soho clubs, where it was the name ultimately arrived at to describe an informal musical interlude—or "breakdown"—performed by the string section of a full jazz band. Its provenance is murky. One explanation has it deriving from "scuffle," a word understood to be commonly used by African Americans in the sense of "scuffling for a living." The performance of this informal and impromptu music, making use of basic instrumentation, flourished in the States during the Great Depression, at house parties where neighbors and friends would get together and all contribute money to pay the host's rent. But how it got its name is less important than what it came to be thousands of miles away, and what it was musically is less important than what it came to mean in that same British context. As Ian Whitcomb freely admits:

> We cared little about the painful American origins of this music—of down-trodden blacks and hillbillies, of murderers (Lead Belly) and Communist dupes (Woody Guthrie). We just liked the slashing rhythm that got faster and faster and the fact that this was DIY music involving household objects: a tea chest, a broom handle and string for the bass and washboard and thimbles for the drums, plus Uncle's cast-aside guitar for the chords. There weren't many chords needed—three would do nicely. The hitherto unbreachable gates of popular music, guarded by double-breasted dance band leaders and sneering, slouching jazz musicians were at last opened to a merry band of amateurs, fuelled by folksy enthusiasm and Merrydown cider. ("Chas McDevitt")

Skiffle was played fast and rhythmical. Where any purchase was necessary, its instruments were cheap to buy. As Whitcomb confirms, it required minimal musical expertise, utilizing few keys and chords. A skiffle lineup typically featured acoustic guitars and an acoustic washtub or tea-chest bass, often augmented by banjo, washboard, and even kazoo.

At its peak, between 1956 and 1958, there were estimated to be anywhere from five thousand to upward of forty thousand groups enthusiastically plying their rudimentary trade across Britain. The vast majority of these never graduated beyond their own living rooms, but those with confidence and the right connections could find themselves playing local church halls and summer fetes. The very pinnacle of achievement for any skiffle group would be to perform in a coffee bar— a venue that attracted and catered to a very different clientele than that served by the dance bands of the pop mainstream, which played larger, industry-sanctioned concert halls and ballrooms.

A full twenty years before punk is claimed to have achieved this, skiffle sparked a DIY musical revolution, as thousands of young Brits without any formal knowledge or training threw themselves enthusiastically into it. Yet, although skiffle's significance should perhaps be best measured as live, participatory performance, its recorded examples undoubtedly helped widen its reach and so helped to further agitate British youth culture. Recorded in July 1954 and released in the wake of

Haley's success on major label Decca, Lonnie Donegan's skiffle version of "Rock Island Line" spent a total of twenty-two weeks on the best-seller list and peaked at number eight in February 1956, beating Elvis Presley to the British chart by four months. All told, it spent eight months on the singles chart and became the first debut 45 rpm disc in British recording history to sell more than five hundred thousand copies. With estimated global sales of three million, "Rock Island Line" signaled British rock's awkward adolescence, if not quite its coming-of-age. Although its American roots unquestionably showed, this jaunty tale of a freight train driver and his smuggling runs along the Chicago, Rock Island, and Pacific Railroad still oozed Britishness. "Rock Island Line" had been ham-fistedly adapted from the repertoire of the American blues singer Huddie "Leadbelly" Ledbetter. One acerbic critic described Donegan sounding more like northern English music-hall comedian and ukulele player George Formby than Leadbelly, as his accent continually slips from a frankly risible approximation of a Southern accent to something much closer to home. Yet the key to understanding this particular and peculiar record's cultural import lies in recognizing the extent to which it sparked a genuinely empowering grassroots and participatory musical practice. "Rock Island Line" was a catalyst, an enabler, planting the thought in the minds of British teens that they could do something similar. It is not coincidental that annual guitar sales rocketed from around five thousand in the early 1950s to more than a quarter of a million in skiffle's annus mirabilis, 1957.

However derivative and clunky his performance on "Rock Island Line," Lonnie Donegan still offered up something infinitely more credible than the likes of the Deep River Boys, Tony Crombie, or even Tommy Steele—and the majority of British teens knew it. And "Rock Island Line" resonated even deeper because it was apparently attainable, because it could be replicated. In *The Restless Generation*, Pete Frame notes how skiffle's fan base was "top-heavy with teenagers who regarded 'Rock Island Line' as a project, a blue-print. . . . It was *Boy's Own* paper, it was Saturday morning pictures at the flea-pit, it was Americana, it was history, it was romance, it was off-beat and rebellious, it was unpalatable and incomprehensible to old fogies, a generation gap widener. . . . It was exciting, even though no sex or dancing was involved. We could do this! The wash-board was the key. Plenty of them lying around. Let's have a go" (94).

With its slashing rhythms and manic tempo shifts, "Rock Island Line" literally and symbolically shredded the bland fare served up in the schmaltzy name of pop at this time. However, a combination of industry unease and the relatively short-lived nature of a moment whose significance was more in the *making* than the consuming meant that there were few other big skiffle hit records. The five-piece Vipers had formed in London in the spring of 1956 and soon earned a residency in Soho's 2i's Coffee Bar, which became a crucible for skiffle in the capital. They eventually signed with EMI imprint Parlophone in September 1956, on the recommendation of future Beatles' producer George Martin. Peaking at number ten in 1957, the Vipers' "Don't You Rock Me, Daddy-o" reworked "Sail Away Ladies," a 1920s rural Tennessee string-band hoedown, into contemporary skiffle. Thanks in no small measure to the studio efforts of the sympathetic Martin, the record managed to capture and communicate the raw, loose, and unrestrained excitement of a live performance—making it a more credible (and creditable) effort at encapsulating the spirit of rock 'n' roll than the likes of the Rockets and the Deep River Boys had managed thus far. Its remodeled chorus now featured the title that was gleefully embraced by Pete Frame, Ian Whitcomb, and thousands of others as some kind of teenage war cry, while, elsewhere in the song, the raw and shouty lyric went to places that British youth could not help but find liberating and exhilarating in equal measure: "Mister leave that girl alone / She got what she wants at home" or "Goin' upstairs to pack my trunk / Find me a bar and get me drunk." Sex, intoxication, and mobility—what's not to like?

Where skiffle is concerned, however, record sales and chart statistics are less important than the fact that this was a popular music whose significance would ultimately rest on its ability to inspire participation. As Ian Whitcomb points out, "Skiffle was an excuse for a knees-up in our grey shorts, a way to enjoy the excitement of Bill Haley–style rock 'n' roll without the expense of electric guitars, saxophones and Scotch plaid dinner jackets" ("Chas McDevitt"). Skiffle's rise in Britain had a powerful and lasting impact on a generation's pop musical aspirations. For this reason, many have made the case, with good cause, for Lonnie Donegan to be considered the founding father of British rock music. When Donegan performed a show at Liverpool's Empire Theatre on November 11, 1956, an enthralled fourteen-year-old Paul McCartney was in the audience; and, a few months later, in July 1957, McCartney would be invited to join the Quarrymen, who billed themselves as "Country and Western, Rock 'n' Roll, *and Skiffle* Performers." Other musicians who began their careers playing skiffle include Van Morrison (the Sputniks), the Rolling Stones' Ronnie Wood (the Candy Bison Skiffle Group) and Mick Jagger (the Barber-Colyer Skiffle Group), the Hollies' Graham Nash and Allan Clarke (the Two Teens), Deep Purple's Ritchie Blackmore and Roger Glover, Dire Straits' Mark Knopfler, Led Zeppelin's Jimmy Page, and the Beatles' George Harrison (the Rebels and the Quarrymen). "All you needed was an acoustic guitar, a wash-board with thimbles for percussion, and tea-chest," Harrison explained at the height of the Beatles' fame. "And you just put a broom handle on it and a bit of string, and you had a bass. You only needed two chords . . . and I think that's basically where I've always been at. *I'm just a skiffler, you know. Now I do posh skiffle, that's all it is*" (qtd. in Maconie 33, my emphasis).

While Lonnie Donegan reportedly loathed rock 'n' roll, and would tell anyone who would listen that it was a gimmick that would not last, it hardly mattered what Donegan said or thought. Fans of skiffle were more often than not fans of rock 'n' roll, too; and, in common with most practitioners of the former, we know that the Quarrymen's leader John Lennon, for example, was listening to the likes of Presley and Chuck Berry at the same time. This connection was made easier by the fact that skiffle and rock 'n' roll shared three key traits: an exaggerated use of guitars, an exaggerated use of the offbeat, and an exaggerated style of mouthing the words. Lonnie Donegan often used electric guitars and drums as he toured Britain's bigger venues in the wake of his skiffle hits. Whether forced into amplification or not, he found himself playing with rock 'n' rollers, and so cementing the bond of exaggeration that existed between the two forms. For the majority of skifflers, though, there were no precious principles to swallow, since—if they thought about it at all—the fact was that both styles drew from similarly exotic African American source material and so mixing the two seemed pretty natural. However, the two forms could not ultimately coexist. Skiffle fizzled out, while rock 'n' roll triumphed. Something that has been put down to largely industry-generated pressures: because skiffle did not produce a marketable teen idol, because skiffle's rough-and-ready music lacked appealing guitar wizardry and sax work, and because the business was simply more comfortable with adolescent lyrics and tamer sounds. Yet, whatever the reasons for it, it was clear that skiffle's "death" had not been in vain. In retrospect, it did not matter that skiffle failed to last. It had done its job. With the funds to purchase more expensive equipment and a need to reach growing audiences in larger venues, it is not surprising that skiffle bands should mutate into rock 'n' roll bands. For those that stuck with it, the limitations of skiffle proved surmountable, as musical ranges were expanded.

Skiffle was symbolic, symptomatic, and a driver of change that was manifest nationwide, on a number of levels. With musical amateurism now firmly established, British teens who were dissatisfied with industry-sanctioned pale imitations and polished imports went looking for live music with a stronger beat. While a handful of credible British rock 'n' roll records did emerge in the years after skiffle's demise, tracks such as Cliff Richard's "Move It" (1958), Vince Taylor and the Playboys' Parlophone single "Brand New Cadillac" (1959), and especially Johnny Kidd and the Pirates' "Shakin' All Over" (1960) represented no more than a very thin and rickety bridge to the beat boom that in turn spawned the Invasion. By 1961, the rock 'n' roll boom looked like a lucrative fad that had pretty much run its course. Just as the British pop music industry had hoped it would. One of the year's biggest pop hits was avuncular West Country jazzman Acker Bilk's soporific "Stranger on the Shore," which occupied the UK singles chart for fifty-five weeks. However, appearances could be deceptive. In April 1960, the American pop idol Bobby Darin told *Melody Maker* that "I'll never tour Britain again in a rock 'n' roll package show [because] I have found British audiences the noisiest I have played to anywhere in the world," suggesting the existence and persistence of something notably outside of the dominant show business model that held sway at the time. Just as with skiffle, what came to be known as beat music thrived in the provinces.

While the transformation of rock 'n' roll into pop has been recognized as also occurring at pace in the United States during this period, there is a crucial difference in terms of each nation's response to this industry-sponsored dilution—and one that would ultimately help explain why the British Invasion hit America so hard in early 1964. Put simply, catalyzed by skiffle, in Britain music *making* became prominent. Beat was initially a regional and local dance club alternative to national, officially sanctioned forms of popular music backed by the music business and organs like the BBC—representing, like skiffle before it, a genuine outburst of grassroots music making. It was a muscular response to the music industry's failure to give many British teens what they craved, the net result being that, in the early 1960s, it continued skiffle's project of actively using popular music as means of personal expression. Driven by the music of the British Invasion, this is a function that would consequently transform the American pop scene, too.

Beat music emerged as young Britons sought to honor their American favorites, while making a living playing in raucous clubs with enough loud energy to simply be heard. As a solution to these problems, beat developed the standard, and enduring, rock group format—lead and bass guitars, with a third rhythm guitar, drums, and vocalist, sometimes augmented by piano, organ, or harmonica—and here drew direct inspiration (and material) from a carefully selected pool of American artists. Principal among these influences was Buddy Holly and the Crickets, whose successful British records importantly showcased this rock group dynamic. Through 1958 and 1959 Buddy Holly and the Crickets enjoyed considerable British chart success with "Maybe Baby" (no. 3), "Rave On" (no. 5), "Heartbeat" (no. 30), "It Doesn't Matter" (no. 1), "Love's Made a Fool of Me" (no. 26), and "Peggy Sue Got Married" (no. 13). There is plenty of evidence, in fact, to suggest that they were, if anything, more popular in Britain than in their native United States. The Beatles named themselves after Holly's band, with John Lennon changing the "ee" to "ea" to make a punning reference to beat—"First hearing Buddy absolutely knocked me for a loop" (John Lennon qtd. in Miles, *British Invasion*, 24). Lennon and many other aspiring beat musicians responded to the liberating antivirtuosity in the music of the Crickets. Hits like "That'll Be the Day"—which quickly became a fixture in the Quarrymen's set—communicated this in spades, and so of course had an obvious appeal for young Brits schooled in skiffle. In marked contrast to the post–Sun Records Elvis Presley then, Holly—and Eddie Cochran, too—came across as mere mortals. It was important that heroes should be within touching distance: "The very first tune I ever learned to play was 'That'll Be the Day.' . . . My mother taught me to play it on the banjo, sitting there with endless patience until I managed to work out the all the chords" (John Lennon qtd. in Black 25).

Brian Poole, beat group front man and future British Invader, confirms that Buddy Holly's influence was widespread at the time:

> Buddy Holly and the Crickets were the loudest thing we'd ever heard. It was a small band but they made such a crack when they came on and it was very, very exciting. We were doing Buddy Holly songs for the next five years. At one stage there was nothing in our act that wasn't a Buddy Holly song. We were so much into Buddy Holly that I had hair and glasses just like him. (Qtd. in Miles, *British Invasion*, 24)

Furthermore, Holly's impact transcended such strenuous efforts to slavishly cover his material. "The big attraction with somebody like Buddy was that he wrote his own stuff and it was three chords. For people looking at the idea of writing their own stuff, it was great, because we didn't know more than four or five chords" (McCartney qtd. in Black 25).

Alongside Buddy Holly, Chuck Berry was almost as important as a catalyst. His influence was felt particularly strongly in the UK, as he toured there more frequently than any other American rock 'n' roller. Between 1957 and 1966 the Beatles performed more songs penned by Chuck Berry than anyone. (They performed more songs sung by Elvis than anyone, but of course Presley did not write his own material.) Berry's influence is also heard in Beatles' compositions like "I Saw Her Standing There" (1963), for example, which appeared to lift its bass line from Berry's "I'm Talkin' 'bout You." Eddie Cochran was also highly influential. His "Twenty-Flight Rock" was the song Paul McCartney auditioned to join the Quarrymen back in 1957. Hits like "Summertime Blues" (no. 18, 1958), "C'mon Everybody" (no. 6, 1959), and the 1960 UK number one "Three Steps to Heaven" made Cochran—much like Holly—arguably a greater success in Britain, where his vocal and guitar styles were particularly well received.

With beat, it appeared that its practitioners had found an effective and culturally specific way of packaging much of rock 'n' roll's original threat and promise, so that, although this music might still have been about the leisure, values, and pleasures of U.S. high school teens, it also managed to communicate a meaningful resonance for its predominantly working-class constituency of young Brits. In this, beat music represented precisely the sum of that process of adaptation and appropriation discussed earlier in terms of the strategic uses to which U.S. popular culture might be put. Like skiffle before it, the beat scene was very much about *making* and doing, not simply the essentially passive (though still potentially empowering) activity of consuming, listening, or even dancing. It has been estimated that there were thousands of amateur beat groups in Britain from the late 1950s on, with several hundred graduating to semi- or full professional status. George Tremlett, for example, has claimed that there were twenty thousand beat groups by 1963, with four hundred alone operating in the Liverpool area (qtd. in Bradley 73). Such numbers are difficult to confirm, but what was clear was that—at least until the Beatles came to nationwide prominence in early 1963—virtually all these groups existed on the very margins of British mass culture. For the time being, there were to be no recording contracts with the Big Four, and no television or radio appearances.

Musically, beat was marked by flexibility and versatility. Rhythm guitar chords were typically broken up into a series of separate strokes, often one to the bar, backed by a regular, plodding bass and crisp drumming. The defining "beat," then, was a product of the interplay between all three instruments, and the flexibility was demonstrated by the incorporation of a greater range of time signatures and song structure than the normally monolithic rock 'n' roll had embraced thus far. Although working under the influence of American models, British beat groups were not slavish copyists. Indeed, their output—honed live and subsequently recorded—revealed the extent to which willful adaptation and necessity combined to produce something rather different. Ironically, as Gordon Thompson has pointed out, the fact that beat groups were often still consciously imitating American musical models that had been discarded by the U.S. pop mainstream—such as, for example, the guitarcentric rockabilly stylings of the Crickets, Berry, and Cochran—only contributed positively to the music's development. Here, then, the time delay or lag under which British beat musicians were forced to operate was actually a source of strength. As the Beatles' first UK album *Please Please Me* (1963) would illustrate, beat groups shoehorned all the sounds they heard on their favorite American records into the two-guitar, bass, and drums format, remodeling those brass solos, string arrangements, and even female vocals as they did so. Thus, *Please Please Me* featured a beat reworking of the Shirelles' B-side "Boys"; the

McCartney-penned "P.S. I Love You," which had been written as a companion piece to the Shirelles' "Soldier Boy"; and a similarly beat-y cover of the Isley Brothers' "Twist and Shout."

The Beatles had played their first show as the Beatles on February 9, 1961, at Liverpool's city-center Cavern Club. As their reputation as a live act grew, they became figureheads of the beat subgenre, Mersey-beat—a mix of black-influenced pop songs with faster, more aggressive rock 'n' roll. In the early 1960s, Liverpool was noted as a musical melting pot, where country, jazz, and other genres freely mixed. However, what was happening on Merseyside was certainly not unique. So, while Liverpool could boast a large number of beat groups, things were no different elsewhere in the UK. The Beatles stood out because, quite simply, they were talented, driven, canny, and lucky—and their success radiated outward, inevitably leading the way for other Liverpool bands, then other beat bands, then other "Invaders," and even American musicians. In February 1963, John Lennon told *Melody Maker*: "We don't play real rhythm and blues. . . . Our musical tastes are various—we like a little bit of classical music, a bit of modern jazz, a bit of everything. . . . One artist I like is Arthur Alexander—you don't hear much of him over here."

In the same interview, Lennon also claimed the Beatles' distinctive sound stemmed from working "without echo"—because "we didn't like it." Later that same year, in August, Lennon was forced to defend the band's sound: "I know what the critics say—that we don't play rhythm and blues. I've never thought we did. We just play rock as far as I'm concerned—in our way. We have nothing to do with rhythm and blues in a strict sense."

This defense in the name of eclecticism was borne out on the band's first album. Half the tracks on *Please Please Me* were covers of African American ballads and soul songs by the likes of the Marvelettes, the Drifters, and the Miracles, with only "Twist and Shout" qualifying as a bona fide rhythm and blues song. Of the early self-compositions, Beatles scholars have identified an original like "Ask Me Why" as an example of Lennon consciously composing in the style of Motown's Smokey Robinson. As his cowriter Paul McCartney freely admits, "We started off by imitating Elvis, Buddy Holly, Chuck Berry, Carl Perkins, Gene Vincent . . . the Coasters, the Drifters—we just copied what they did" (qtd. in Wicke 64).

Between 1961 and 1964, with hundreds of Liverpool groups competing for attention, the scene was recorded in a local paper. On July 6, 1961, Bill Harry published the first edition of *Mersey Beat*, which featured John Lennon's piece "On the Dubious Origins of the Beatles." It sold five thousand copies. The second edition, published two weeks later, featured the Beatles on the cover, and has been credited with encouraging Brian Epstein to visit the Cavern Club to see what all the fuss was about. That the rather starchy figure of Epstein should be drawn to the Cavern demonstrated beat music's deep impact. It also implied a significance that, even in 1962, threatened to transcend the level of mere entertainment. As the Beatles "delivered their American obsessions with infectious verve [they] also reflected British youth's joyful sense of being cultural outsiders, ready to seize everything new, and everything that their surrounding society tried to prohibit them" (Gilmore 26); and because BBC radio continued to largely ignore it, it was down to ITV's newly minted *Ready Steady Go!* to capture and project this potentially revolutionary energy by showcasing British pop culture, and beat music in particular. To do this, of course, the show needed a ready supply of beat product if it were to credibly bottle the zeitgeist. In January 1962 the Beatles had unsuccessfully auditioned for Decca. Although by their own admission they did poorly, this rejection illustrated just how entrenched and out of touch the mainstream pop music business was at this time—Decca famously declaring that guitar groups were on the way out. Having been reluctantly signed up by EMI—but pointedly contracted to what was essentially its novelty imprint Parlophone—the Beatles' first single was released in October 1962. "Love Me Do" had been written while Paul McCartney was playing hooky from Liverpool Institute in 1958. Although McCartney has claimed that he was trying to "do the blues," it is arguably closer to skiffle in sonic character. Unsurprising, given its genesis. However, given the vogue for echo-laden melodramatic pop that held sway at the time, "Love Me Do" stood out as willfully primitive in late 1962. It has more in common with a track like the skiffle classic "Don't You Rock Me, Daddy-o" (1957), its breezy, casual, and unpretentious charms complemented by a superdry George Martin production. For this reason alone, then, while an unremarkable debut in many respects, the track still stands as the earliest indication of the "free-spirited un-orthodoxies" that would characterize so much of the band's recorded output

(MacDonald 77). While the song's vocal harmonizing might have been modeled on that of the Everly Brothers—another of the Beatles' American favorites—it is evidently rough hewn. Yet this did not ultimately prove to be a weakness. Far from it. The northern vowels of "Love Me Do"—its unapologetically provincial delivery, its conscious denial of mid-Atlantic phrasing—contribute greatly to an honesty that did not go unnoticed at the time. Andrew Loog Oldham said in *Mojo*, "I thought the record was amazing, it had space, mood and sex . . . something British pop records didn't often do. . . . It had certainty and attitude, something which I'd previously looked for Dion and the Belmonts and Eddie Cochran to provide."

The modest chart success enjoyed by the Beatles' first single—which peaked at number seventeen in the winter of 1962—nevertheless confirmed that beat music had finally broken through nationally; and so, now convinced that there was a reassuringly limited but lucrative future for guitar groups, the British pop music business took note, caught up, and rapidly transformed the existing scene, by signing up bands and swamping the market with beat product.

The Beatles' next UK single, "Please Please Me" (1963), noticeably upped the ante—being more definably and definitively beat in character than its rather skiffle-y predecessor. Eschewing pop's usual appeal to puppy love, the song's lyrical content aligned it with the grown-up sexual politics of rhythm and blues—particularly when Lennon rasps out the simultaneously pleading and lascivious "c'mons" in the chorus. Possibly drawing on James Brown's "Please Please Please" (1956) for inspiration, there is a palpable sexual tension and frustration in this song that is absent from "Love Me Do"—"Please please me / like I please you." Yet it could have been very different. "Please Please Me" had been initially presented to George Martin as a languid Orbisonesque ballad, which the producer had declared "dreary." Speeded up and beefed up with urgent chord changes, a harmonica part, and some muscular drumming, the track was transformed. Although not quite the "fifth Beatle" as some have claimed, this early example of George Martin's creative intervention nevertheless emphasizes his importance. As so many self-composed songs do, particularly in the band's early output, "Please Please Me" betrays its obvious American influences—with a call-and-response chorus in the classic rhythm and blues dance style and falsetto parts that are arguably indebted to one of their other American musical idols, Little Richard.

Please Please Me was also the title of the Beatles' first UK album, released in March 1963. For many British teens now with the funds to support the habit, it provided an introduction to the world of the album—sparking an important shift that would eventually transform the production and consumption of pop music on both sides of the Atlantic. *Please Please Me* was the nation's best-selling album for an unprecedented thirty weeks. In fact, it took the Beatles' second UK album, *With the Beatles*, to finally knock it off the top spot in late November. *Please Please Me*'s impact, though, was not confined purely to the level of the commercial. This record played a major part in establishing the idea that the pop album was more than the sum of its individual parts—more than randomly sequenced singles, B-sides, and filler. Many of the tracks featured on *Please Please Me* had been honed live. In this way, the album is effectively a performance for tape—or "recital" as Martin has referred to it—reflecting the band's accumulated knowledge on how to structure this performance drawn from hundreds of gigs. With their very first long-form record, the Beatles were looking to consciously fashion the pop album into a kind of artistic statement. On *Please Please Me*, then, "each of the two sides . . . is structured like a suspension bridge, with firm footings at the ends supporting a thinning span toward the middle" (Gould 147–48). So it is that the strongest tracks open and close each side ("I Saw Her Standing There" and "Please Please Me" on side one, and "Love Me Do" and "Twist and Shout" on side two) with the remaining ten tracks in the "thinning span" composed of beat rockers (like "Boys") and ballads (like "Anna"). The decision to position the band's highly successful single "Please Please Me" at the end of side one of the album represented a noteworthy departure from the usual company-dictated practice of (over)loading the hits at the record's start. Yet more evidence of the group's bravery and self-confidence.

Please Please Me's fourteen tracks were recorded in just twenty-five hours, with ten of the songs taped in an exhausting twelve-hour session on February 11. Remarkably, eight of the tracks were self-composed—something unheard of on either side of the Atlantic at that time, and especially noteworthy coming as it did from a pop band at the very start of their recording career. *Please Please Me* then marked the dawning of the age of the self-sufficient pop group whose members would generate most, if not all, of their own material, and therefore represented the first of a number of key moments peppering the Beatles' life span that would inspire others to actively create rather than passively consume. In this way, *Please Please Me* marked the beginning of a fundamental shift in the "status and subjectivity of the pop musician" (Blake, *Land*, 92). With their very first album release, the Beatles carved out space in which creative autonomy could be exercised, and thus made a game-changing contribution to popular music practice. With this record, then, a "comfortable and insular system was interrupted . . . principally by the establishing of John Lennon and Paul McCartney as songwriters as well as performers. This marks a most important interruption both in the way in which the music business worked (i.e., in terms of the flow of capital) and in the relationship between British pop and the American model. . . . [And] because of this redirection of earnings the writer-performer became more important in the political economy of music-making, and potentially at least, a more independent figure" (Blake, *Land*, 90–91).

The album opens with the brash rocker "I Saw Her Standing There"—a track whose rough blues changes encapsulated the grooves British pop music would be moving in from now on, as it announced emphatically the distance traveled from Tin Pan Alley. Producer George Martin reportedly retained Paul McCartney's live introductory count-off because he felt it was redolent of Beatles gigs at Liverpool clubs like the Cavern and the Casbah. Martin had initially wanted to record a Beatles gig and release it as an album. This idea had to be shelved—Martin said of the Cavern that it had the "acoustic ambience of an oil tank" (qtd. in Gould 147)—but technological and time limitations, together with the band's energy and rawness, made this studio-produced album (with all its bum notes and wonky harmonies) close to "live" as was possible. "All we did really," Martin recalls, "was to reproduce the Cavern performance in the relative calm of the studio" (qtd. in Riley 58), and it is *Please Please Me*'s first and last tracks that most effectively capture and communicate on vinyl what the Beatles could achieve as live performers. This was a strategy deemed to be so effective that it would be employed several months later on the Beatles' second studio album, which opens with the self-penned "It Won't Be Long" and closes with the band's cover of "Money."

While some consider the count-off that opens "I Saw Her Standing There" to be as portentous and exhilarating as Elvis Presley's "Well, it's a-one for the money" (with which he had kicked off his first album seven years earlier), for many it was the album's closing track, an utterly unselfconscious version of the Isley Brothers' 1962 American hit "Twist and Shout," that is the highlight. Lennon's shredded vocal—which to George Martin sounded "rather like tearing flesh"—delivered a climax that arguably comes closest to fulfilling Martin's intention to capture the band "as live." It is raw, urgent, and explosive—a one-take affirmation of rock 'n' roll's threat and promise that transformed the Isleys' loose-limbed original into a beat-ified wall of noise. Emphasizing the bass line, doubling it up with Harrison's guitar, and then augmenting it with some seriously meaty drumming produced an ur-beat track, the likes of which had not been heard up until now in British pop.

Through the summer and fall of 1963 Britain experienced a home invasion. The Beatles' third single, "From Me to You," was the UK's best-selling single for seven weeks through May and June, while "She Loves You"—the band's fourth single—hit number one in September 1963, selling an unprecedented 750,000 copies in its first month on release to make it Britain's fastest-selling record in any format to date. Written and recorded in the space of one week in July, "She Loves You" was organized chaos as pop noise, a thrilling jumble of percussion, guitars, voices, hooks, and harmonies that exploded into life in arresting fashion with the chorus, and simply did not stop exploding thereafter. Rich, sugary, and addictive, "She Loves You" was dessert-only songwriting. As the sessions for *Please Please Me* had demonstrated, "getting a really loud rhythm sound" (qtd. in Gould 157) was key to George Martin's aim to capture and effectively communicate the band's live sound on record. With this record, it would appear that his mission had been accomplished. If "Twist and Shout" was ur-beat, then "She Loves You" was ur-*Beatles*.

On vinyl and particularly when performed live, "She Loves You" incited rapture. A bemused Lonnie Donegan—now well and truly usurped in the affections of young British pop fans—observed at the time, "A strange bedlam was taking over which had nothing to do with anything we had previously known" (qtd. in Chambers 50). Donegan might not have named it as such, but this was Beatlemania. Early Beatles songs, of which "She Loves You" remains arguably the ultimate example, joyously and brazenly "celebrated the pleasures of getting through, of listening, being heard, telling and touching" (Bromell 30)—vital connective prerequisites for Beatlemania, which combined opportunity for expression and release. In "She Loves You," calculated moments of direct address abound. It is "fresh"—a descriptor fans on both sides of the Atlantic would frequently apply to explain the band's appeal—because it is so inclusive, because it is about a triangular relationship sung in the third person, with the Beatles playing the role of the caring, mediating friend—"You think you've lost your love" but if you "apologise to her," then you'll find that "she loves you / and you know you should be glad."

"She Loves You" possessed an astonishing unity of purpose, in which the music energetically embraced its listeners from the opening bar and was quickly joined in this work by its superinclusive lyric. In its formal and thematic perfection, then, it proved to be a most effective carrier of the UK strain of Beatlemania. When the song was performed live, the fans seemed to match the band scream for scream. "She Loves You" was a primer in Beatlemania—an audio instruction manual, if such a text were really needed by this time, that enabled and encouraged fans to identify both with the Beatles and each other.

Although the epidemic had spread to millions of British teens through the summer and early fall of 1963, first mention of Beatlemania did not occur until October. On October 13 the Beatles had appeared on ITV's *Sunday Night at the London Palladium*—a performance watched by fifteen million that climaxed with "She Loves You." The next day, in the wake of this appearance and reports of the screaming fans that had greeted the band outside the theater, the British press declared the nation to be in the grip of "Beatlemania." A few weeks later, the Beatles featured on the bill of the prestigious *Royal Variety Show*, which subsequently drew twenty-six million viewers, approximately half the population, when televised. They performed four songs, including "She Loves You," which returned to number one on the UK singles chart as a result. In the royal box, Princess Margaret reportedly led the enthusiastic applause, while the Queen Mother smiled as Lennon delivered his famous invitation to those in the posh seats to "rattle yer jewelry" if clapping was beneath them. This performance was also noticeable for an example of Beatles' savvy, as they included a cover of the Broadway standard "Till There Was You" in their miniset in a calculated appeal to a wider audience. They were to do something similar on their *Ed Sullivan Show* appearances three months later.

By the end of 1963 it was as if—in Ian MacDonald's memorable phrase—"the nation's centre of gravity slipped from upper lip to lower hip" (60)—a transformation fueled and documented by beat music that could be further gauged by reviewing the year's singles chart. Whereas the weeks between January and May 1963 had seen pangenerational, sing-along best sellers from Cliff Richard ("Summer Holiday" and "Bachelor Boy"), Frank Ifield ("Wayward Wind"), and the instrumental group the Shadows ("Foot Tapper"); the second half of the year had witnessed a significant changing of the pop guard, as Liverpool bands—produced by George Martin, managed by Brian Epstein, and performing songs published by Dick James—held the number-one position in the UK singles chart for a total of thirty weeks through the spring, summer, and fall, supplying eight of the nation's twelve best sellers. At Christmas, there was nothing to suggest that the beat boom had run its course. On the eve of the British Invasion, the Beatles' "I Want to Hold Your Hand" was the nation's best-selling single.

2

"WE'RE OUT!"

1964

By the summer of 1964 the Beatles would prove themselves the first notably non-American act to achieve international stardom in the mass media age. Of course, key to achieving this global superstar status was conquering the American market—an unprecedented feat for a British pop act. Explanations for how and why they managed this success are generally regarded by critics like Millard, for example, as the result of that unique combination of being in the right place at the right time (41). Certainly, basic demographics pointed to an opportunity to exploit the mass consumption of pop music. "By 1964, about 40 percent of all Americans were aged twenty or less, and seventeen-year-olds were the largest age cohort in the United States, a lucrative market for a range of consumer goods and services including records" (Millard 138). But even demographics cannot explain why *the Beatles* should sell so many records to American teens. True, timing cannot be discounted as a critical factor in their success, but it was not by any means the only one. You only had to attempt to comprehend the hysteria they generated in Britain to see this.

However, although it is perhaps too simplistic to argue that Beatlemania was firmly rooted in the cold and clinical realm of economics, it is equally pat to suggest that it was purely a manifestation of American youth's desperately romantic need of the good times that only the Beatles could promise and deliver. Indeed, this explanation has become a near cliché. And so it is, for the Grateful Dead's Jerry Garcia, for example, that the Beatles supplied "a happy flash . . . like the first good news" (qtd. in Millard 39), while even the normally temperate Ian MacDonald has suggested that they pulled the nation out of its post-Kennedy-assassination slough of despond like so much pop musical Prozac. Yet, a cliché achieves its status as a cliché presumably only because it has some basis in a—if not necessarily the—truth. American Beatlemania was undeniably unprecedented. Some pop acts may well have rivaled or even surpassed the Beatles in terms of units sold, "but *without getting under people's skins, or provoking anything like a collective swoon. . . . It was as if*," James Miller writes in his memoir, *Almost Grown*, "a large segment of the population had fallen suddenly, and hopelessly, in love—the feeling of shared pleasure was that intense" (213, my emphasis). Clearly, the nature and depth of this relationship would not have developed in the way it did had it not been for a variety of key determining factors. So, for example, the Beatles could be seen to have functioned as a relief from unspecified if still palpable Cold War anxieties. As noted above, it has been suggested that they offered potentially more targeted relief from the collective depression that is commonly believed to have afflicted the nation following Kennedy's assassination. Furthermore, at a time when rock 'n' roll's originators had been sidelined and pop seemed self-absorbed, stale and lifeless, and largely driven by fads and craze, their joyous and exciting music is said to have reinvigorated the mainstream, making them "Elvis to the power of four" (Miles, *British Invasion*, 8). So, while Andre Millard has argued that "you don't need a degree in Sociology or Psychology to understand why the Beatles conquered America in 1964, all you have to do is understand how all the new machines worked in their favour, and then do the Baby Boom math" (137), it does not seem unreasonable to suggest that "math" alone cannot fully explain the Invasion.

The U.S. media first took note of Beatlemania in the late fall of 1963, when *Time* magazine ran a short piece entitled "The New Madness" on the excesses of the fans. This was quickly followed by a similarly pitched and focused piece in *Newsweek*. On December 1 the *New York Times Magazine* featured an article headlined "Britons Succumb to Beatlemania," which was supported by photos of the band meeting royalty and their fans clashing with police, and through the rest of the month and into the new year *Life* magazine also ran a number of photo stories on

Beatlemania. December also saw the first TV feature, when CBS News aired a three-minute story on "adolescent adulation." The first media feature on the *music* appeared in a December edition of *Variety*, whose front page announced that "I Want to Hold Your Hand" had become the first 45 rpm record to achieve prerelease UK sales of more than a million copies. This was deemed particularly noteworthy, as it was something that had only happened once in the much bigger U.S. market, with Elvis Presley's "Hound Dog" in 1957. It was also reported that, in a market a third of America's size, "She Loves You" had also sold more than a million copies in the UK and that the Beatles' second album *With the Beatles* had sold half a million copies in a week. The message delivered loud and clear to America, then, was that "I Want to Hold Your Hand" was quite simply the fastest-selling single ever released anywhere in the world.

By Christmas 1963, Capitol Records—who had the distribution rights to Beatles product in the United States—had evidently received this message, and so were finally and fully on board with the Beatles project, agreeing to release and promote "I Want to Hold Your Hand" prior to the band's first visit. Capitol would then release and promote an album in tandem with the band's planned TV appearances in early February. In the event, that first U.S. album *Meet the Beatles* was actually rush-released and in stores by the third week of January. An estimated $40,000 was earmarked for a publicity campaign concentrated in the New York metropolitan area, which included the distribution of half a million stickers, flyers, and even a mock newspaper. This represented a financial outlay that eclipsed anything Capitol had committed to a single release thus far, and was certainly unprecedented in its hefty backing of a nonnative act.

Capitol's newfound ardor was of course motored by the promise of fat profits, but the company should perhaps have been reassured that their considerable investment would reap handsome returns in a cultural climate in which there was a healthy, well-established Anglophilia fostering favorable conditions for the reception of "Invasion" product. These were sympathetic circumstances further enhanced by the close and long-standing ties between the two nations that had been strengthened by both war- and peacetime alliance. (Of course, "funny" accents and haircuts notwithstanding, the Beatles looked smart and evidently worshipped at the American pop culture altar.) The strength of this fascination with, and the extent of the influence of, all things Brit could be seen in the late '50s success of the Broadway production of *My Fair Lady* and the five-million-plus original cast recordings sold, and in the stateside popularity of movies like *Around the World in Eighty Days* (1956). In 1963, half the big Broadway hits were British imports, while *Lawrence of Arabia*, *Tom Jones*, and the second James Bond outing, *From Russia with Love*, had been sizeable American box-office hits. Perhaps of greater significance given its class focus, sexual content, and apparent parochialism, *Room at the Top* had been a surprising U.S. hit in 1959—its success confirmed by a Best Actor Oscar nomination for Laurence Harvey and a win in the Best Actress category for Simone Signoret. In 1962 British director David Lean had won the coveted Best Director and Best Picture Oscars for *Lawrence of Arabia*, and his British leading man, Peter O'Toole, had also been nominated in the Best Actor category. In 1963, British director Tony Richardson picked up the Best Director Academy Award for *Tom Jones*, which also won the Oscar for Best Screen Adaptation and saw Albert Finney nominated in the Best Actor category. The unexpected Broadway success in 1962 of the Oxbridge satirical review *Beyond the Fringe* could well be viewed as a sign of things to come. Its mix of irreverence, satire, and surrealism arguably prepared the ground for one of the Beatles' key qualities— specifically, the refreshing humor and wit that would be communicated through their music, their jousting with the press, and of course through the movie *A Hard Day's Night*.

Recognizing this receptive American context, the Beatles' shrewd manager, Brian Epstein, knew that if he could create a stir in New York City, then there would be a good chance that the rest of the nation would follow if the right media channels could be exploited. In preparation for an assault on the U.S. market, it is sometimes claimed that Epstein had urged the Beatles to write with America in mind. However, their producer, George Martin, has always denied that "I Want to Hold Your Hand" was tailored for the United States. So it is more likely that Epstein simply claimed this to be the case in an effort to add weight to his strenuous efforts to persuade a reluctant Capitol to back the record.

At the time, Capitol was America's third-largest record company and since 1955 had been a subsidiary of the Beatles' label EMI. Yet it had passed on "Please Please Me" in spring 1963 and on each subsequent UK release. As a result of this, prior to December 1963, Beatles' singles were released without fanfare in the United States under license to small, independent labels like Chicago's African American–owned Vee-Jay and the Philadelphia-based, Dick Clark–owned Swan Records. Despite evidence in related cultural fields that should perhaps have suggested to them that Brits were "going down rather well" in the States, Capitol dragged its corporate feet on the Beatles through virtually all of 1963 for several reasons. Principal among these was conventional record business wisdom, which had it that the transatlantic trade in popular music moved in one direction, from west to east. In fairness to Capitol, the Beatles themselves appeared to share in this belief—"They've got their own groups," Paul McCartney is reported to have said. "What are we going to give them that they don't already have?" (qtd. in Gould 221). Even on that first flight to New York, with "I Want to Hold Your Hand" sitting at number one on the Billboard chart, the group had continued to express serious reservations and doubts about their chance of real success in America. Furthermore, like most of the country's major labels, Capitol also possessed an undisguised distaste for rock 'n' roll, which was demonstrated and (presumably) vindicated by its existing and commercially successful roster featuring Frank Sinatra, movie and Broadway soundtracks, classical musicians, and a Nashville-based country division. Capitol was also the home of the folk group the Kingston Trio, who had crossed over to enjoy mainstream pop success with over a dozen Top 10 albums in the late '50s and early '60s. The label's executive-led contempt for rock 'n' roll notwithstanding, it also had the Beach Boys on its books. For Capitol, the Beach Boys represented teen-pop pay dirt. With two hit singles and a hit album in 1963, it seemed reasonable for the company to conclude that it had successfully plugged that particular gap in the market. With Brian Wilson writing the apparently corporate-compliant, conformist anthem "Be True to Your School," Capitol's reluctance to back a relatively unknown pop commodity was perhaps even more understandable.

The Beatles flew to the United States for the first time on February 7, 1964, with modest ambition and expectation. Yet with hindsight, perhaps they should have been more confident of the likelihood of achieving success in America. "I Want to Hold Your Hand" had reached number one on January 17, 1964. Although Top 40 stations undoubtedly played their part, the record's success—and indeed all that followed—was not simply attributable to committed marketing, since it was clear that American teens genuinely wanted to hear Beatles music. In this, there were some obvious parallels with the function, appeal, and impact of "She Loves You" in Britain a few months earlier. Coming on like "She Loves You *Part Two*," "I Want to Hold Your Hand" communicated the Beatles' appealing brand of energy and attitude with particular effectiveness in an American context. Just as "She Loves You" had, the track packaged "their belief, voiced again and again, in the redemptive possibilities of communication. Of love" (Bromell 29). And just as it had done for British teenagers with "She Loves You," this played a vital role in the development of that pretty unique bond between the band and their young American audience that was a prerequisite of Beatlemania, as they continued to make explicit contact with "You." Just as "She Loves You" had been, "I Want to Hold Your Hand" was stuffed to the musical gills. It also exerted a similarly powerful connective embrace—establishing what Tacchi has called an "affective dimension" via consumption that might supply a sense of belonging. Not by any stretch is "I Want to Hold Your Hand" a deep lyric, as its many detractors gleefully pointed out. However, these critics were surely missing the point. For, the song's simplicity—its banality even—was actually a source of its power, particularly in its highly receptive American context. For there was "comfort, reassurance, and even consolation" to be found in the "image of holding hands" that might see it function "as a common denominator of human connection between friends and lovers alike" (Gould 214).

In order to fully work its transformative magic, the Beatles' music undoubtedly required a highly specific context. This had been duly shaped by the murder of John F. Kennedy. In the month or so between their manager making his first business trip to New York and the release of "I Want to Hold Your Hand," America had lost its president to an assassin's bullet and had been mourning his death. While not consciously exploiting this situation, the Beatles' status as "outsiders" surely granted them license to commit acts in the name of joy that homegrown pop acts may have felt uncomfortable dealing in so soon after the national tragedy. Although, as a nation, America overcame its collective grief fairly swiftly, Martha Wolfenstein and Gilbert W. Kliman's 1965 study, *Children and the Death of a President*, confirmed that its teenagers proved a notable exception to this. More than anything, the study highlighted this group's depth of feeling—an intensity of grief that neither diminished nor resolved as quickly as it did among other demographic groups; Wolfenstein and Kliman concluded that it was the strength of this emotional connection that led teenagers to experience Kennedy's passing so keenly. So, while homegrown pop respectfully stood back, for the Beatles there was to be no such sensitivity. "I Want to Hold Your Hand" granted grateful American teens cathartic release, permission to "Let go—feel how good it is" (MacDonald 79).

By the first week of February "I Want to Hold Your Hand" had sold one and a half million copies in the United States, with estimated sales of half a million in the New York area. While, on one level, the song may have helped alleviate the pain of loss, in other respects it clearly *brought* pain. For it is often pointed out that the Beatles were a traumatic shock to a moribund American music scene; and though this critical consensus is arguably oversimplified—partial even—there can be no doubting its broad brushstroke veracity with teen idols like Frankie Avalon, Fabian, and Bobby Rydell in the ascendant, performing bland material with little of the raw charge of midfifties rock 'n' roll. For many observers, the final straw had been the rise of the Singing Nun's "Dominique" to the very top of the Billboard chart late in 1963.

By 1964, rock 'n' roll was firmly established on the American popular music landscape. So well established, in fact, that it seemed to have become just another highly lucrative arm of the mainstream entertainment business. Those ingredients that first attracted teenagers to the music in the mid-1950s—the excitement, the sexual energy, the fact that your parents did not like it, the threat it carried—appeared to have been discarded or suppressed in favor of an altogether safer recipe. In its purest incarnation, rock 'n' roll represented "a real threat to sobriety, virginity, wholesomeness, structure, Republicanism," making it "by genetic inheritance, completely outside of, and somehow threatening to, mainstream American culture." But that was then. Presumably, in a time before it had been "plucked from Long Tall Sally's alley, scrubbed up, and decked out in clean clothes" (Pichaske 25, 37, 47). Yet this process had in fact begun almost as soon as the music of Little Richard, Chuck Berry, and its other originators had appeared, leading to wholesome, "white-bread" performers like Pat Boone offering anemic covers of their songs. Little Richard has recounted the story in numerous interviews of how teenagers would smuggle his originals into their homes, while pretending to their parents that it was only the also-purchased safe, invariably Caucasian versions that interested them. As the late fifties gave way to the early sixties, in addition to these rather tame covers, the teen market was swamped by well-crafted songs with the flavor of rock 'n' roll but with more in common with the professional songwriting tradition of Tin Pan Alley. Indicatively, the addition of strings and smooth backing vocals to many of Elvis Presley's early recordings for major label RCA-Victor also apparently signaled rock 'n' roll's journey to the very heart of the pop mainstream. The distance and difference between "Heartbreak Hotel" (1956) and "Wooden Heart" (1961) seemed to demonstrate not only that Elvis had been defanged but that the threat and promise he and his music symbolized had been well and truly nullified.

As the industry wised up to the lucrative potential of rock 'n' roll, it quickly moved in to the package the music and its performers for mass consumption and big financial reward. The homogenizing and standardizing undertaken by the record companies meant that the neutralizing of rock 'n' roll could not be blamed on moralists, racists, politicians, educators, or even concerned parents. Although many at America's major labels endorsed Frank Sinatra's memorable and much-quoted dismissal of rock 'n' roll in the *Los Angeles Times* as "brutal, ugly and desperate" music for "cretinous goons," they were often more than willing to overcome their own prejudices, being reassured that it was just a passing fad and fully aware of the money to be made by capitalizing on its obvious teen appeal. Executives, like Columbia Records' Mitch Miller for example, openly detested rock 'n' roll. In the pursuit of profits that promised to come quick and easy, however, these key industry players dropped any personal objections in the name of the almighty dollar, and so set about making the music safe, acceptable, and marketable. This was a process that left rock 'n' roll pioneers like Jerry Lee Lewis understandably frustrated: "We . . . kept cutting rock records, though nobody would play them. . . . Elvis started singing like Bing Crosby. Don't get me wrong, I love Elvis and he's a great talent, but I think he let us down. All you could hear was Bobby—Bobby Vee, Bobby Vinton, Bobby Denton, Bobby Rydell, Bobby Darin. There was nothing but Bobbies on the radio" (qtd. in Palmer 222).

The net result was that, post-1958, rock 'n' roll appeared to have mutated into high school pop—a powder-puff variant in which rebellion had been replaced by industry-endorsed sentimentality, empty posing, and teen histrionics. Further proof of this transformation—if it were needed—could now be *seen* as well as heard. Although initially wary of rock 'n' roll as befits this most conservative of media, television came to offer another outlet for this new musical phenomenon. Yet, crucially, a show like *American Bandstand* would only accommodate a sanitized version, suggesting that the music could only take its place in the entertainment mainstream at a price. Effectively, rock 'n' roll's TV appearances were nothing more than proof of its containment. On *American Bandstand*—which had premiered on ABC in August 1957— producer-presenter Dick Clark's "good looks, neat clothing, and civil- ised manner helped reassure American parents that rock and roll was not a barbarian invasion that was turning the young into juvenile delin- quents" (Oakley 281). Clark ran a tight ship, working tirelessly to keep his TV product clean, actively enforcing a strict "code of conduct" that deemed "impulsive and overtly demonstrative behaviour [to be] grounds for expulsion: waving to the cameras was forbidden, and so was chewing gum" (Miller 146). *American Bandstand* had an under-eight- eens-only policy for its studio audience and ensured that rock 'n' roll's wilder performers were not invited to the carefully controlled party.

While the years between 1958 and 1964 were neither marked by the *complete* dilution of rock 'n' roll's threat nor did they signal popular music's *total* incorporation, in terms of the music that the majority of young, white Americans were listening to, things had indeed gotten very flat. Although this was also the period that witnessed the emer- gence of soul music, it was perhaps only producer Phil Spector's "little symphonies for the kids"—built around his fabled "wall of sound" and featuring memorable hooks and massive driving rhythm parts—that represented truly nonbland pop fare for teen America at this time. John Lennon recognized this when he reportedly told Phil Spector, "You kept rock 'n' roll alive while Elvis was in the army" (qtd. in Miles, *British Invasion*, 42). Spector-produced singles like the Ronettes' "Be My Baby" and the Crystals' "Da Doo Ron Ron" enjoyed massive com- mercial success, reaching number two and number three, respectively, on the Billboard chart in 1963.

The American success of "I Want to Hold Your Hand" demonstrated that the Beatles were operating against a sociocultural backdrop that, if anything, was even more medicated than in their home country. As Brian Epstein never tired of telling anyone who asked him to explain the Beatles' appeal, they were simply "being themselves"—a quality that surely accounted for a large measure of their appeal on both sides of the Atlantic. It was clear then that, for many of its afflicted, Beatlemania was not simply and solely about acts of empty consumption. A lot of this did go on, of course—there was a lot of "stuff" to buy. Beatlemania, though, did help many young fans to define both who they were and, perhaps more crucially, who they wanted to be. Here, initially through their music and then via a variety of other expressive outlets, the Beatles led by example. By apparently doing and saying whatever they liked, the band extended the invitation to their fans. "I tasted something"—one American teenager explained when trying to put her Beatlemania into words—"I was totally going outside myself. It was total freedom. Once you tasted it, you had to have more" (qtd. in Millard 133). According to poet Allen Ginsberg, the Beatles should be credited with nothing less than "chang[ing] American consciousness": "introduc[ing] a new note of complete masculinity allied with complete tenderness and vulnerability. And when that note was accepted in America, it did more than anything or anyone to prepare us for some kind of open-minded, open-hearted relationship with each other and the rest of the world" (qtd. in Bromell 26).

As Ginsberg called it, the Beatles initiated and encouraged through word and deed a change in what it meant to be a young man, with songs like "She Loves You" and "I Want to Hold Your Hand" functioning as primers for a new sexual politics. Both nameless teenager and famous poet, then, united in their assessment of the potential power of the Beatles in 1964.

Complementing this aural freshness was a visual freshness that was reinforced by the band's appearance and behavior. Not only did the Beatles sound fresh to American ears, they *looked* fresh to American eyes. When they stepped from the plane onto American soil for the very first time, they were dressed in European-sourced "mod" suits, sported black ties on crisp white shirts, and wore three-quarter-length dark, A-line overcoats, Cuban-heeled boots, all topped off with that memorable haircut. As one of their earliest American advocates, the DJ Murray "The K" Kaufman, confirmed the Beatles "were utterly different from any other musical, or even movie, stars that America had ever seen" (qtd. in Palmer 234). Notwithstanding a certain trepidation about their chances of stateside success, the band shared this appreciation of difference, and its potential power. "We were new," Lennon noted. "When we got here, you were all walking around in fuckin' Bermuda shorts with Boston crew cuts and stuff on your teeth" (qtd. in Fricke 89).

However, televised press conferences, newspaper articles, and photographs could only achieve so much in exposing America to this alien look and attitude. In this respect, "I Want to Hold Your Hand" had proved to be the noisy advance guard sent on ahead of the band's first sighting in the flesh. The Beatles had flown into New York on February 7, 1964, to be greeted by more than five thousand screaming fans and two hundred journalists, the primary objective of this short visit being their live TV appearances on *The Ed Sullivan Show* on consecutive Sunday evenings on the ninth and sixteenth—performances that would both galvanize their teen appeal and make them a genuinely pangenerational phenomenon.

Broadcast on CBS from 1948, this variety showcase had a track record of promoting British pop acts. Cliff Richard, Acker Bilk, and Helen Shapiro had all appeared on the show in October 1962. So, Sullivan could not be accused of being resistant to featuring the best of British pop, and, in the case of the Beatles, any reservations he might have had would presumably have been wiped when he witnessed Beatlemania firsthand as he was passing through London's Heathrow Airport in October 1963. Brian Epstein had hoped the slots that he had negotiated on the show would persuade Capitol Records to get behind the Beatles' records. With this in mind, he had insisted on and was granted "top billing" for the Beatles' three contracted appearances. "Top billing"—secured by Epstein's willingness to accept just $10,000 in total, when acts typically received $7,500 *per appearance*—would ensure that the band featured prominently in any advance publicity, and, much like his booking of New York's Plaza Hotel as the band's base, reflected the manager's rather old-school but in retrospect entirely justified belief in the Beatles as the real show business deal rather than here-today-gone-tomorrow pop novelty. It was this belief that had also convinced him to book the band for two shows at the prestigious but traditionally nonpop Carnegie Hall on February 12.

On January 3, 1964, Jack Paar's had been the first American TV show to feature Beatles' music, when the host introduced a BBC clip of the band performing "She Loves You." However, in common with the way they were treated in the American print media at the time, Paar had framed the Beatles as a novelty and gently mocked their British fans. Just a month later, things would be very different. The Beatles now had the nation's best-selling 45 and were a bona fide pop phenomenon. Sullivan had received fifty thousand applications for the paltry 728 tickets available to watch the band as part of the live studio audience. In the event, nearly seventy-four million viewers—or a third of the total population—tuned in to that first appearance. This represented comfortably the largest TV audience in American broadcasting history, symbolically dwarfing the sixty million who had watched Elvis Presley when he first appeared on the show. The Beatles' TV appearances were undoubtedly the culmination of their first triumphant visit to the United States, as the nation—or at least a third of it—received its first, heavy dose of pure-grade Beatlemania.

The Beatles performed five songs on the February 9 show, split into three-song and two-song minisets. In the first of these, the melodious "All My Loving" was followed by a version of the Broadway ballad "Till There Was You"—a "legitimate" popular song that Brian Epstein had urged the band to play in its TV appearances to presumably maximize appeal. "She Loves You" closed the brief set. In the second half of the show, the band performed two more songs—"I Saw Her Standing There" and "I Want to Hold Your Hand," the A- and B-sides of their current single. Most in the studio audience screamed throughout. At the end of the show, Sullivan read out a congratulatory telegram purportedly from Elvis Presley but penned by his manager Colonel Tom Parker, which seemed to mark the passage from one rock 'n' roll era to another. Yet the significance of this moment transcended the level of musical turf wars, for it could also be claimed that the period of national mourning was well and truly over.

"Let the feasting begin!" George Harrison had cried at the band's first press conference—an invitation the Beatles now extended to all. Much like their first movie would later in the year, these early U.S. TV appearances helped seal the deal, in allowing the Beatles to be both *seen* and *heard*. Furthermore, their transformative power was not simply registered in, and so limited to, the supposedly passive arena of teen consumption. For, echoing skiffle's effect on British youth, it was evident that seeing and hearing the Beatles could inspire active music making. As one member of the many thousands of long-forgotten-be-cause-they-never-made-it bands explained, "I was inspired by the Beatles like everyone else. I remember seeing them on *The Ed Sullivan Show* and thinking, 'Neat tunes. Simple. I can do that'" (qtd. in Hicks 25). Watching the Beatles perform on TV, thousands of future musicians were inspired to form a band. Some of these—like Bruce Springsteen, for example—would go on to achieve great success, but of course most would not. However, for all, the Beatles signposted the route for a personal journey on which they were no longer to be passengers.

Two days after their first appearance on *The Ed Sullivan Show*, the Beatles attended a party at the British embassy in Washington, D.C. Here, Lyndon Johnson is reported to have said to the British prime minister, "I like your advance party but they need a haircut." The British Invasion was under way and even the president knew it. On February 19, just a few days before the Beatles returned home, *Variety* ran a story headlined "Rocking Redcoats Are Coming—Beatles Lead Massive Drive." Yet, did the "Rocking Redcoats" ultimately triumph? In strictly beat musical terms, it might well be accurate to identify British-style dominance lasting no more than twelve months. Furthermore, it has been argued that the Invasion was "more symbolic than actual—the high profile appearance of a new dynamism rather than a literal occupation of the American charts" (MacDonald 77). This is an assessment that urges perspective while simultaneously (and quite rightly) emphasizing that the Invasion's injection of dynamism might ultimately be more significant than its sales.

This same critical consensus, however, has viewed the Beatles-led Invasion as driving a wholesale and rapid changing of the American pop guard. This is an impression given some substance by the disappearance of well-established chart regulars in 1964. Here, the dethroning of Bobby Vinton—whose single "There I've Said It" had held the number-one spot in the first weeks of January 1964—has assumed both literal and symbolic significance, as he was knocked off the top by the Beatles. In fact, Bobby Vinton enjoyed a highly respectable total of five Top 40 hit records through 1964. It was just that the Beatles had nineteen hits in that year. As the shell-shocked Vinton himself recognized, "Times were changing. I couldn't believe it" (qtd. in Di Martino 107). Vinton, though, was down but not out, returning to the top of the Billboard singles chart in December 1964 with "Mr. Lonely," and the eleven months that had passed between his number-one records had seen Louis Armstrong, Dean Martin, and even Lorne Greene have best sellers. Other homegrown number-one records in 1964 included Mary Wells's "My Guy," the Dixie Cups' "Chapel of Love," the Shangri-Las' "Leader of the Pack," the Beach Boys' "I Get Around," the Four Seasons' "Rag Doll," Roy Orbison's "Oh! Pretty Woman," and three Supremes' 45s, "Where Did Our Love Go," "Baby Love," and "Come See about Me."

While some perspective on the Invasion is clearly needed, it cannot be denied that Billboard chart placings for British pop acts were often eye-catchingly vertiginous. In 1964 and 1965 British-made 45s occupied the number-one spot on the Billboard chart for a total of fifty-two weeks. British acts were at number one on the Hot 100 in 1964 for twenty-four weeks, with the Beatles accounting for eighteen of those—"I Want to Hold Your Hand" (seven weeks in February/March), "She Loves You" (two weeks in March), "Can't Buy Me Love" (which had unprecedented advance orders of over two million copies and spent five weeks at number one in April), "Love Me Do" (one week in May), "A Hard Day's Night" (two weeks in August), and "I Feel Fine" (one week in December). The band's first American album, *Meet the Beatles*, had sold 3.6 million copies by mid-March, when it kept its follow-up *Introducing the Beatles* waiting at number two. At least in the first half of 1964 when they reportedly accounted for an astonishing 60 percent of all recorded music sold in the States, these statistics suggest that Beatles *were* the Invasion. Indeed, if further proof of the force of the band's impact were required, there were even four Beatles tribute records that charted in the spring of 1964, too—one of these, the Carefrees' "We Love You Beatles," was at number forty-two in the momentous week in early April when the band had the five best-selling singles in America.

As the Invasion's "advance party," the Beatles had dominated the market through the early months of 1964 but were quickly joined by a number of British acts. Although the subsequent successes of Petula Clark (whose "Downtown" reached number one in early 1965), Dusty Springfield, and the Bachelors might have suggested that the Invasion was musically heterogeneous, the most penetrative of the "Invaders" were purveyors of beat music. In February, the Dave Clark Five reached the Top 10 with "Glad All Over." Although quickly followed by a duo of Epstein-managed acts—Billy J. Kramer and the Dakotas and Gerry and the Pacemakers—London's Dave Clark Five (DC5 for short) were therefore the first British act to achieve American success in the

Beatles' wake. "Glad All Over" and its equally successful follow-up "Bits and Pieces" were archetypal, even cartoonish beat-by-numbers with the loud, stomping drum sound that typified their output. Dave Clark was clean cut and good looking—something that helps explain why and how his band made a record eighteen appearances on *The Ed Sullivan Show* and enjoyed fifteen Top 20 hit records over a three-year period including eight in 1964 alone. Clark was also the group's principal songwriter, manager, and producer. He financed the recording sessions and paid the other band members a weekly wage—"We're all in it to try and make money" (qtd. in Miles, *British Invasion*, 83). The fact that he was a very shrewd operator was demonstrated, for example, in his use of the saxophone on DC5 records, which may have been a conscious concession to American tastes and one that marked the band as different from the rest of the Invasion groups. Between 1964 and 1968, the DC5 enjoyed eight hit albums in America. The band had just two big-selling albums in Britain in the same period.

Through the spring and summer of 1964 the Invasion acts kept coming. The Searchers, the Swinging Blue Jeans, Billy J. Kramer and the Dakotas, Gerry and the Pacemakers, and the Kinks all broke into the Billboard Top 20. However, the first Brits to reach number one other than the Beatles were Peter and Gordon, who had America's best-selling single in May with "World without Love." While they were clearly not the Beatles, Peter and Gordon were a folk duo turned pop act that evidently benefited from its strong connections with the Invasion's kingpins. Peter Asher was the brother of Paul McCartney's actress girlfriend, Jane; but, more importantly, McCartney had written the decidedly un-beat ballad "World without Love" and would also supply the duo's two follow-up singles. In total, Peter and Gordon placed fourteen singles and seven albums on the Billboard charts; and, like the Dave Clark Five, they enjoyed noticeably greater success in America, where they managed to sustain a career as a viable pop act long after their commercial sun had set in the UK.

In the fall, the Animals ("House of the Rising Sun") and Manfred Mann ("Do Wah Diddy") joined Peter and Gordon to form a trio of non-Beatles Invasion acts who reached number one in 1964. At this time, "I'm Into Something Good" also represented the first flush of American success for Herman's Hermits that would stretch over several years. It has been suggested, quite plausibly, that the Hermits' U.S.

success was largely attributable to the teen appeal of its toothsome front man Peter Noone. Noone had been a child actor, familiar to Britons from his many TV appearances including a decent run in a popular soap opera. He, in particular, was aggressively sold to prepubescent American girls. "I'm Into Something Good," which peaked at number thirteen, was written by American pop writers Gerry Goffin and Carole King, recorded in a mere two-hour session, and structured around the kind of harmonies now familiar from Beatles' records. Subsequent hits—many of which were actually performed by top British session musicians like future Led Zeppelin members Jimmy Page and John Paul Jones—demonstrated the full extent of the band and producer Mickie Most's conscious targeting of the American market. The Hermits had two U.S. number-one singles—"Mrs. Brown, You've Got a Lovely Daughter" (1965) and "I'm Henry VIII, I Am" (1965)—that were not even released in Britain. In the case of "Mrs. Brown," it was pressure from American fans that reportedly led to the track being released as a single as it had generated a million in presales, and its subsequent success undoubtedly, and perhaps understandably, persuaded the Hermits to exploit their Englishness and draw heavily on an English music-hall tradition for future material.

Initially, the Beatles' core support was similarly composed in terms of age and gender to that of the Hermits'. A fan club poll conducted in the first flush of Beatlemania revealed that the typical American fan of the group was a thirteen- to seventeen-year-old, white, female, middle-class, Christian, B-grade student with a personal radio; and it is true that, while subsequent tours in 1965 and 1966 would see more males in attendance, audiences for the Beatles' first U.S. tour in the summer of 1964 were indeed overwhelmingly female in composition. However, even at this early stage, it was also clear that the band's fan base was widening at pace, accumulating more males and more post-teens (and maybe even more beat poets) almost daily. Of course, television appearances had helped in this, but it was the movie *A Hard Day's Night* that represented the single most important driver for the expansion of the Beatles' constituency, cementing the band's status as global superstars in the process. It enabled the Beatles to engage a wider demographic. The panmedia project *A Hard Day's Night*—which incorporated the movie, its soundtrack album, and related artwork—was the distillation not only of all the Beatles meant at that point but much of what they would come to mean. It showcased, for example, their ability to keep several steps ahead of the game, to innovate and extend the meaning of pop, while taking their massive fan base with them on the journey. Across each media platform, it highlighted their "ability to be two contradictory things at once—comfortably safe and exhilaratingly strange" (MacDonald 82). On vinyl and celluloid, the Beatles were cheeky and irreverent but never downright insolent or offensive. In the movie, when a journalist asks Ringo whether he is a mod or a rocker, he replies that he is a "mocker." As their publicist Derek Taylor perceptively notes, they "turned on millions of adolescents to what had been hurting all the time . . . but the young never did want it raw, so they absorbed it through the Beatle filter" (qtd. in Palmer 230). With *A Hard Day's Night*, the Beatles opened up the mainstream, but to a degree and at a pace that would not risk alienating their fans.

In the first few years of their recording career, Beatles' music was consistently described as "fresh" and "exciting," not "alien" and "offensive," offering "an altered perspective, not a foreign landscape" (Chambers 63). Listening to the Beatles in 1964, Greil Marcus has recalled how the music struck him as *simultaneously* "instantly recognisable and like nothing we had ever heard. It was joyous, threatening, absurd, arrogant, innocent, tough" (qtd. in Bromell 13). *A Hard Day's Night* honed and dosed this paradox to perfection. Under the direct influence of not only the Beatles themselves but also of those who, duly inspired, followed in their wake, the pop mainstream would never be the same again.

The soundtrack album was released in June, several weeks before the movie premiered. It featured seven songs from the movie padded out with some instrumental arrangements of the same material credited to George Martin and His Orchestra. Following this, Capitol Records—who owned the rights to all Beatles' recordings in any format but the soundtrack—began releasing some of the same material as singles and, with considerable chutzpah, also promoted an album called *Something New* (which of course it patently was not). Although there has been a tendency to identify "modest evolution" in and across early Beatles' albums—as the band steadily developed its artistic depth and range supported by improved technological resources—*A Hard Day's Night* arguably represented a more substantive forward leap than is commonly allowed. Whether in its UK or U.S. incarnation, the album was composed entirely of the band's own compositions. This was almost as shocking a proposition for the American music business as it was for its British counterpart. The album was also notable for its effective use of multitrack recording. Although the rudimentary studio facilities available to the Beatles on their earlier records had proved a source of strength in approximating the band's pulsating live performances, the recording process was greatly enhanced with four-tracks now at their disposal. On *A Hard Day's Night*, multitracking allowed for the use of overdubs, which thickened the band's sound by layering instrumental and vocal textures. It also encouraged the use of a greater range of instrumentation. In addition to the standard beat group lineup of guitars and drums, *A Hard Day's Night* featured the acoustic guitar, the twelve-string electric guitar, a variety of percussion instruments—for example, the Latinate "And I Love Her" featured claves and bongos—the piano and organ, and even orchestration. Technological developments undoubtedly played a part, then, in helping the Beatles to extend their musical range, supplying the hardware to complement artistic ambition.

Although noteworthy for its deployment of the Rickenbacker twelve-string, *A Hard Day's Night* could not be said to have heralded the arrival of folk rock. Lyrically, all of the album's tracks were still determinedly pop in their sensibility and scope—so that, for example, "I'm Happy Just to Dance with You," a song written for George Harrison to sing, is rather throwaway beat-by-numbers. However, the album was arguably and audibly more "relaxed," as perhaps befits a record that is often viewed as reflecting both the Beatles' discovery of Bob Dylan and the marijuana the American singer is believed to have introduced them to. John Lennon, in particular, was apparently taken with Dylan, and while the latter's influence cannot necessarily be heard lyrically on *A Hard Day's Night*, it was certainly traceable in both the music and the introspective, intimate mood or vibe of many tracks on an album dominated by Lennon compositions. The romantic ballad "If I Fell"—perceptively described by George Martin as "reflective" rather than "dreary"—sees the narrator open up emotionally, revealing a hitherto unheard vulnerability that would of course become characteristic of the passive-aggressive Lennon: "If I fell in love with you / Would you promise to be true / And help me understand." Furthermore, the line that follows in which Lennon sings "I found that love is more / Than just holding hands" appear to pointedly replace the sparkling confidence of their breakthrough American single of just six short months earlier with the beginnings of mature doubt.

The most memorable single track, however, was the album's explosive opener "A Hard Day's Night," which as a single became the band's fifth Billboard number one in August 1964. A Ringoism eagerly adopted as the movie's title, the track was written and recorded to order in the space of just a single week in April. With an explosive opening salvo easily the equal of "She Loves You" in its force and impact, its unusual chiming first chord—a most un-beat-like G eleventh suspended fourth—gave yet another sonic demonstration of the Beatles' cultural power and ambition. Though initially wary, the ever-astute George Martin recognized the appropriateness of what he has referred to as the song's "instant combustion": "To this day, I still don't know what that chord was. But it was a very good one. And it set the tone for the song and the whole film. Because we knew that what was going to follow was going to be dramatic, wonderful, funny, exciting and everything else" (qtd. in Du Noyer 70). Motored by some ridiculously high-speed percussion, this caricature of life in the fast lane would also effectively function in two and a half minutes as the movie would over its full eighty.

Eight of the songs—including "Can't Buy Me Love" and its B-side "You Can't Do That"—were completed in a single week following the Beatles' return from their first trip to the States. America's best-selling single for five weeks in April and May, McCartney's "Can't Buy Me Love" is an optimistic and upbeat track that—as its phenomenal sales suggest—had genuine pangenerational appeal. By way of contrast, its B-side was the Lennon composition "You Can't Do That," a darker, more adult track that was pointedly omitted from the movie. Frank and autobiographical, where "Can't Buy Me Love" was blithely universal, the chugging groove of "You Can't Do That" perfectly complemented its lyrical coverage of grown-up themes like sexual jealousy and self-loathing. Here then, the two sides of the 45 not only reflect the distinctive personalities of their principal authors, they also illustrate the contradiction that lay at the heart of the Beatles' cultural power.

Anticipating easy profit, United Artists had offered the Beatles the opportunity to make a movie as early as October 1963. United Artists were interested in the Beatles where Capitol Records were not, simply because they had had a production office in London since 1961 and so were well aware of the band's phenomenal success in their home country. So, United Artists duly gave the green light to a low-budget project, to be headed by expat Walter Shenson, an independent producer who had produced a successful movie called *The Mouse That Roared* (1959) starring the British comic actor Peter Sellers.

Just as the music had done, so the movie packaged the Beatles as gentle revolutionaries. For all its satirical swipes at various targets—teen culture included—*A Hard Day's Night* still remains recognizably a genre picture in which our young heroes strike a series of blows against adult authority. Yet another instance of the Beatles offering their growing army of fans "an altered perspective" rather than a "foreign landscape" (Chambers 63), *A Hard Day's Night* was a teen movie, but all was not quite as it seemed. As its scriptwriter Alun Owen points out, "We're not going to have a story that ends up at the Palladium with the vicar smiling and giving the thumbs-up sign from the stalls. Nothing like that" (qtd. in Du Noyer 74). The movie would also make few concessions to the American market. Despite its considerable U.S. connections, it was very "British" (or perhaps "European"). In this, it marked a departure from the usual pop-music-and-film fare normally served up to America teens. Reviewing *A Hard Day's Night* for *Village Voice*, Andrew Sarris goes so far as to call it "the *Citizen Kane* of jukebox musicals" (175). Here, credit for this should go to both the Beatles and those around them who worked on the film—including United Artists, Walter Shenson, and, in particular, its American director Richard Lester. Yet more evidence, if it was needed by now, of the importance of timing and collaborating with the "right" people.

United Artists had wanted the movie to be made quickly and cheaply to capitalize on the Beatles' now near-global success, which—in common with Capitol Records—it was nevertheless convinced was a moment that would soon pass. In the early 1960s, a typical Hollywood feature would cost around $1.5 million. *A Hard Day's Night* cost approximately £180,000, with the Beatles paid a modest £25,000 between them. Here then, the much-lauded break with the glossy look of the standard teen movie was the product of both conscious strategy and stringent budgeting—the same twin drivers that had combined to such startling effect on the Beatles' first two UK studio albums. So, while the decision to film in black and white was one dictated primarily by finan-

cial necessity, it actually helped transform the movie into a genre masterpiece because, as Paul McCartney observed of the use of monochrome, "It just seemed harder, more artsy. We liked all that stuff"
(qtd. in Du Noyer 76). Shot over a period of just six or seven weeks in
the early spring of 1964 at studios in Twickenham and various locations
in and around London, the movie grossed a phenomenal $1.3 million in
its first week on release in the United States.

On one level, *A Hard Day's Night* could be viewed for what it quite
evidently was: a B movie with the flimsiest of plots. Yet, although there
was *apparently* little to elevate it above the generic norm, the movie
had edge. This is one that might well have suggested a culturally specific theme confined to British youth and its struggles. However, there
was plenty to suggest that the movie's apparently parochial concerns
played out just as powerfully with American youth. For one thing, just
like the music that had preceded it, the movie radiated an infectious
positivity that appeared to have a quantifiable impact. In fact, more so
than in response to any single Beatles' track, album, or even televised
performance, countless American musicians, filmmakers, and artists
have reported the movie's life-changing effect—inspiring them to pur-
sue their dreams, to "light out" Huck Finn–style down their own path
and ignore doubting voices. Here, the words of David Crosby attest to
both this cultural power and to the vital hypodermic function *A Hard
Day's Night* performed in dosing it: "I knew right then what my life was
going to be. I wanted to do that. I loved the attitude and the fun of it,
there was sex, there was joy, there was everything I wanted out of life"
(qtd. in Echols 24).

Those earlier *Ed Sullivan Show* appearances had of course sparked a
similar desire—confirming that the Beatles' impact was not simply confined to the arena of passive teen consumption, but could signpost a
route for some young Americans on which they would no longer be
mere passengers. *A Hard Day's Night* delivered this potentially empowering message in a much more sustained and concerted fashion, to a
much wider catchment. For in the summer of 1964, the Beatles existed
in no more fully realized form than *on-screen*; and so, through the
powerful filter of *A Hard Day's Night*, this fully dimensional presence
enabled them to effectively communicate their meaning on both sides
of the Atlantic. As the director Richard Lester notes, in *A Hard Day's
Night* the Beatles "sent the class thing sky-high; they laughed it out of

existence" (qtd. in Miller 217), and this played out with equal force in the less class-obsessed, but no less conformist United States. In America, the Beatles "laughed" conformity "out of existence."

A comparatively youthful thirty-one-year-old in 1964, American Richard Lester had moved to London nearly ten years earlier, keeping company with Britain's preeminent comedy team, known collectively as the Goons, and working on various TV shows. In 1962 he had directed a budget, teen, B movie called *It's Trad, Dad*, which featured the teenage pop singer Helen Shapiro along with a number of Britain's then very popular trad jazz acts like Acker Bilk (who had enjoyed a number-one single in America with "Stranger on the Shore" in the same year) plus a smattering of American artists like Chubby Checker and Del Shannon. Although in many respects a perfectly ordinary teen picture, *It's Trad, Dad* featured some memorable musical sequences, and was marked by traces of satire and surrealism that preempted *A Hard Day's Night* and demonstrated Lester's affinity with anarchic comedy. On *A Hard Day's Night*, Richard Lester broke with the long-take tendency to experiment with faster, flashier editing. In perhaps the most positive review at the time, Andrew Sarris summarized the movie as a "brilliant crystallisation of such diverse cultural particles as the pop movie, rock 'n' roll, cinema verite, the nouvelle vague, Free Cinema, the affectedly hand-held camera, frenzied cutting, the cult of the sex-less adolescent, the semi-documentary, and studied spontaneity" (175).

Going into the Beatles' movie project, Lester's directorial resume included *The Running Jumping and Standing Still Film* (1960), a ten-minute "short" filmed over two weekends at a total cost of just £70 that had been devised by the British comedian and actor Peter Sellers. It featured Sellers and fellow *Goon Show* comedian Spike Milligan in various wordless sketches, most of which were shot al fresco in the English countryside. An absurd and surreal homage to silent comedies, it was reportedly one of John Lennon's favorite films and earned cult status both in Britain and America, where it received an Academy Award nomination for Best Short Film. Not only did *The Running Jumping and Standing Still Film* feature personnel who would go on to work on *A Hard Day's Night*—such as the actor Norman Rossington, who played the group's much-hassled manager—there were also stylistic similarities between the two in terms of sight gags and editing.

Shooting the movie in black and white gave it a documentary feel, and here, Richard Lester was also directly influenced by documentary filmmaking traditions, and in particular British free cinema. Spearheaded by filmmakers like Tony Richardson and Karel Reisz, the British free cinema movement produced a number of short films in the second half of the 1950s, which drew on the techniques of documentary realism allied to a strong sense of social justice. With his genuine regard for the Beatles as people, Richard Lester shared in the free cinema's empathy for its subjects. *Momma Don't Allow* (1956) and *We Are the Lambeth Boys* (1959) were representative of a filmmaking agenda committed to "the importance of people [and] the significance of the everyday" (qtd. in Dupin), often with an unabashed provincial gaze and featuring British youth smoking, talking, flirting, and dancing in clubs and pubs. Exactly the kind of activities the Beatles would engage—and take great delight in—in *A Hard Day's Night. We Are the Lambeth Boys*, part of the Ford-sponsored *Look at Britain* series, was directed by Karel Reisz and shot in characteristic vérité style. This fifty-minute documentary offered a sympathetic take on young, working-class life in South London. Despite a rather paternalistic, and at times intrusive, voice-over—which at one point identified the young Britons featured as a "rowdy generation," and at other times tried a little too hard to present them as really rather "nice"—the teenagers were allowed to speak for themselves, expressing their aspirations, dreams, frustrations, and fears via internal monologue, conversations with one another, and interviews. Particularly noteworthy here—because it would turn out to be pertinent to an assessment of *A Hard Day's Night*'s politics—was how the monotony of young working lives was pointedly contrasted with the release achieved through the teen rituals of dancing, drinking, and courting.

A Hard Day's Night was scripted by Alun Owen, a Liverpool native then in his late thirties who had written for the popular British TV series *Z Cars*, which featured policing in a northern, working-class locale as realistically as the BBC would allow in the early 1960s. Owen was charged with producing credible dialogue, and he had researched this by trailing the Beatles on a tour of Ireland in November 1963, where he witnessed firsthand not only the oppressive nature of their fame but also, importantly, how each member of the group dealt with it. From this field trip, Owen created the exaggerated, distinct personalities of each band member that would endure. It was Owen who contributed greatly to the movie's Mersey vérité. Contrary to the impression given, there was very little improvisation. According to Shenson, only somewhere between 5 and 10 percent of the dialogue was improvised. Despite striving for a "natural feeling" and encouraging ad-libbing, Lester himself confirmed that "virtually every line was scripted and rehearsed" (qtd. in Du Noyer 74). The Beatles did not have the time or, for that matter, the inclination to exert a great deal of influence on the script but, equally, were determined not to make themselves look silly, and so were just as eager to avoid the embarrassing contrivances of the typical teen movie. "Rock 'n' roll films," explains McCartney, "were traditionally bad vehicles . . . so we had this idea that it would be great to be in something that was actually a decent film and had music" (qtd. in Du Noyer 72–73).

While the "razor-slashing wit" (Sarris 175) was largely of Owen's making then—exploiting Scouse slang that, in many instances, the Beatles themselves did not use in real life—the band still sounded believably young and northern. Throughout the course of the movie, they punctured class pretension and the older generation's hypocrisy. Indeed, *A Hard Day's Night* is built around a number of duels between north and south, young and old, working and middle class. The first of these confrontations occurs as the band makes its way on a train down to London and clashes with an irate city gent—something each Beatle had experienced in real life and Owen then incorporated into the screenplay. In highlighting generational and class tensions, the Beatles deployed their own language and humor to resolve things in their favor—a notable feature of a movie in which the "depravity of such honest frankness [was] worth a hundred pseudo-literary exercises like Beckett" (Sarris 175). As the bowler-hatted Blimpish passenger attempts to enforce *his* rules—shutting the window the lads would prefer left open, commanding Ringo to turn off his transistor radio—the Beatles use both words and deeds to register their resistance. So, for example, when the city type predictably mobilizes his war service to simultaneously assert his rights and deny those of the Beatles, Ringo delivers the sarcastic one-liner "I bet you're sorry you won," while Lennon's response to this lecture is to simply flutter his imaginary eyelashes and ask the man to "give us a kiss." As Arthur Schlesinger notes in *Show*, the movie reveled in its presentation of "a conspiracy of delinquency against pomposity" (qtd. in Gould 244). This particular sequence ends surreally with the Beatles running alongside the train, banging on the compartment window, mugging furiously, and shouting at the older passenger like four scampish eight-year-olds ("Hey mister, can we have our ball back?")—enacting a distinctive brand of "delinquency" that drew much of its energy and power from the simple pleasures of being childish and childlike. An early example of protest through festivity that would, of course, become the trademark practice of a generation just a few short years later.

Just as it had been in other formats—and just as Epstein and Martin had recognized from very early on in their dealings with the group—the strategy of "being themselves" was key to the movie's success. ("All I gotta do is act naturally," Ringo would sing a year later on *Help!*) *A Hard Day's Night* had in fact started out life as pure documentary, provisionally titled *Beatlemania!* This idea was quickly shelved, as real-life Beatlemania had made it impossible. Yet, even as a fiction, the movie had comparatively little of the genre's typical fakery and cynicism. Aided by the band's charisma, it was palpably different because it gave the impression that here was an insight into the Beatles' lives. Perhaps ironically, it was the mock documentary approach that enabled much of this to shine through, focusing on the Beatles as prisoners of their success—or, in Shenson's words, "convicts in transit"—and the various strategies adopted to cope with this.

The American satirist Mark Twain once wrote that "against the assault of laughter nothing can stand"—a manifesto to which Richard Lester clearly subscribed. "Although we did it in a light way," he said of *A Hard Day's Night*, "I still feel there is a serious purpose to the film. The Beatles told everybody, 'You can do anything you damn well like.' Just go out and do it. There's no reason why you can't" (qtd. in Miller 216–17, my emphasis). Filmed on April 23, 1964, in Isleworth, just outside London, the movie's most acclaimed scene enacted a variation on similar set pieces from *The Running Jumping and Standing Still Film*. It represents a moment of *Goon*-ish unconditional release, a literal escape from a succession of tight, restrictive spaces that have hemmed the Beatles in—train compartments, low-ceilinged corridors, crowded hotel lobbies, and backstage stairwells. Throughout *A Hard Day's Night* relief—and with it the possibility of joyful transcendence—has come via musical sequences and interludes. Andrew Sarris describes the "open-field helicopter-shot sequence of the Beatles on a spree [as] one of the most exhilarating expressions of high spirits I have ever seen on the screen" (175). With a cry of "We're out!" and to the bounce of "Can't Buy Me Love," the band "invades" the playing field like four hyperactive children, careening manically around, pinballing off each other, their gleeful escape captured by some equally kinetic camera work. One moment looking up from the floor, the next looking down on the action from a helicopter.

Similarly—although with possibly less impact—at the "live gig" that closes the movie, a squad of cameramen were given directorial license to work multiple angles and succeeded in capturing the smallest of details from unusual perspectives (a boot heel, fingers on a fret board, the view from Ringo's drum riser). According to one cameraman who worked on the movie, the net result of this was that "we established a style that's still used today when they photograph rock groups" (qtd. in Du Noyer 82). Certainly, the use of wordless scenes backed by pop songs that work to generate insight and meaning sparked a vogue that could be seen and heard, for example, in Mike Nichols's masterful opening sequence to *The Graduate* just three years later—which deployed Simon and Garfunkel's "The Sound of Silence" to great effect as Benjamin Braddock journeys through LAX—and, twenty years later, almost everywhere one looked on MTV.

In *Revolution in the Head*, Ian MacDonald has written perceptively of the Beatles "suffusing the western world with a sense of rejuvenating freedom comparable to the joy of being let out of school early on a sunny afternoon" (1). As the breakout scene demonstrated, no single text—certainly not in 1964 at any rate—so comprehensively and graphically bottled this "joy" as did *A Hard Day's Night*. In this, it was genuinely era defining, for the "joy" was to be most effectively communicated via a kinetic charge that would help shape the very meaning of the times for many. While defining the sixties has inevitably proved problematic, if there is such a thing as a critical consensus it has tended to focus on movement. As David Pichaske notes, then, "The Sixties may have said no to everything including itself, but the greatest no of all was to stasis. On that everyone agreed. It was *motion* and *change*, constant change, change now that made the Sixties as heady and terrifying as they were" (xvii, my emphasis). As vanguards of the "Invasion," the Beatles broke through convention to sound "real" and "fresh." Significantly, in *A Hard Day's Night*, the band not only sounded "real" and "fresh," but *looked* (and so *behaved*) this way, too. It has been argued that it was in fact the Maysles brothers' documentary of that first American visit—*What's Happening! The Beatles in the USA*—that confirmed as much, but the more widely viewed movie surely proved more effective in this regard. In the words of the movie's director of photography, Gilbert Taylor, "we disturbed people to some extent, didn't we?"

On August 11, 1964, *A Hard Day's Night* was premiered in seven hundred movie theaters across North America. On August 12, it opened on twenty-one screens across New York and raked in an impressive $75,000 in a single night. Predictably, it became the top-grossing movie of the summer, setting a record for "return on investment" that would stand for years, as young Americans watched it over and over. It would end 1964 as the seventh-ranked grossing movie—in a year marked by a *cinematic* "Invasion" of sorts in which seven of the top ten grossing movies in North America were either British made or featured British talent. Although *Time* had previewed the movie on August 7 as "rubbish to be avoided at all costs," a review in *Newsweek* was typical of more favorable press reaction to the movie. It reported that "the legitimacy of the Beatles phenomenon is finally inescapable. With all the ill-will in the world, one sits there, watching and listening—and feels one's intelligence dissolving in a pool of approbation and participation." The *New York Journal—American* was similarly generous in its praise, if not quite so perceptive in summarizing the movie (and the band's) social significance: "The picture turned out to be a completely whacky, off-beat entertainment that's frequently remindful of the Marx brothers comedies of the '30s" (qtd. in Miles, *British Invasion*, 68).

In mid-August the Beatles embarked on a monthlong, thirty shows in twenty-three cities North American tour—supported by the Bill Black Combo, the Exciters, the Righteous Brothers, and Jackie De Shannon. On this tour the Beatles were making a minimum of $50,000 every night, in addition to generating impressive and unprecedented amounts of revenue from record sales, movie tickets, and merchandising. Having arrived in San Francisco on August 18, where an estimated nine thousand fans met them at the airport, the Beatles opened their tour at the city's Cow Palace on the nineteenth, where they played to an audience of 17,130 and grossed $92,000. As reported in the *San Francisco Examiner*, the screams were so loud that the band could not hear themselves sing or play: "Although it was publicised as music, all that was heard and seen of the Mersey Sound was something like a jet engine shrieking through a summer lightning storm because of the yelling fans. It had no mercy, and afterwards everyone still capable of speech took note of the ringing in the ears which lasted for as long as the Beatles had played" (qtd. in Miles, *British Invasion*, 105).

Later in the month, at a Chicago show, a policeman on security detail reported that "it was kind of like Sinatra multiplied by fifty or a hundred" (qtd. in Miles, *British Invasion*, 111). Bringing *A Hard Day's Night* to life in Pittsburgh, thousands lined the route from the airport to the Beatles' hotel, and an estimated five thousand fans surrounded the city's Civic Arena hours before they were due onstage.

By the end of 1964 the Beatles had sold an estimated twenty-five million records in America. "Can't Buy Me Love" alone had sold nearly a million copies on the first day of its release and three million copies by year's end. According to the ever-skeptical Michael Kelly, it was "at this point [that] the newness of the invasion had certainly worn off [and its] groups were no longer a novelty" (45). While Kelly has a point in suggesting that by December 1964 the Invasion was "no longer a novelty," its effects had by no means "worn off." Even self-professed myth buster Kelly has had to concede that "perhaps the most important legacy of the invasion of 1964 was that, for the first time, the suits at the record companies, television executives, and adults in general finally took rock 'n' roll seriously" (Kelly 45). If it was the Invasion that persuaded "adults in general" to take rock 'n' roll "seriously," then an obsession with chart placings—or any other empirical weight and measure—as a marker of its significance should not be allowed to obscure the full, enduring force and range of its transformative power. As later chapters of this book will demonstrate, the Beatles had a key role to play in not only presaging but actually shaping what was to come as far as rock music's contribution to the sixties was concerned. Of course, but for a few million "Ringo for President" badges, the link between the "real" America and the Beatles was not immediately apparent in the summer of 1964. Even though Beatlemania was newsworthy, the idea that it might possess meaning and significance over and above that of the latest in a long line of teen crazes did not occur to many observers. Yet perhaps it should have. Andrew Sarris was among a select few who did "get it." In his praise-ful but prescient review of the movie, he concludes that "the Beatles are a sly bunch of anti-establishment anarchists, but they are too slick to tip their hand to the authorities" (Sarris 176).

Persuading the skeptical here was problematic, not least because Beatles' songs did not openly address current affairs. Yet, early Beatles' output certainly touched American lives in myriad ways. Besides, it was also the case that the Beatles did get involved at a more direct level. After a show in Philadelphia on September 2, they mentioned in a radio interview that they were dismayed, in the wake of recent race riots in the city, to see their audience was almost exclusively white. On the eleventh they played Jacksonville, Florida, only after having been assured that their audience would not be segregated, as they had insisted in an early press release. Small steps, maybe. But it was clear that, even at this relatively early point in their career, the Beatles were aware that their fame afforded them a platform to exercise power that would take them beyond the banal realm normally mapped out for pop stars.

In the second half of the sixties, America's sociopolitical context was primarily motored by generational conflict. While there were numerous movements for change under way and causing considerable friction— civil rights, antiwar, feminism, environmental—it was generational tension that played a vital, defining role in each of these. Roy Shuker has defined the counterculture as a "loose expressive social movement . . . an integrative label for the various groups and ideologies present," but—most importantly—best viewed "as a generational unit, the youth culture, challenging traditional concepts of career, education, and morality, and seeking an identity outside an occupational role or family" (Shuker 70–71). *A Hard Day's Night* carried this challenge and activated this search. As the band's publicist Derek Taylor points out, the Beatles "represented hope, optimism, lack of pretension, that anyone can do it, whatever their background" (qtd. in Palmer 233).

So, although countercultural dissent was neither being widely practiced nor debated in the summer of 1964, the Beatles—and their "good little movie"—did plenty of groundwork. In this way, the opening chord in "A Hard Day's Night" was as portentous as the snare shot on Dylan's "Like a Rolling Stone" (1965)—simultaneously tolling the end of something and heralding the start of something else. While it is clearly no *Easy Rider* (1969), *Five Easy Pieces* (1970), or even their own *Magical Mystery Tour* (1968), mobilizing Shuker's definition of counterculture, it is possible to see how and why the *A Hard Day's Night* package anticipated many of the movement's concerns and rehearsed many of its practices and behaviors. It is a "primer in Beatlemania" (Millard 131). However, it was arguably a "primer" of potentially greater import, as many young fans found it immensely empowering. In presenting the Beatles as careless and carefree, it delivered a message that resonated powerfully with American youth. Just as "I Want to Hold Your Hand" had done, the movie reinforced the absolute imperative to live for the moment, carpe diem—a total commitment to *nowness* that should sit at the very heart of any credible attempt to grasp the meaning of the counterculture.

In their sheer ubiquity, via both music that expressed this fearless commitment to change and by constantly changing themselves, the Beatles did more than any one single artistic entity to open eyes and ears to new exciting opportunities and possibilities. "They were amazing people," recalled the actor Victor Spinetti, who played the touchy TV director in *A Hard Day's Night*, "and they were curious, they wanted to learn. They didn't have the laddishness you get now, this wanting to be ignorant" (qtd. in Du Noyer 78). In Nick Bromell's view, "Revolutionary music delivers life as something fresh and anarchic from the grip of the past, habit, convention" (23–24). The cultural power wielded by the Beatles in 1964 was rooted in the band's absolute and refreshing indifference to ridicule, in their contagious uber-self-confidence. This could be seen and heard in the shaking of their mop tops and the distinctive tailoring, in the "yeah yeah yeahs" and the swooping "oohs" and "aahs," in the high jinx and making faces and Lennon's invitation to the city gent on the train to "give us a kiss," in those "outrageous" chord progressions singled out by Bob Dylan. In *A Hard Day's Night*, through word, song, and deed, the Beatles wrested power and space away from adult control, and in the process preempted those more explicit countercultural protests that would achieve greater visibility and impact on the nation's college campuses and main streets in the decade to come. "Sorry we hurt your field, mister," Harrison offers by way of apology, as the four Beatles are chastised by yet another representative of adult power. He did not mean it.

On December 26 "I Feel Fine" reached number one on the Billboard singles chart, capping a phenomenal year for the Beatles. It had also been a year of unprecedented American success for a host of other British pop acts. The second half of 1964 had seen the first U.S. hits for the Animals, the Kinks ("You Really Got Me" and "All Day and All Night"), the Zombies ("She's Not There"), and the Rolling Stones, whose three minor hits had announced in uncharacteristically low-key fashion the coming of the Invasion's second wave. Clearly, the American popular music landscape was not the same as it had been on December 26, 1963. The droney feedback that opens "I Feel Fine"— and that the song's composer, John Lennon, claimed to be the first time the effect was used on a pop record—confirmed as much, making it the band's most radical musical proposition to date. However, as with so much of their work before and after, it also highlighted that "ability to be two contradictory things at once—comfortably safe and exhilaratingly strange" (MacDonald 82). Composed quickly in the recording studio, it was positive pop with an ostensibly familiar, even banal message— "I'm in love with her / And I feel fine." Once again, the music offered its millions of young listeners "an altered perspective, not a foreign landscape" (Chambers 63).

3

"LIKE A ROLLING STONE...
OR A BEATLE"

1965

The British Invasion pretty much *was* the Beatles in 1964. Yet, it is evident that, while the band had a defining role to play, they did not and could not transform the '60s pop soundscape single-handedly. As the second half of 1964 proved, the Beatles opened up the American market for other British acts; and, going into 1965, not only would this continue to be the case, but the Invasion's influence would also be clearly heard (and arguably of equal importance, seen) in homegrown artists who regularly bothered Billboard's upper reaches. The biggest-selling American pop act of 1965 was Gary Lewis and His Playboys, who had hit number one on the singles chart with the anodyne "Diamond Ring"—a song that sounded like the Beatles crossed with the Hermits.

While the Playboys' success might well suggest that American pop had swiftly and smoothly moved to absorb the latest novelty into its repertoire—just as it had done with various crazes prior to the Invasion—it would be a mistake to draw such a conclusion. Very few "insiders" had failed to notice that the Beatles' creativity and fluidity, their boundary stretching, had brought them *more* fans—something that seemed to grant permission to other musicians to be similarly adventurous in a field where change was now less likely to meet with industry resistance. This was felt instantly and at the sharp end of American pop.

There were twenty-seven number-one singles in 1965—a rapid turnover that saw just two records occupy the top spot for more than three weeks. The overwhelming majority of Billboard number ones—twenty-two, in fact—were at the top for one or two weeks only. This telling volatility was one indication of pop music's vitality in 1965—a year subsequently regarded by some as "more profoundly pivotal and more genuinely fertile" than either the more commonly feted 1967 or 1976. Recalling how it felt to be a young pop fan in 1965, Richard Williams notes that "things changed fast. It just happened. You didn't even have to try. . . . Because in 1965, change was expected: every month, every week, almost every day. Every time you walked into a record shop, opened a book, bought a magazine, turned on the TV" (80–83).

In this pop annus mirabilis, it appeared to be business as usual for the Invasion. There was of course more success for the Beatles, who by year's end would have sold two hundred million records and so surpassed Elvis Presley (who had had an eight-year head start on the Brits). In 1965, the Beatles generated an estimated $100 million. So, in many respects, these figures form the headlines of a continuing story, suggesting that 1965 could be read as a carbon copy of the previous year. There was a similar volume of Invasion hits. There were five number-one singles for the Beatles, holding the top spot for a total of twelve weeks. There were an impressive seven number-one singles for British Invasion artists, totaling twenty-eight weeks. Invasion acts like Herman's Hermits enjoyed continued success with two number ones in 1965, "Mrs. Brown, You've Got a Lovely Daughter" and "I'm Henry VIII, I Am." While the band had a total of eighteen U.S. hits, 1965 saw the Hermits at their commercial peak, with seven Top 10 singles including those two best sellers. The Hermits appealed to American teenyboppers like irresistible catnip. Peddling music-hall Englishness channeled through the Beatle filter, the band's two American number ones were shameless novelty records that were not even released in their native Britain.

Other "first-wave" Invasion acts that reached number one in 1965 included Merseybeat opportunists Freddie and the Dreamers ("I'm Telling You Now"), actress and occasional singer Petula Clark ("Downtown"), and the still-popular Dave Clark Five, who had the Christmas best seller with "Over and Over." The Kinks had three more hit singles in 1965: the downright melancholic "Tired of Waiting for You" (no. 6, spring), the surprisingly avant-garde "Set Me Free" (no. 23, summer), and the rather misnomered "Everybody's Gonna Be Happy" (no. 34, fall). The diminishing returns here, however, were not so much to do with the use of the sitar, the change of pace, and reduction in noise, or even songwriter Ray Davies's increasingly parochial lyrical focus, as the various issues his band was having with the unions at this time. In what could best be described as an act of halfhearted protectionism, in January 1965 the U.S. Labor Department had put a block on visas for UK pop groups, effectively stranding a number of British acts—like the Zombies who were then riding high on the back of their successful single "She's Not There"—in midtour. Although the Kinks had not been helped by their own poor behavior on tour, there can be little doubt that the band's prospects were adversely, if not fatally, affected by this act of federal trade restriction. The fact that the Invasion had made the federal government nervous and, more importantly, act on those concerns could of course be viewed as a backhanded compliment. There were, after all, thirty-six UK-produced Top 10 Billboard hits in 1965, up four on the previous year. This did not go unrecognized on either side of the Atlantic. Back home, the Beatles were being feted for almost single-handedly opening up a global market for British pop music. The four musicians would each receive an official honor, the Member of the British Empire (MBE) in 1965 in formal acknowledgment of their contribution to the nation's coffers.

The year 1965 even had an Invasion banner chart-week to match that much-celebrated week in April 1964, when the Beatles were at numbers one through five. On May 8, 1965, nine of the Billboard Top 10 singles were of British origin. In that same month, "Ticket to Ride" became the last of an unbroken run of four Invasion singles to top the Billboard chart—following a run of three number ones by Manchester acts (the Dreamers, the Hermits, and Wayne Fontana and the Mindbenders). To cap it all, those two aforementioned singles that managed to hold down the top spot for more than three weeks were Invasion tracks—the Beatles' "Yesterday" and the Rolling Stones' "Satisfaction" both spent a month as the nation's number one. However, digging just a little deeper reveals some crucial differences with the previous year. Even Billboard's apparently incontestable truths might be challenged. There were two number ones for folk-rock pioneers the Byrds ("Mr. Tambourine Man" and "Turn Turn Turn"), a chart-topping single for ex-folkie Barry McGuire with "Eve of Destruction," and even garage rock's first number one in the form of the McCoys' "Hang On Sloopy." Alongside this native pop success, Billboard also showed that a number of Invasion acts who had ridden in on the Beatles' coattails were struggling. Billy J. Kramer and the Dakotas, Gerry and the Pacemakers, the Searchers, and the Swingin' Blue Jeans all faded badly.

There was, though, a "second wave" of British acts that broke through commercially in 1965. Perhaps surprisingly, given the band's audible Beatles-esque use of jangly guitar, beat rhythms, and vocal harmony, the Hollies were not among them. Their UK number one "I'm Alive" had only made number 103 on Billboard, and it would not be until early 1966 that the band scored its first substantial U.S. hit with "Look through Any Window" (no. 32). Neither did the Who make any significant commercial inroads in 1965—"I Can't Explain" limped to number ninety-three in the spring, "Anyway Anyhow Anywhere" failed to even chart, and "My Generation" peaked at a lowly number seventy-four at year's end. These were all Top 10 singles in Britain. However, in contrast, the Yardbirds, featuring Eric Clapton on lead guitar, enjoyed their first U.S. hit in the spring of 1965 with "For Your Love" (no. 6), and then followed this up with another Top 10, "Heart Full of Soul," in the fall and the Top 20 hit "I'm a Man" later on. Although usually identified as part of the Invasion's first wave, the Animals' fall 1964 number one "The House of the Rising Sun" was in fact the earliest indication of this second wave's bluesy musical styling and its accompanying attitude. In 1965, the Animals enjoyed a run of five hit singles in the States, which included the raw and pleading "Don't Let Me Be Misunderstood" (no. 15, spring) and "We've Gotta Get Out of This Place" (no. 13, summer), a Brill Building confection that in the group's hands carried such emotional power that it became connected with the then-escalating Vietnam War and in particular the U.S. soldiers' desire to escape its horrors.

Though not anywhere near matching that of the Beatles—or even the Dave Clark Five or the Hermits, for that matter—the commercial successes of the Yardbirds and the Animals in America nevertheless still gives lie to the perception that the music of the British rhythm and blues groups was somehow too extreme for mainstream tastes. However, this rawer, blues-based sound was undeniably at odds with the Beatles' more polished, melodic pop, and, in the hands of the second wave's most successful band, its musically generated threat was compounded by equally uncompromising behavior, onstage and off. For the musicians, though, like the Rolling Stones' guitarist Brian Jones, it all started—and, for a time at least, finished—with the music: "The essential difference between ourselves and the British groups that are well-known in the United States at the moment is that we're the first to have a really strong Negro rhythm and blues influence. We haven't adapted our music from a watered down music like white American rock 'n' roll. We've adapted our music from the early blues forms" (qtd. in Miles, *British Invasion*, 129–30).

When he gave this interview in 1964, the Stones played rhythm and blues with the fanaticism of religious zealots. It was a self-consciously noble project, as the equally fanatic Eric Clapton explained: "It was very clear that it wasn't showbiz. It was not pop. . . . I could tell you by ear what was being done for the love of it and what was being done for money. But hearing something as extreme as that may have been the reason I could tell. Because that was extreme" (qtd. in Simmons 70).

Of course, the Beatles and other beat groups had drawn, and would continue to draw, inspiration and—albeit less frequently—material from American rhythm and blues. However, this influence was often filtered through skiffle, rock 'n' roll, rockabilly, or the pop-soul of Motown. Acts like the Rolling Stones took it all in unfiltered. On *Beatles '65*, released in December 1964, the cover versions betrayed the band's influences (Chuck Berry's "Rock 'n' Roll Music," rockabilly superstar Carl Perkins's "Honey Don't" and "Everybody's Trying to Be My Baby," Arthur Alexander's soft-soul "Mr. Moonlight"); while their Christmas number-one single "I Feel Fine" *was* based on the basic blues template of Bobby Parker's "Watch Your Step" but with the melody and lyrics changed. Compared to this kind of freewheeling musical eclecticism, the Rolling Stones were representatives of a rather ascetic scene that can be dated from British musicians Alexis Korner and Cyril Davies' first live encounter with Chicago bluesman Muddy Waters, who had toured the UK in the late '50s. Suitably inspired, Korner and Davies formed Blues Incorporated, and the growing popularity of this band subsequently gave rise to London's early 1960s blues explosion. Blues Incorporated afforded Mick Jagger, Charlie Watts, and future Cream bassist Jack Bruce early opportunities to perform, and future incarnations would also feature Rod Stewart and Elton John.

So, by the early 1960s a blues-oriented scene had emerged in and around London that operated concurrently with the more provincially motored beat boom. It was a scene fueled by collectors and enthusiasts, many of whom were products of an art school education. In late 1950s and early 1960s Britain, art schools played a crucial role in the development of homegrown pop music. As Keith Richards told *Rolling Stone* magazine in 1971:

> It was somewhere they put you if they can't put you anywhere else. If you can't saw wood straight or file metal. It's where they put me to learn graphic design. . . . Fifteen . . . I was there for three years and meanwhile I learned how to play guitar. Lotta guitar players in art school. A lot of terrible artists too. It's funny. (Qtd. in Brackett 183)

Bands with art school pedigree included some of the Rolling Stones, the Who, the Kinks, the Yardbirds (whose vocalist Keith Relf and guitarist Chris Dreja both attended Kingston Art School), and the Animals. Typically, the art school's unofficial musical syllabus included Ray Charles, Chuck Berry, Bo Diddley, Muddy Waters, Charles Mingus, Thelonius Monk, and Robert Johnson. Although apparently leading two distinctive movements at this time, the Beatles and the Rolling Stones still shared a mutual interest in, and love of, rock 'n' roll, especially as practiced by Chuck Berry and Buddy Holly. The Stones covered Holly's Bo Diddley–esque "Not Fade Away" and Berry's "Come On," for example. However, the Stones dug much deeper with archaeological care, constructing a reverential repertoire of cover versions by Chicago blues artists like Muddy Waters and Howlin' Wolf, and Detroit- and Memphis-based soul musicians like Solomon Burke, Marvin Gaye, and Otis Redding. The band's first American LP, *England's Newest Hit Makers*, included "faithful"—for which read, painfully deferential—covers of Slim Harpo's "I'm a King Bee," Chuck Berry's "Carol," Willie Dixon's "I Just Wanna Make Love to You," and Jimmie Reed's "Honest I Do." Both the band's first UK number-one single "It's All Over Now" and their first substantial American hit, "Time Is On My Side," were the products of a pilgrimage to Chicago's Chess Studios.

As Greil Marcus perceptively observes, "It was the Beatles who opened up the turf the Stones took as their own—there was no possibility of a left until the Beatles created a center." This relationship was shaped by a number of literal connections between the two, as the

Stones' manager Andrew Loog Oldham had briefly worked for Brian Epstein, George Harrison's endorsement helped get the Stones their recording contract with Decca, and the Stones' first UK hit was a cover of Lennon and McCartney's "I Wanna Be Your Man." As savvy as his mentor Epstein, Oldham—memorably described by Nik Cohn as "the most anarchic and obsessive and imaginative hustler of all," who "loathed slowness and drabness, age and caution and incompetence, mediocrity of all kinds" (148, 149)—became the Stones' manager at just nineteen in April 1963. He was instrumental in marketing the band as the antithesis to the Beatles: "The overall hustle I invented for the Stones was to establish them as a raunchy, gamy, unpredictable bunch of undesirables. . . . Rejecting matching clothing was one step, emphasising their long hair and unclean appearance was another, and inciting the press to write about them, using catchy phrases that I had coined, was yet another. . . . I wanted to establish that the Stones were threatening, uncouth and animalistic" (qtd. in Szatmary 118).

Although consciously crafted as the anti-Beatles, what Oldham had clearly learned from his time with Epstein was the importance of the combined clout of image and sound. Thanks to Oldham's media savvy and the Stones' compliance, the band projected an ironic detachment, arrogance, and aggressive sexuality that stood in apparent contrast with the Beatles—qualities that were part PR puff and part genuine but that would be amply rewarded.

When the Beatles were breaking all kinds of records on their triumphant summer tour of 1964, the Rolling Stones had played to a largely indifferent America. Stones bass player Bill Wyman notes how dispiriting it was to play to near-empty venues. "We all wanted to pack up and come home," he writes (qtd. in Miles, *British Invasion*). This first tour had kicked off inauspiciously when, even before they had played live, they had been openly mocked for their appearance by host Dean Martin on his *Hollywood Palace* TV show. However, by the time they returned to the States for a second tour in the fall of 1964—having enjoyed their first number-one single in Britain with a cover of Howlin' Wolf's "Little Red Rooster"—the band found that interest (and, thankfully, ticket sales) had most definitely picked up. Off the back of three minor hits—"Not Fade Away," "It's All Over Now," and "Tell Me"— that had each marked a steady if unspectacular upward chart trajectory, the Rolling Stones played to enthusiastic crowds as "Time Is On My

Side" climbed to number six on Billboard and so gave the band its first genuine hit record in the United States.

As they became more successful, the Rolling Stones found to their delight that they were routinely billed in the American press as "the ugliest band from England." *Newsweek* called the band a "leering quintet," while a letter published in *Time* described them as "garbage" and "sick." The Beatles had of course met with some adult disapproval, but this had quickly dissolved in the face of a charm offensive rooted in their odes to joy. The Stones' young manager, Andrew Oldham, did nothing to counter their press image. He welcomed it, knowing only too well that it would push American teens—freshly liberated by the Beatles and the Invasion's first wave—firmly into the Stones' camp. The band's first appearance on *Ed Sullivan* in October 1964 had drawn numerous complaints. Future rock critic Anthony DeCurtis recalls how his schoolteachers had lectured the class on the Stones' awfulness in the days immediately after this TV appearance—condemnation that drew much of its fire from the band's physical appearance, and in particular front man Mick Jagger's decision to wear a sweatshirt. Their hair was long and unkempt and they wore mismatched clothing. The Beatles' mop tops and smart (if European) tailoring had not prepared America for this. Yet, only serving to convince Oldham that his approach was working, this controversial TV appearance gave sales of "Time Is On My Side" a real boost; and, while Ed Sullivan publicly promised that the Stones would never appear on his show again, he conceded privately to Jagger that the show had been a great success with his young audience. The Rolling Stones would be back on in May 1965.

The Rolling Stones sealed their American success with a less bluesy sound and a lyrical content squarely aimed at white youth. It had become apparent to Andrew Oldham that retaining a purist's outlook and repertoire would not deliver mainstream pop success. When the same thought occurred to the musicians, the reaction of some was understandably quite different to that of their managers. Eric Clapton, for example, quit the Yardbirds after the release of "For Your Love" because he was—and wished to remain—a purist:

> We never played pure blues. With the greatest respect to those guys, that was not a possibility for them. We played versions of blues. We'd play "Smokestack Lightning" . . . but they were poppified and they'd have these extended solos that were essentially crowd pleasers. It was

theatre. . . . It was when they just tore the root up and threw it away and became like Dave Dee, Dozy, Beaky, Mick and Tich—that was it for me. (Qtd. in Simmons)

All the British acts speeded up the tempo of their blues covers and played louder, but the decision to write their own material was a step too far for some. Initially even the Stones. "Can you imagine a British-composed R&B song?" Jagger said in 1963. "It just wouldn't make it" (qtd. in Clarke 463). Oldham tells the tale of how he had to force Jagger and Richards into composing by locking them in the kitchen of their dingy London one-bedroom apartment and not releasing the duo until they had come up with something. While this may well be yet another example of the manager's (self-)mythologizing, compositional self-sufficiency undoubtedly secured the band a longevity and influence that others, by accident or conscious design, would not match. As the Animals' drummer John Steel notes, it was not only mismanagement that led to his band's eventual implosion: "We never had the writing talents of the Beatles or the Rolling Stones. Maybe if we had, that would've been the glue to hold us together" (qtd. in Light 54).

The Rolling Stones' first self-composed track deemed worthy of being an A-side was still audibly influenced by Chicago urban blues, which supplied not only the template for "The Last Time" (no. 9, spring '65) but the riff-based sound that girded much of the band's future work. "The Last Time" was recorded in the United States, at RCA's facility in Los Angeles, with arranger and Spector acolyte Jack Nitzsche. Unlike the Beatles—who would remain loyal to Abbey Road Studios—the Stones recorded extensively in America, and undoubtedly benefited from the expertise and technological opportunities this afforded, as the band's next U.S. single release demonstrated. Although "The Last Time" had possessed musical and lyrical bite, it was still work in progress. "Satisfaction," however, arrived fully formed. It was the "perfect synchronization of sound and spirit" (Egan, *Rolling Stones*, 49). Driven by what Keith Richards had first envisioned as a Memphis-style horn riff but what was now drenched in fuzz and ably backed by a Staxy drumbeat, the menacing but thrilling noise of "Satisfaction" was matched by its equally unpop message. Lyrically, "The Last Time" had perhaps only tentatively explored less pop subject matter, as its narrator casually (even callously) debates whether to give his unfaithful lover another chance. In the end, he resolves to give his "girl" a second chance, having come to the conclusion that she will now have the necessary sexual experience to "please him." "Satisfaction," though, abandoned even the dark side of romance to deliver an angry, scattergun broadside of frustrations. There is no coherent political manifesto here. Jagger's lyric rails against the "useless information" and hypocrisy of an out-of-touch mass media, but the narrator also appears to regret that he cannot "make some girl" because she is menstruating. Mick Jagger notes that the song channeled his "frustration with everything" and that it was "simple teenage aggression" (qtd. in Szatmary 120). "Satisfaction" was openly contemptuous and confrontational. It was also America's best-selling single for a month. This meant that it was pretty much unavoidable in the summer of 1965.

Its follow-up single, "Get Off My Cloud," also reached number one in the fall. While it is sometimes dismissed as a cynical "Satisfaction" cash-in, "Get Off My Cloud" is actually a sequel, exploring the same thematic field and expressing similar sentiments. Clearly, there is still no "satisfaction." "Cloud" offered another example of the Stones' ability to synthesize music and lyric, sound and stance. It has a stomping soul beat, a memorable riff, and delivered its litany of annoyances—pushy marketeers, overzealous traffic wardens, and complaining neighbors— with characteristically sardonic humor. As linked expressions of consciousness, both singles seemed to fully justify the words of an article that had appeared a year earlier in the British music paper *Melody Maker*, in which the Stones had been described as "symbols of rebellion against the boss, the clock, and the clean-shirt-a-day routine." If both "Satisfaction" and "Get Off My Cloud" had offered this diagnosis— telling us what the band did not like—then perhaps a track like "I'm Free," which featured both on the B-side of "Cloud" and on the band's first American number-one album *Out of Our Heads*, could be taken as the possible cure. On "I'm Free" the Stones' young fans were given hedonistic license, urged to act and think for themselves, to do exactly what they "want, any old time" with whomever they "choose."

The Beatles first came across Bob Dylan on record in January 1964, when George Harrison had purchased a copy of Dylan's *Freewheelin'* LP while the band was in Paris on the eve of their inaugural visit to the States. This was around the same time that Dylan would have no doubt become aware of the Beatles, with "I Want to Hold Your Hand" all over

American radio and having taken up residency in Billboard's upper reaches. However, the earliest example of a concrete Dylan-Invasion relationship can be traced to the first two 45s by the Animals—"Baby Let Me Take You Home" and the number-one single "House of the Rising Sun"—which were versions of songs found on Dylan's eponymous first LP for Columbia Records. Though not written by him, the Animals' interpretation of "House of the Rising Sun" was directly inspired by Bob Dylan's treatment of it—and Dylan, in turn, was reportedly impressed and suitably inspired by the Animals' version: "It's fuckin' wild. [It] blew my mind." Dylan, though, reserved his most fulsome praise for the Beatles. "In my head the Beatles were it," he recalls:

> They were doing things nobody else was doing . . . but I just kept it to myself that I really dug them. Everybody else thought they were just for teenyboppers, that they were gonna pass right away. But it was obvious to me that they had staying power. I knew they were pointing the direction that music had to go. . . . It seemed to me a definite line was being drawn. This was something that never happened before. (Qtd. in Gilmore 27)

Even allowing for some judicious revisionism here, it was clear that, as early as 1964, Bob Dylan understood the Beatles' game-changing cultural import. He has also freely acknowledged the spirit of creative inspiration, liberation, and competition that they sparked.

Yet, if the Beatles helped change the face and direction of popular music in the 1960s—and, in the process, arguably even American culture itself—then they could not have single-handedly accomplished this. The impact of that triumvirate of Rolling Stones' singles in 1965 demonstrates this. But the Beatles also found a principal ally—maybe even a partner of equal stature—in Bob Dylan. Although undeniably oversimplifying its emergence, rock music could still be usefully viewed as the sum total arrived at when you add these two artists together. For, in tandem with Bob Dylan, the Beatles helped make popular music "become . . . pregnant with ideas and innovations" (Wicke 109). The eighteen-month period through 1965 and 1966 saw the release of LPs like *Bringing It All Back Home, Help!, Highway 61 Revisited, Rubber Soul, Blonde on Blonde,* and *Revolver;* and 45s like "Ticket to Ride," "Like a Rolling Stone," "Day Tripper," "Paperback Writer," and "Positively 4th Street."

By 1964 the Beatles and Bob Dylan were in comparable positions following their breakthrough year in '63—possibly another reason they were acutely sensitive to each other, and so developed a kinship, a mutually beneficial creative bond. Their status as artists operating with unprecedented leverage and autonomy, for instance, must surely have made this relationship, if not inevitable, then highly likely. While the Beatles were conquering their homeland, *The Freewheelin' Bob Dylan* had been released in May 1963 and peaked at twenty-two on the Billboard album chart. Though only a modest commercial success, as Sean Egan notes, *Freewheelin'* "struck a chord": "In 1963 it was a huge blast of fresh air: young and vibrant when society and culture was usually middle-aged and staid, irreverent when that was uncommon, informal (right down to the artfully dropped title 'g') when that was synonymous with radical/degenerate, risqué when open sexuality was frowned upon and unremitting in its condemnation of the faults of society when that society was still presented to itself in chocolate-box terms" (*Bob Dylan*, 20).

One track in particular had significantly raised Dylan's national profile. "Blowing in the Wind" had been adopted as an anthem for the civil rights movement, and, in the hands of Peter, Paul, and Mary had reached number two on the Billboard chart in July with sales of over a million. In August, Dylan—who had campaigned tirelessly for civil rights—had appeared alongside Martin Luther King in Washington, D.C., at the high-profile demonstration at which King delivered his "I Have a Dream" speech. As further confirmation of his impact and import, Bob Dylan had been written up in both *Newsweek* and *Time*.

However, by 1964 Dylan had grown resentful of what he perceived to be folk music's limitations, its seriousness, its worthy commitment to cause. He felt trapped by the massive expectations of, and hence demands placed on him by, an audience that saw him as some kind of prophet. In his mind, he was in danger of becoming folk's "hired gun"—expected to trot out to-order polemical masterpieces on every social and political ill or outrage, wheeled out at every rally, demonstration, and fund-raiser to perform his earnest songs of protest.

In early 1960s America folk music was enjoying a rare moment of credibility and popularity. But for all its engagement and profile, folk was still a music of the past that neither sought to embrace or understand youth. Rigidly acoustic, musically direct, and lyrically declamatory, folk—as Dylan and others knew only too well—could be effectively employed as a vehicle for social commentary, urging change and voicing dissent. Folk music worked to solidify collective identity and individual belonging, acting as a kind of glue that bound performers and audiences to causes and movements. Even allowing for its unprecedented commercial appeal in the late 1950s and early 1960s, though, folk had remained very much a minority taste, typically consumed by young, often college-educated adults. It was "grown up" in comparison to pop music and especially rock 'n' roll, which seemed to revel in its immaturity. This meant that the Beatles and Bob Dylan had two very separate audiences at the beginning of 1964, shaped by often big differences in age, class, gender, and education. However, in a classic pincer movement that would collapse this difference, through 1964 Bob Dylan would bring his audience to the center field, just as the Beatles would begin taking theirs from the pop mainstream to its fringes.

Dylan had begun this journey in earnest with the release in early 1964 of *The Times They Are A-Changing*. Although in many respects his most "civil rights" record, on which he urges his listeners from the outset to "gather 'round" him apparently without irony to receive his message, the *Times* arguably kick-started his tumultuous transformation to fully fledged pop star through its reception and acclaim. The June release of *Another Side of Bob Dylan* offered unequivocal proof that Dylan's modus operandi had shifted. Its title said as much. With *Another Side* Dylan had effectively declared his intention to quit folk protest. On one track, "My Back Pages," he sings of the "lies that life is black and white," distancing himself from the earnest certainties of folk protest. As Dylan told *New Yorker's* Nat Hentoff, when the journalist visited him during the album's recording sessions:

> There aren't any finger-pointing songs in here, either. Those records I've made, I'll stand by them, but some of that was jumping into the scene to be heard and a lot of it was because I didn't see anybody else doing that kind of thing. Now a lot of people are doing finger-pointing songs. You know—pointing to all the things that are wrong. Me, I don't want to write for people anymore. You know, be a spokesman. . . . From now on, I want to write from inside me, and to do that I'm going to have to get back to writing like I used to when I was ten—having everything come out naturally. (Qtd. in Egan, *Bob Dylan*, 31)

These were not recognizably pop or even rock 'n' roll arrangements. Songs were still performed solo and acoustic. However, they were love songs, albeit ones with lyrics that avoided pop's tendency for the facile and sentimental. Written and recorded in just one week, it is willfully slapdash, sloppy, and immediate. It has a palpable energy and joy that comes across as something of a relief after the grim, seriousness of *Times*. "Insubstantial" it might have been, but it was still momentous, a sure sign that something had shifted quite dramatically. Having freed himself from the burden of being folk's messiah, on "My Back Pages" Dylan sings, "I was so much older then, I'm younger than that now." A unilateral declaration of independence. He was with the "now" lobby. He was with the Beatles.

If *Another Side* articulated anything, it was an embrace of rock 'n' roll's urgency and commitment to the present. Furthermore, in the characteristically gnomic sleeve notes, Dylan writes: "You tell me about politics an' I tell you there are no politics. . . . I know no answers an' no truth." As a teenager growing up in Minnesota, Dylan had been in a rock 'n' roll band, and so the music was not alien to him. His first Columbia single in December 1962 was a track called "Mixed Up Confusion," a self-penned rock 'n' roller that was withdrawn soon after its release, most likely because the record company felt it compromised his carefully constructed image (and marketability) as a folk-protest singer. Like the Beatles, Dylan was immersed in rock 'n' roll. He shared with them a mutual admiration for Elvis Presley, Little Richard—playing with whose band Dylan listed as his ambition in his 1959 high school year book—and Buddy Holly. Dylan has (in)consistently maintained through the years that he used folk music as a means to get into rock on his own terms. This is not as disingenuous as it might seem. Folk gave him autonomy, opportunity, and mobility. But rock 'n' roll was there first. He has also claimed that he only became successful as a folk artist because "I played . . . with a rock 'n' roll attitude" (qtd. in Egan, *Bob Dylan*, 3), and it is also likely that he abandoned rock 'n' roll "when the music died" in the late 1950s—when it was "taken over by some milk," as he put in a 1966 interview.

The year 1965 represented the moment at which Bob Dylan became central to the development of American popular music, but, in order to arrive at this point, he had to embrace and then somehow process the invigorating, liberating effect of the British Invasion. Proof of this came in the early months of 1965, when he recorded the semirock album *Bringing It All Back Home*—whose title might well have referred to its creator's conscious decision to return to the preferred music of his youth in realizing an intention announced on "My Back Pages." With this record "Dylan had stopped pretending that he was rambling through the 1930s with Woody Guthrie, and recognised instead that his time was Now—he was thirty years younger in an instant" (Storey 145). On half of the album's tracks Dylan embraces rock 'n' roll's visceral rhythms with the aid of a ramshackle amplified band. Significantly, though, while folk's musical frames may have been abandoned, its lyrical emphases were not. Indeed, if anything, here Dylan ramped up the complexity, as words tumbled out, overloading where folk had tended to favor the power of declamatory understatement and simplicity. In all respects, the final track on the album's "electric" side, "Bob Dylan's 115th Dream," offered listeners the perfect opportunity to gauge the distance its author had traveled in just twelve short months. "I have given up at making any attempt at perfection," Dylan writes in the sleeve notes; and, true to his word, the false start as the band misses its cue and collapses into a (drug-induced?) collective giggling fit is pointedly retained. Thereafter, what follows—embedded in a chugging rock 'n' roll beat—is a rambling, sardonic rereading of the discovery myth, complete with references to "Englishmen" who say "Fab!" and the kind of sight gags and *Goon*-ish pratfalls seen in *A Hard Day's Night*—at one point, for example, the narrator is on the telephone when "a foot comes down the line." All a very long way, then, from the high seriousness of folk, but of course equidistant from pop's crafted clichés.

Bringing It All Back Home was recorded very quickly in the early months of 1965, with the bulk of the work done between 13th and 15th of January. While it peaked at number six on Billboard, it rather symbolically dislodged *Beatles for Sale* from the top spot in the UK's album chart. Yet—as "Bob's 115th Dream" demonstrated—it also confirmed the extent to which the Invasion, and in particular the Beatles, had shaped Dylan's startling new music. While he appeared to have abandoned the simplicity and purity of the acoustic folk sound for something altogether dirtier and messier, *Bringing It All Back Home* made it abundantly clear that Dylan had no intention of giving up folk's lyric intelligence. His new material wedded folk's emphasis on the "message"—or perhaps, in this specific case, more accurately the lyric, since it was not always entirely clear what a song was "about"—to the urgency and excitement of rock 'n' roll now reanimated by the Invasion. Dylan's lyrics stretched to the breaking point rock 'n' roll's—and particularly mainstream pop's—"moon/June" banalities. Yet he also recognized that these musical fields had much to offer. "They were doing things nobody was doing," he said of the Beatles. "Their chords were outrageous, just outrageous, and their harmonies made it all valid. *You could only do that with other musicians. It started me thinking about other people"* (qtd. in Miller 218, my emphasis).

In July 1965, Dylan would book the Butterfield Blues Band to back him in his epochal "electric" performance at the Newport Jazz and Folk Festival in an effort to re-create the plugged-in sound he had enjoyed while jamming with John Mayall's Bluesbreakers on tour in Britain earlier in the year. In the album's sleeve notes Dylan writes that "my poems are written in a rhythm of unpoetic distortion." In one very important respect, then, *Bringing It All Back Home* was a concerted and conscious effort to simultaneously channel and surpass all that Beatles energy.

When the album's opening track, "Subterranean Homesick Blues," was released as a single in May it became Dylan's first American hit 45. Although only reaching a modest number thirty-nine on Billboard, it deployed rock 'n' roll's weapon of choice to confirm that Dylan was now a pop star, but that he had achieved this status on his own terms. While it appeared to be modeled on Chuck Berry's "Too Much Monkey Business," its bitter but hip and humorous lyrical exposé of establishment hypocrisies and false promises—a world of "eleven-dollar bills"—took it to a dissenting place that rock 'n' roll had not been before. Fully two months before the Rolling Stones' "Satisfaction" hit number one, here was a pop song expressing similar youthful contempt for the adult mainstream, but with arguably greater force and focus. There were slogans, for sure, but not empty ones. Young Americans were doomed to the scrap heap after "twenty years of schooling" or, worse still, would end up as cannon fodder ("Join the army if you fail").

In the combined wake of the single and album's success, Dylan experienced what it was like to be a pop star. However, he was a new kind of pop star, as his next single would emphatically demonstrate. Memorably described by its author as "really vomitific in its structure," the six-minute-long "Like a Rolling Stone," which reached number two in the summer of 1965, "sounded simultaneously young and adult" to a receptive Bruce Springsteen. "It was revolutionary," he recalls. Dylan "freed your mind the way Elvis freed your body." "Like a Rolling Stone" effectively granted American pop license to roam. Columbia Records had initially balked at releasing a track that was twice as long as the average chart single, but Dylan insisted there be no edits. He won. So the song's commercial success was both personal vindication and, importantly, it supplied leverage. In this way, it was "not a record, it was an event" (Marcus 34). In addition to its length, it also broke new emotional ground, as Dylan howls "How does it feel?" But who is he so disgusted with? His girlfriend? The government? Himself? All three? This then seemed to mark the moment when something as previously ephemeral and trivial as pop mutated into something enduring and significant. Here, a track like the eleven-minute-long "Desolation Row" on Dylan's second studio album of the year, *Highway 61 Revisited*, appeared indicative of this transformation. According to Philip Ennis, 1965 saw rock 'n' roll "maturing into rock," achieving "a minimal level of maturity when it stretched beyond its teenage concerns and constituency, past the trauma of puppy love and the problems of parental authority" (Ennis 313). As the admiring Bruce Springsteen confirms, listening to Bob Dylan was "like somebody'd kicked open the door to your mind."

If 1964 had belonged to the Beatles, then it could be argued that—while he did not match the Brits' five number-one singles—1965 was surely Dylan's year. In addition to the still highly impressive commercial success enjoyed by his own singles and albums, the Turtles had placed their cover of Dylan's "It Ain't Me, Babe" in the Top 10, while both the Four Seasons'—under the unlikely (and unnecessary) *nom de disque* the Wonder Who?—reworking of "Don't Think Twice, It's All Right" and Cher's of "All I Really Wanna Do" made the Top 20. However, the most noteworthy cover was undoubtedly the Byrds' version of "Mr. Tambourine Man"—a track that offered conclusive proof that American pop had been transformed due to the combined influence of Dylan *and the Invasion*. While "Mr. Tambourine Man" would be marketed as folk rock, and so as America's answer to the Invasion—coinciding as it did with those federal acts of protectionism—there was considerable irony in the fact that folk rock was shaped and fueled by that same Invasion. So, even though it was a credible rival to the Invasion, it was by no means "indigenous." Indeed, the two pop movements were bound tightly together.

The Byrds were a Los Angeles–based band led by a former folkie, Roger McGuinn. He had performed with folk groups like the Limeliters in the early 1960s, but like many thousands of young Americans had experienced a Beatles epiphany, which led to him initially performing their songs solo in Greenwich Village clubs. After seeing *A Hard Day's Night*, however, he determined to form a band. This band was quickly signed to Elektra Records as the Jet Set but had a flop single under the Invasion cash-in name of the Beefeaters and the label dropped them. They were then picked up by Dylan's label, Columbia; and, now renamed the Byrds in the quirky manner of the Beatles' deliberate, punning misspelling, they also acquired the services of the latter's former publicist, Derek Taylor. They recorded their version of "Mr. Tambourine Man" with session musicians in April 1965, a few weeks before Dylan recorded the acoustic version of the song that found its way on to *Bringing It All Back Home*. It was Columbia's PR department that dubbed it folk rock, as it brazenly and simultaneously marketed the five long-haired, Cuban-heeled, good-looking young men as America's Beatles. Yet this was not all empty marketing puff. "I saw this gap"—Roger McGuinn confesses—"with Dylan and the Beatles leaning toward each other in concept. That's where we aimed" (qtd. in Inglis, "Synergies," 66).

Significantly altered from Dylan's LP version, the Byrds' reworking has been condemned as a bowdlerization of the original, and it is true that the band did use only one of the four verses while shamelessly emphasizing the chorus. It was certainly different but not necessarily the worse for it. McGuinn's twelve-string electric guitar, his conscious Beatles-esque stylings in terms of beat and, most distinctively, vocal harmony, combined to produce superior pop product that was the equal of anything the band's British heroes had produced thus far. It was also evident that the Byrds were not empty headed, either. When asked about the "teenage revolution" in an interview with *Beat* magazine in November 1965, David Crosby opines:

> Over half of the people in the country are under 25. The country isn't being run as they know and feel it should be. The discrepancies are too obvious. The wrongness and the corruption disturbs and upsets them. And the uncertainty of the nuclear thing, which is

something we've lived with since we were born. They definitely want to change this and a lot of other things. . . . They're interested, as far as I've been able to discern, in the possibility of love as opposed to war. (Qtd. in Feigal 247)

Barry McGuire's "Eve of Destruction" provided still more evidence of Bob Dylan's transformative power in 1965. It was a million seller that was number one for a week in the fall. Complete with perfunctory, Dylanesque harmonica parts that only served to reinforce the impression that here was folk-rock-by-numbers, its splenetic, bilious, scattershot denunciations of various injustices undoubtedly struck a chord. (It did not mention Vietnam directly, for example, but it did highlight the hypocrisy of being "old enough to kill, but not for votin'.") Written by the then nineteen-year-old P. F. Sloan, formulaic pastiche or not, it proved so controversial and impactful that it prompted a conservative "answer" song—a sure sign of its ability to get under people's skin. The "Dawn of Correction" by the Spokesmen delivered an uncompromising anticommunist, anti-Vietnam protest, pro-American message. It did not achieve anywhere near the sales (and reach) of "Eve of Destruction." There were also semisuccessful attempts to get "Eve" banned, largely on the grounds of its "unhealthy pessimism." As a result, the record was not played on ABC stations.

Barry McGuire was an ex-folkie, and so it was not surprising that the lyric, structure, and sound should reflect and project a familiar folk-protest anger, aimed with sarcasm at various social ills. In fact, there was a direct lineage traceable to Bob Dylan's preelectric "finger-pointing" songs here. Activist turned social historian Todd Gitlin has described the track as "brooding," carried by McGuire's "surly" delivery. For all its formulaic histrionics, Gitlin contends that there had been "no song remotely like this one in the decade-long history of rock music" to that point. Audience research, however, perhaps suggested otherwise, as it confirmed that only a very small percentage of listeners was "tuned in" to the song's apparent critique of homegrown and worldwide ills, with only a similarly small number admitting to all but a partial grasp of its message and meaning. Yet Gitlin is adamant that this did not matter because young listeners responded to the song's mood, regardless of whether they fully comprehended its lyrical content or not. For Gitlin, then, the "sound carried the point"; and so, as a result of this faith, some would hear "Eve of Destruction" as evidence that a "mass movement of

American young" was on the march, its commercial success "signall[ing] a new mentality on a grand scale" (Gitlin 196–99).

Others were more skeptical, even dismissive. For some of its critics, it was perceived as Madison Avenue pop. More audience research from the time confirmed that you did not have to be politically radical—or even engaged—to consume folk-rock music—because "most of the record-buying kids of today are about as aware as eggplants" (qtd. in Anderson 52). Folk singer Phil Ochs dismissed the song as a "vague philosophical point that can be taken any way by anybody" (qtd. in Pichaske 61). The real "destruction," he concluded with bitterness possibly leavened by jealousy, was that inflicted upon the genuine folk-protest song. A track like "Eve of Destruction" was ambiguous, where traditional folk protest dealt in certainties. It also lacked Dylan's verbal wit and play.

While Dylan was controversially abandoning folk for rock 'n' roll, it appeared that the Beatles were moving in the opposite direction, producing in the process something Roger McGuinn called "electrified folk music." (McGuinn has in fact identified the Beatles' use of folk's passing chords on earlier records such as "I Want to Hold Your Hand" and the Rickenbacker-soaked *A Hard Day's Night*. This suggests that the Beatles' "journey" might have begun before any close encounter with Dylan and his music.) Beatles' American "headlines" from 1965 would appear to suggest a continuation of the band's 1964 story. There were five number-one singles and four number-one albums; and, on their summer tour, the band played Shea Stadium to fifty-five thousand fans, establishing a new record for attendance and receipts (and therefore a completely different business model). This tour comprised just ten dates—half of 1964's number—but these gigs took place in venues typically twice the size. The MBEs the Beatles collected at Buckingham Palace—as mentioned earlier in this chapter—were both recognition of the b(r)and's economic value to Britain and a means by which the newly elected Labour government could bathe in some reflected glory.

The Beatles had first met Bob Dylan in late August 1964 at the Hotel Delmonico in New York, when the latter famously introduced the former to marijuana. For the Brits, this was to prove a revelatory experience, as a reliance on the "superficial states of mind"—and behavior—"induced by drink and 'speed' gave way to the more introspective and sensual moods associated with cannabis" (MacDonald 99). Paul

McCartney, for example, reported that, under marijuana's influence, he was "thinking . . . really thinking for the very first time." "Being a musician means getting to the depths of where you are at. And most any musician would try anything to get to those depths" (qtd. in Miller 222). Recorded in the fall of 1964 but featuring on the early '65 release *Beatles VI*, "What You're Doing" offers early proof of its songwriter McCartney's engagement with pot. Although by no stretch experimental, it does have an unorthodox musical arrangement and sonic texture—embedded in an unusual, unpropulsive, lazy beat—allied with an equally uncharacteristic (for McCartney) tone of sardonic, slow-burning anger: "Would it be too much to ask of you / What you're doing to me?"

However, as was noted in the previous chapter, it was John Lennon whose creative output was most evidently affected by contact with Dylan. Although Perkins-esque in its rockabilly rhythms, "I'm a Loser"—from *Beatles '65*—explored lyrical territory opened up by Dylan. When Lennon sings, "I'm not what I appear to be," this suggests a pointedly unpop degree of self-scrutiny, self-ridicule, even self-loathing. There is a confessional honesty here ("Is it for her or myself that I cry?"); and, while such autobiographical conviction was evident in his '64 output, it is difficult to miss in Lennon's work over the next eighteen months. Typically, though, Dylan's influence is more usually to be found in a song's "mood," attitude, or tone than in any direct lyrical or (even less likely) musical specifics. With its bossa nova rhythms, "No Reply" (*Beatles '65*) could also hardly be identified as folk protest in musical lineage. However, it has a lyric that bucks pop's default "happy endings" setting. Indeed, by the end of the song, nothing has progressed. We are back where we started. We are also unlikely to empathize with the song's narrator. Is the girl—the real victim here—avoiding him with good reason? Our narrator is an unattractive obsessive, a stalker perhaps.

Under the combined influence of Dylan, marijuana, and their own fame (which brought with it creative confidence and autonomy), the emotional range of the Beatles' songwriting had widened considerably over the course of 1964. Six of the eight self-compositions on the band's UK LP *Beatles for Sale*, for example, had explored darker themes, sometimes in darker musical tones; but, through 1965, the Beatles' music started to lose its "innocence" at pace. This was not hidden away on albums, either. In May, "Ticket to Ride" became the band's seventh American number-one single, and marked both musically and lyrically the Beatles' boldest incursion into alien pop territory thus far. "Ticket to Ride" features Lennon the "loser" at his self-lacerating worst/best—"The girl that's driving [him] mad is going away," but, since we also learn that "living with [him] is bringing her down," our sympathies lie with "her." The song is emotionally deeper and more psychologically complex than anything the band had released up to this point—a depth and complexity augmented by its musical frame. The lyric highlights the narrator's essential passivity—the "girl" is "going away" but there appears to be no effort expended to prevent her imminent departure—and this is perfectly complemented by the loping, stuttering midtempo rhythm, its tempo shifts, and by the song's decidedly unemphatic closure, which sees it stuck in a groove, leaving us in an appropriately liminal musical space that matches the narrator's similarly puzzling and puzzled state of betweenness. While "Ticket to Ride" did indeed reach number one, it is tempting to conclude that its uncharacteristically brief single-week stay at the top might well have been the result of the very evident artistic distance traveled by the Beatles in little more than a year.

In September, "Help!" held the number-one spot for three weeks. In some respects, its longer run at the top of the Billboard singles chart could be seen as a reflection of its obvious return to less risky musical territory. In fact, "Help!" had first been presented to the band by its author John Lennon as a midtempo ballad that lyrically distilled his misery. A song about the fallacy of success, it emerged from what Lennon referred to as his "fat Elvis" period as he struggled with fame. Even when speeded up, the song's rockabilly stylings could not obscure the high levels of anxiety found within. "I meant it," Lennon said of this track, and his personal investment shone through in a mature, genre-stretching lyric of which he was clearly proud ("My independence seems to vanish in the haze"). "Help!" was also noteworthy, then, for its confessional honesty. "Help! I need somebody!" Lennon cries in desperation from the start; and indeed his situation is so painful, his emotional state so fragile, his need for aid so urgent that he is prepared to take it from "anybody."

The folky "You've Got to Hide Your Love Away," which featured on the *Help!* album, represented the kind of naked honesty the title track's musical structure had perhaps "obscured." "That's me in my Dylan period again," explains its author, Lennon. "I am like a chameleon, influenced by what is ever going on" (qtd. in Inglis, "Synergies," 64). Yet, although this acoustic track—a Beatles' first—might well have been folk flavored, no amount of Dylanesque vocalizing could disguise the fact that Lennon is emotionally open and scrutable here. The track is typically transparent, where Dylan was given to opacity. The narrator is being "laughed" at, and it clearly hurts. While there is a halfhearted effort to expose love's empty platitudes—"How could she say to me, love will find a way?"—it is only semisuccessful, as Lennon is simply not concerned with the "game." Bob Dylan's "I Don't Believe You (She Acts Like We Never Met)" (*Another Side of Bob Dylan*) was apparently a Beatles' favorite; and there are certainly lyrical similarities between it and "You've Got to Hide Your Love Away" that can be found particularly in the first three lines of the latter—in its rhyming of "hand" and "stand" and the phrase "facing the wall." So it could be viewed as homage. But it was not a copy. Musically, it featured a flute solo, where a harmonica might reasonably have been expected of a straight copy; lyrically, as noted above, there is none of Dylan's characteristic evasion.

Somewhat lazily but understandably, *Billboard* magazine had identified "Yesterday" as "Dylan styled" when it was released as a single in the late summer of 1965. It was at number one for four weeks; and this level of commercial success might, perhaps counterintuitively, indicate what the record was *not* rather than what it was. It was *not* the band's first romantic ballad. It was *not* the first pop record to make heavy use of strings. It was *not* a major compositional leap forward. It highlighted what the band was capable of and, even to a certain extent, what they had been doing for quite a while. As was common with much earlier Beatles material, it was both "comfortably safe and exhilaratingly strange" (MacDonald 82). It was noteworthy for the fact that, of the band, only McCartney performed on it—something that undoubtedly helped supply it with its raw emotional honesty. George Martin's string score ensured that it was not cloying, schmaltzy, or melodramatic, and perfectly complemented McCartney's restrained vocal. While not directly a product of the latter's engagement with Bob Dylan, maybe *Billboard* magazine had been inadvertently onto something when it noted the ballad's Dylanesque quality. Entering a space that Bob Dylan seemed to have carved out almost single-handedly, "Yesterday" proved that "introspective self-absorption" was now right at the very heart of the American pop mainstream—a sure sign that its range had been expanded, so that it might now be a "medium fit for communicating autobiographical intimacies, political discontents, spiritual elation, inviting an audience, not to dance, but to listen—quietly, attentively, thoughtfully" (Miller 227–28).

This transformation in pop's range and reach was confirmed on the Beatles' late 1965 album *Rubber Soul*. Clearing a path for the genre-stretching experimentation of the second half of the 1960s and beyond, it demonstrated the band's willingness to deal in more edgy topics with greater lyrical maturity and musical sophistication. The greater risk, experimentation, and intelligence found here were fearlessly communicated to their vast young audience, most of whom went along for the "ride," and many of whom became open and receptive to the even weirder sounds that followed. Recorded over a period of one month in the fall, *Rubber Soul* was as much a product of the time the band's success had earned them as it was of their contact with Dylan. Capitol's American version of *Rubber Soul* featured twelve Beatles compositions—ten new tracks and two from earlier UK albums. Yet, despite the label's best efforts to package the album as "folk rock"—demonstrated in its substituting of the intended opener "Drive My Car" with the decidedly jangly "I've Just Seen a Face"—the overriding impression was still that here was a major creative breakthrough. The album featured exotic instrumentation like the sitar and bouzouki ("Girl"), distorted timbres ("The Word"), and acoustic instruments and plush harmonies ("Michelle"). "Norwegian Wood"—which understandably became a firm favorite with American folkies—was much closer in spirit to Dylan than anything the band had recorded thus far. Supposedly about an affair Lennon had with a journalist, it is nevertheless lyrically oblique, elusive, and sardonic—as its narrator comically "crawls off to sleep in the bath" in trademark Dylanesque fashion. Predominantly acoustic, "Norwegian Wood" was also colored by mainstream pop music's earliest use of the sitar, as Lennon played a sustained E major to approximate the drone of Indian classical music. In yet another example of transatlantic exchange, it has been pointed out that Harrison and Lennon had first picked up the sitar in the summer of 1965 when jamming with the Byrds' Crosby and McGuinn.

Although the tempo-shifting *Anthology* take of Paul McCartney's "I'm Looking Through You" better suits the song's lyrical ambiguities, the *Rubber Soul* version remains indicative of a more "grown-up," even cynical reading of relationships: "You don't sound different, I've learned the game." Here, the narrator is both perceptive and paranoid—his lover's "voice" might be "soothing" but her words "aren't clear."

According to producer George Martin, *Rubber Soul* presented "a new, growing Beatles to the world. For the first time we began to think of albums as art on their own, as complete entities." Meeting up with the audibly and visibly changed Beatles in London in 1966, Bob Dylan commented: "Oh I get it—You don't want to be cute anymore" (qtd. in Miller 230–31). Yet, as their 1965 output had demonstrated, the Dylan-Beatles relationship was a genuine dialogue, a transatlantic exchange, a shared project. "I think it was mutual admiration," Paul McCartney notes. He then adds modestly: "Certainly from our side, there was admiration. I mean . . . he influenced us and a lot of people. He showed all of us that it was possible to go a little further. . . . But the nice thing about Dylan for me was that he brought back poetry. . . . We got so huge that that kind of student thing got cut short, but Dylan re-introduced that into all our lives" (qtd. in Inglis, "Synergies," 72).

While Bob Dylan could never be categorized as a mere Invasion copyist, others emerging in 1965 would make little attempt to deny such a label. Even the Byrds' "Mr. Tambourine Man," Roger McGuinn conceded, could accurately be described as a Beatlesed-up version of a Dylan song. One rather unlikely but high-profile side effect of the Beatles' unprecedented level of success in America was the appearance of thousands of groups made in their image. Copycat bands emerged, reinforcing their Invasion sound and "look" with nomenclature that was supposed to give them an aura of fashionable Englishness. The earliest of these was the Beau Brummels, a San Francisco band named after a Georgian dandy whose Top 20 single "Laugh Laugh" owed much to Merseybeat and to the Dakotas' "Bad to Me" in particular. Thereafter, they were joined by the Knickerbockers, the Brogues, the E-Types, the Squires, the Clefs of Lavender Hill, the Beefeaters (who subsequently became the Byrds), and the Palace Guard (who went so far as to wear red British guardsmen's uniforms). However, the strangest case of all surrounded the Sir Douglas Quintet, a band formed at the instigation of Texan record producer, Huey P. Meaux. Anxious to capitalize on the Invasion, Meaux called in local musician Doug Sahm and told him: "Get me a tune, grow some fuckin' hair, and let's go cut some of this shit" (qtd. in Stax 64). The product of this creative union was "She's About a

Mover," a Top 20 hit in the spring of 1965 that bore more than a passing resemblance to the Beatles' "She's a Woman" (the B-side to "I Feel Fine"). Unfortunately, by this time the Quintet's faux-British cover had been comprehensively blown, as publicity photographs (though not the deliberately silhouetted still on the LP cover) and related media work following the nationwide success of the single had revealed the band to be of Hispanic rather than English stock.

In late 1964 the Gestures' "Run Run Run" (no. 44) had emerged as one of the very earliest examples of copyism. However, it was the Knickerbockers' late '65 hit "Lies" (no. 20) that represented the apotheosis of American attempts to recreate the Invasion sound, distilling all those ingredients it was believed to comprise: the Lennonesque lead vocal, the lively harmonies, the distinctive Ringo-style drumming, even McCartney's Little Richard–inspired screaming. The Knickerbockers' less commercially successful follow-up, "One Track Mind" (no. 46), continued to showcase the band's Beatles' influences.

Over and above such artless efforts to reproduce the Invasion sound, one important way to evaluate the Invasion's cultural impact is to understand it as an empowering agent, inspiring American youth to *make* music. In this respect, its influence was akin to that of skiffle in late 1950s Britain. It is no coincidence to find that guitar sales peaked in America between 1964 and 1967, just as they had in the UK during skiffle's heyday. Thousands of amateur and semiprofessional bands, largely composed of teenage males, strove to sound like British Invaders. It has been estimated that 63 percent of American males under the age of twenty-three were active members of rock bands in 1966; and, more so than the creatively ambitious and melodic Beatles, it was the Rolling Stones, the Kinks, and the more-surly-than-the-Stones, Northern Irish band Them that were particularly influential here. These were the bands American teens copied, particularly in their use of fuzz and power chords, in vocal styling and attitude. So, there were, for example, countless rudimentary covers of "Gloria," which had originally featured as the B-side to Them's minor hit single "Baby Please Don't Go" (no. 93, March 1965).

There are those who have worked hard to bust the myth that the Beatles and the Invasion they spearheaded "saved" American rock from total incorporation. Richard Aquila, for example, has argued that this myth "oversimplifies a complex process [as] attempts to standardise rock and roll did occur but the homogenisation process was never complete." "Early 1960s rock and roll" he has contended, "remained as diverse and vital as its predecessor" (Aquila 269). Here, both the emerging black pop sound that would become known as soul and the work of record producer Phil Spector might be taken as proof of American rock 'n' roll's rude health during this supposed fallow period. There were also other American popular music forms that stood up to the British Invasion. There were thousands of what Charlie Gillett has called "rough and ready" groups, performing in local bars and dance halls, many of which *predated* the Invasion and flourished in its wake. Sometimes referred to as garage bands, the most resolute often found themselves simultaneously threatened and empowered by the British Invasion.

As a descriptor, garage is "indispensable, [but] it is also difficult to pin down" (Hicks 23). If it refers to a group that typically practices in a garage, then most bands would qualify. If it refers to a group that records in a garage, then most bands that make a demo recording would qualify. However, the term applies to a range of bands enjoying wildly varying levels of commercial success—a few consistent hit makers, some one-hit wonders, and a host of no-hit wonders. It is, though, at the level of metaphor that the term "garage" works best. For, as Michael Hicks has observed: "A garage is a rougher, dirtier place than where humans typically reside; a place to store heavy machinery and marginally useful possessions. It is a place of noise and alienation, a psychological space as much as a physical one. In this light, 'garage band' implies a distancing from more respectable bands (and from respectable enterprises in general)" (25).

Here the association with the garage is particularly significant, because this was a marginal space—in most cases consciously chosen—where American youth might revel in its outsider status. Regardless of whether they had any direct influence on the music that eventually emerged from the garage, the Beatles and other Invasion acts undoubtedly inspired many young Americans to form a band, to "take up arms"—largely by demonstrating a kind of protopunk attitude. However, it would be a mistake to assume that these garage bands only appeared after the Brits arrived in force. In fact, many garage bands were playing to packed houses before February 1964. Crucially, though, what most of these bands were not achieving was nationwide radio play or the kind of major-label record deals that would guarantee such extensive coverage. But for a few notable exceptions, the garage bands of the early to mid-1960s achieved localized levels of success—flourishing as live acts and so often building healthy local or regional followings. It is this local dimension—the establishment of small but perfectly formed networks, scenes, or communities—that connects 1960s garage rock to later outbreaks of punk in New York and Los Angeles in the 1970s, and even to grunge coming out of the Pacific Northwest in the late 1980s.

So while mainstream pop culture was hard at work filtering and separating, diluting, refining, and homogenizing those elements that had made rock 'n' roll such an exciting and heady brew in the midfifties, out in the provinces the raw sounds that characterized the early rock 'n' roll of a setup like Memphis's Sun Records, for example, survived. As Gillett has pointed out, "Every time the record industry thought it had come to grips with rock and roll's elusive spirit the thing evaporated and went to play in some obscure place out of public view" (Gillett 349). As we have seen earlier, one such backwater was England, and more specifically Merseyside. Yet, there were pockets of resistance closer to home, and one noticeable place where this "elusive spirit" went to play in the early to mid-1960s was up in the Pacific Northwest, in the states of Oregon, Washington, and Idaho. To a certain extent, it is almost as if—in the case of the many bands that emerged out of Seattle, Tacoma, and Portland and other cities in this part of the United States—their unfashionable geographical origins were markers of their outlaw, outsider status. It was as if they could only play the music they did, in the way they did, because they were so far away from the twin centers of America's pop cultural mainstream of Los Angeles and New York.

The most noteworthy of the many Pacific Northwest garage acts was the Wailers. This band from Tacoma, Washington, pioneered the Pacific Northwest sound as a raw, stomping treatment of rhythm and blues. Formed in 1958, the Wailers wrote their own songs, played their own instruments, and even set up their own label—ironically called Etiquette—through which they and other local bands could record and distribute material that no major label would touch. All this several years, of course, before the Beatles came along to supposedly make such autonomy possible. In 1965 the Wailers released the ur-garage track "Out of Our Tree"—a primal, hard-driving, uncommercial noise that complemented an equally unpop lyrical focus on psychosis. Stablemates and fellow Pacific Northwesterners the Sonics' single "Psycho" (1965), much like "Out of Our Tree," failed to chart nationally but was a big regional hit, selling an estimated 25,000 copies. "Psycho" carried the clear imprint of Invasion acts like the Stones, the Kinks, and Them, making it archetypal garage rock. It too is blatantly about psychosis and dementia, subjects that at the time were deemed inappropriate for teen pop music. The track also launched a musical assault on "good taste" that was the equal of its lyrical attack. The band's guitarist, Andy Parypa, described his willfully distorted playing as sounding "like a trainwreck" (qtd. in Hicks 21).

Another Pacific Northwest garage band, Paul Revere and the Raiders, enjoyed considerably more commercial success. Released by Columbia Records and produced in Los Angeles by Terry Melcher, "Steppin' Out" reached number forty-six on Billboard's singles chart in 1965. The backing of a major label, the band's willingness to wear American Revolution uniforms, and a big teenybopper fan base fed by regular appearances as Dick Clark's house band on his TV show *Where the Action Is* might have perhaps suggested that the Raiders were Invasion copyists, but they still produced hard-driving garage rock. "Steppin' Out" fused the Pacific Northwest stomp pioneered by the Wailers and practiced by the Sonics with the kind of casual, threatening misogyny regularly heard in Stones' songs—"Stop your messin' 'round / I'm gonna step on you."

Formed in 1962, the Standells had started out as a smooth supperclub turn. In 1965, inspired by the success of the Rolling Stones and other uncompromising second-wave Invaders, the band was reborn as a garage rock act. This involved not only the adoption of a new "look" and sound but also a new sensibility. "Dirty Water," which peaked at number eleven nationally in late 1965, managed to capture all this, as the band delivered on their promise to tell us a "big fat story" to the backing of a similarly corpulent rhythm and blues beat.

If, aside from that R & B stomp, there was one musical common denominator in the garage rock sound, then it was arguably the fuzz that augmented the distinctive beat. Fuzz had been "created" in the late 1950s, when some guitarists—most notably the surf rocker Link Wray—deliberately damaged their equipment to produce it. In the studio, it was achieved by wounding an amplifier's speaker cone and then turning up the volume as high as it would go, so that the distortion would produce the desired fuzz effect. By 1965, it could be switched on and off at will and had become the principal sonic weapon in the garage band armory, signifying moody, menacing, aggressive power and "attitude." Kinks guitarist Dave Davies had deliberately sabotaged his own amplifiers—reportedly slashing them with a razor blade—to produce the distinctive guitar sound on both U.S. hit singles "You Really Got Me" and "All Day and All Night"—tracks that had also birthed the power chord. However, in the summer of 1965, the Rolling Stones had employed fuzz to memorable effect on "Satisfaction," which became the single most commercially successful example of its usage. Its signature riff needed sustaining, and, while Keith Richards considered fuzz to be a "bit of a gimmick," it undoubtedly contributed in significant measure to the song's force. Inevitably, post-"Satisfaction," fuzz was widely deployed—from the crudest examples of garage rock to the slickest examples of mainstream pop. It was aided in this by the availability of relatively inexpensive, mass-produced amplifier distortion controls and switches, fuzz knobs on guitars, and fuzz effects pedals.

Although garage bands were often united in their profligate use of fuzz, they did not share so much a common sound as a sensibility. This was symptomatic of an affective alliance forged with second-wave Invasion acts like the Rolling Stones and Them. In particular, they shared the belief that anyone could and should play—a belief rooted in notions of participation and inclusion that, in the second half of the 1960s, would eventually run directly counter to the increasing exclusivity of a rapidly professionalizing rock business. While chart success may have eluded most garage acts, the importance of the strong bond forged between the bands and their fans should not be underestimated, as boundaries between musical producers and consumers frequently came close to collapsing. In this way, the music appeared to allow for the construction of identities that validated and celebrated "difference," anticonformity, and even dissent. (This predated recognition of pop music's role in the creation of subcultural identities but also demonstrated it functioning similarly to Beatlemania with its emphasis on connection and communication.) Although it might not necessarily be true of the wholesome Kingsmen—whose version of "Louie Louie" had reached number two in February 1964—or even the McCoys—who had enjoyed the first garage number-one single with "Hang On Sloopy" in October 1965—many garage bands channeled antagonism and dissatisfaction through their "noise." They did so in the wake of the pungent trail blazed by the antisocial Stones, in particular. The Leaves' "Too Many People" (1965), for example, featured similarly generalized "protest" lyrics to "Satisfaction," packaging youthful frustrations with and contempt for the adult mainstream with Stones-flavored guitar and harmonica parts and a snotty Jaggeresque vocal—"Too many people are trying to change me / Too many people are trying to rearrange me." The Leaves, though, will never succumb to the "9 to 5," preferring to "sit and die" rather than "wear a suit and tie."

As the Sonics' "Psycho" and the Wailers' "Out of Our Tree" had demonstrated, garage rock songs could explore "different," darker lyrical territory to the conventional pop record. Tracks like the Raiders' "I'm Not Your Stepping Stone" and "Nothing'll Stand in My Way," the Barbarians' "Are You a Girl or a Boy" (no. 56, 1965), the Lyrics' "So What" (1965), and the Seeds' "You're Pushing Too Hard" (1966) rebuked, despised, bitched and moaned, and menaced. These contemptuous anthems openly challenged mainstream pop's romantic dominant—an antagonistic stance that was often signposted in band names that implied negativity, aggression, and antisocial affiliations. Whereas in the late 1950s and early 1960s band names were typically aspirational (e.g., the Squires, the Dukes, the Sires, the Barons, and the Premiers), by the mid-1960s, garage band nomenclature often suggested a very different set of affiliations and attitudes (e.g., the Bad Seeds, the Primitives, the Charlatans, the Psychopaths, the Barbarians, the Vandals, and the Undertakers).

So, what did 1965 tell us? That the Beatles were a garage band that developed under the influence of Bob Dylan? That Dylan himself was clearly influenced by the Beatles and, as a result, developed a sloppy, garage-y sound? That the American garage bands were inspired in particular by the second-wave British Invasion acts, while benefiting from Dylan's significant rearrangement of the pop landscape? Each of these is true but cannot be treated in isolation or ranked according to importance. Even taken together, they cannot tell the full story of a year in which *rock music* emerged—a complex process driven and defined by all of the movements, moments, and music examined in this chapter.

4

"A SPLENDID TIME IS GUARANTEED FOR ALL"

1966–1967

At the beginning of 1966, the Beatles traded places with Simon and Garfunkel for Billboard supremacy. Through January, "We Can Work It Out" spent a total of three weeks at number one, with its run at the top split in two by the American duo's "Sound of Silence." At the same time, *Rubber Soul* was enjoying a six-week run as the nation's best-selling album. The "story" told by Billboard history, then, might well have suggested one of continuing success for the principal British Invaders, but that Beatles versus Simon and Garfunkel duel hinted at a less straightforward narrative. In purely statistical terms, the story of 1966 indicates that a fight-back was well under way. There were thirty UK-produced singles in the Top 10, down six from the previous year, while there were ninety-seven homegrown 45s, up an impressive twenty-three from 1965. The fight-back might also have been signaled in the number of native pop singles to reach number one in 1966, which included Lou Christie's "Lightnin' Strikes" (one week in February), Nancy Sinatra's "These Boots Are Made for Walking" (one week in February), the Young Rascals' "Good Lovin'" (one week in April–May), the Association's "Cherish" (three weeks in September–October), and even Frank Sinatra's "Strangers in the Night" (one week in July). All told, there were "indigenous" singles at the very top of Billboard for forty weeks in 1966; and the year's biggest-selling single, and its longest-running number one, was Sgt. Barry Sadler's "The Ballad of the Green Berets," an irony-free, superpatriotic paean to all-American heroism.

The Invasion yielded six number-one singles, which occupied the top spot for a total of "just" twelve weeks, sixteen fewer than in 1965. As we have already seen, however, sales and airplay—important though they may be—do not necessarily provide us with the fully dimensional account. We need to look elsewhere then for evidence of the Invasion's meaningful impact. For example, to the continuing commercial and artistic centrality of performers whose careers had been forged by the Invasion. In 1966, folk-rock acts delivered four number-one singles, and this was also garage rock's commercial annus mirabilis, crowned by a number-one single for the Mysterians' "96 Tears." The year 1966 also witnessed the emergence of the "next big thing," acid or West Coast rock, which both drove and benefited from a shift in emphasis from the single to the album. Neither this music nor the format that became its natural home could have happened without the Invasion.

Arguably the most high-profile sign of the Invasion's continuing impact could be seen and heard in the year's biggest pop act—the Monkees, who owed their very existence to a TV show based on the premise of a band that wanted to be the Beatles. Following the success of *A Hard Day's Night*, movie director Bob Rafelson together with Bert Schneider, the son of Columbia Pictures' president, placed an ad in the Hollywood trade papers for "four insane boys, aged 17–21" to star in a TV show shamelessly made in the movie's image. They auditioned more than four hundred young men—including Stephen Stills and Charles Manson—but eventually chose two folkies, Mike Nesmith and Peter Tork, a former child actor, Mickey Dolenz, and an expat Brit, Davy Jones, who had starred as the Artful Dodger on Broadway and appeared on the *Ed Sullivan Show* with the Beatles. By late 1965 Rafelson and Schneider had secured $225,000 from Jackie Cooper at Columbia, and NBC had already purchased the series having understandably anticipated little difficulty selling it to prospective sponsors. The cream of pop's Tin Pan Alley—Goffin and King, Mann and Weill, Sedaka and Greenfield, and Neil Diamond—were mobilized to write the songs, while top session musicians like Glen Campbell and Leon Russell played on the tracks.

Across the project, Beatles' connections were hard to miss. The promotional campaign for the Monkees' debut album aped that of the Beatles in early 1964, with $100,000 being spent as seventy-six staff distributed thousands of posters claiming that "the Monkees are coming!" while preview discs were sent to six thousand DJs, the band's name was misspelled in a similar fashion, and the first single, "Last Train to Clarksville" even included several "no, no, no" choruses to calculatedly mirror the Beatles' "yeah, yeah, yeahs." *Time* declared that "less than a year ago, a team of wily promoters ran the Beatles through a Xerox machine and came up with the Monkees" (qtd. in Szatmary 115).

The TV show debuted in September 1966 and typically drew ten million viewers every Monday evening. At its peak, the band was receiving over five thousand letters per day, and it is estimated that the project generated over $20 million in merchandise. In November 1966, "Last Train to Clarksville" made number one. It bore more than a passing resemblance to the Beatles' "Day Tripper." The Monkees' next single, "I'm a Believer," fared even better, selling in excess of ten million copies worldwide. In February 1967, with twelve million now watching the TV show each week, the Monkees had the number-one single and album on both sides of the Atlantic, and had sold six million LPs and five million 45s in just four months. Through 1966 and 1967, the band had four number-one albums. Released in early 1967, the band's second album, *More of the Monkees*, spent eighteen weeks at number one, which meant that the first two LPs held the top spot for a Beatle-busting thirty-one weeks. Such success indicated that the Monkees, at least for eighteen months or so, could genuinely rival the British group and make a credible claim to be nation's favorite pop act.

Finely crafted though their songs might have been, the Monkees were, as *Time* had suggested, brazen Beatles copyists. However, elsewhere in the pop field, the Invasion had clearly sparked a creative dialogue. This resulted in a transatlantic "trade" that fueled some of the year's most noteworthy output. "There was a constant stream of new material going back and forth," explains the Byrds' Roger McGuinn. "We'd get to hear it before it came out, and when we got together we'd play our new stuff" (qtd. in Heylin 44). "Eight Miles High"—a Top 20 hit for the Byrds in the spring of 1966—was a consciously conceived product of this dynamic interplay between America and Britain. Originally titled "Six Miles High," the song had been written by McGuinn following the band's first tour of the UK in the summer of 1965. "Six Miles High" referred to the cruising altitude of transatlantic airliners— a fact that the aviation-obsessed McGuinn was well aware of. However, fellow band member Gene Clark had persuaded McGuinn to change it from "six" to "eight" because he believed the Beatles' recent hit "Eight Days a Week" had demonstrated that this number had a more "poetic" ring about it.

On its release in May 1966, "Eight Miles High" became a target for what McGuinn called the "establishment over-reacting to the LSD threat" (qtd. in Heylin 46). This "overreaction" had been kick-started by a piece in the subscription trade paper *Bill Gavin's Record Report*, which had identified the song as a "drug record" and had been circulated to thousands of U.S. radio stations. This, in turn, had led to immediate airplay bans in Washington, D.C., Baltimore, and Houston, and had effectively stalled the single's upward chart trajectory, dealing it a fatal blow, in fact. With sales imperiled, a lawsuit was threatened, accompanied by a letter from the Byrds and their management demanding a retraction. In the band's defense, the song's opening line does reference touching down in London—the "rain grey town"—and documents the ensuing feelings of cultural dislocation the members of the group experienced on their first British tour, with McGuinn describing it as a "pretty lyric about an intriguing city" (qtd. in Rogan 255). However, it undoubtedly represented a potentially unsettling sonic departure for a folk-rock band. Indeed, "Eight Miles High" had drawn on progressive jazz, and specifically the work of John Coltrane, for its principal musical inspiration. As McGuinn explains, "We were playing 12-string Rickenbackers to sound like a saxophone. We were translating it into a rock form" (qtd. in Rogan 251). Given the track's aural strangeness, one could perhaps understand how it led to efforts to ban it.

"Eight Miles High" was forged out of a creatively nourishing transatlantic rivalry, which seemed to reach its peak in 1966. It also played its part in disseminating the myth of "Swinging London," which came to prominence in this year. Even though the Invasion had obviously helped to counter it, there was still a lingering sense of cultural inferiority in the UK, and so the British press was "particularly keen to quote Americans announcing that London was now the international capital of youth" (Sandbrook, *White Heat*, 244). American benediction, it seemed, would give the idea of "Swinging London" substance and validity. Appearing in the *Telegraph*'s *Weekend* supplement in April 1965, it was in fact an American, John Crosby, who first told British readers that London was now the "most exciting city in the world." London, Crosby declares, was "vibrating with youth"—and the clubs, cafes, restaurants, and shops of the capital were "just a symptom, the outer and visible froth [of] a sort of English renaissance" (qtd. in Sandbrook, *White Heat*, 244). The most famous example of American enthusiasm for "Swinging London"—and so consequently the single most powerful boost to the myth—found expression in a cover story that appeared in *Time* magazine on April 15, 1966, entitled "You Can Walk Across It on the Grass." Ostensibly referencing the city's many green spaces, its title was also possibly a sly, hip nod to the growing popularity and use of cannabis. The magazine's cover featured a collage mixing images of pop music, pop art, and, perhaps somewhat incongruously, morris dancing. Inside, the reader was left in no doubt about the story's booom'sh intent. "In this century," it declares, "every decade has had its city," and the piece made it perfectly clear that London's time had arrived. According to Andrea Adam, she and the rest of the editorial team at *Time* "were all totally riveted by London. London was special, it had a kind of mystique." While Adam also points out that it was the copyeditor's fascination with the miniskirt that helped put it on the cover, she also concedes that, from an American perspective at least, what was happening in London did appear to "differ from what was going on in the States. . . . I don't think we understood it. . . . We perceived a kind of classlessness that we found attractive. We were fascinated" (qtd. in Green 72). Of course, the story was written in part to appeal to American tourists, and, not uncoincidentally, it was timed to hit the newsstands in the spring, when it was assumed many Americans would be planning a European trip and so might require a more up-to-date guide. Thanks to cheaper air travel, American tourists were indeed flocking to London in increasing volume through the 1960s. In 1965, approximately three million foreign visitors had visited the city, with Americans prominent among this impressive number.

Just as John Crosby's earlier piece had done, the *Time* article focused on "a swinging meritocracy," stressing the apparent classlessness that defined this "scene." London—it claimed—was "a city steeped in tradition, seized by change, liberated by affluence, graced by daffodils and anemones so green with parks and squares that, as the saying goes, you can walk across it on the grass. In a decade dominated by youth, London has burst into bloom. It swings; it is the scene" (qtd. in Sandbrook, *White Heat*, 245).

"Swinging London" was not entirely without substance. It was clear that the Britain of 1966 was, in many important respects, a radically different place from the Britain of 1956, even perhaps of 1963. And of course, its popular music culture had documented and in some cases even driven many of these transformations. However, "Swinging London"—as its name suggested—was a highly localized phenomenon, in which it was clear that not everyone was invited to participate. Indeed, it was sometimes pointed out that there were in reality only a handful of "scenesters," a self-selecting mix of old-moneyed aristos and new-moneyed artists. Allied to this was a growing realization that Britain's boom years were coming to an end. So, flattery aside, perhaps one of the reasons why Britons welcomed the American-patented myth of "Swinging London" so enthusiastically was for the boost it would hopefully deliver to an economy in free fall. Although the Invasion meant that the UK's music business was performing well in the export market, domestically things were not looking so healthy. Year-to-year sales had declined by 25 percent, and no one was immune. The Beatles' 1966 UK number-one single "Paperback Writer" sold fewer copies in Britain than any Beatle single since "Love Me Do," which had only scraped into the Top 20 in late 1962.

Alongside a raft of troubling economic indicators were equally concerning statistics that some were quick to point to as evidence of the high price the nation was paying for its social transformations: a 60 percent rise in convictions for drunkenness, a doubling of illegitimate births, psychiatric hospital admissions up by a third, gambling expenditure increasing by more than 400 percent, incidents of arson up by 250 percent, a tenfold rise in cases of addiction to hard drugs, and a sharp increase in crimes against the person. Whether these figures were conclusive proof of social unraveling or not was hotly debated, but there was no denying that there had been a significant shift in collective mood in the short space of a few years—a waning of national optimism that was only fueled by wave upon wave of poor economic numbers. In such a climate—with domestic spending on leisure in sharp decline—clubs, cafes, restaurants, and fashion shops welcomed the international dissemination of the "Swinging London" myth, believing not unreasonably that it was only foreign, and especially American, spending power that would keep them afloat in these difficult times. And there was reason to be hopeful, particularly when looking west across the Atlantic. The U.S. economy was healthy, and its young were still spending. In contrast to its ailing UK counterpart, for example, the American music business was posting impressive profits that suggested boom rather than bust. Indeed, 1966 witnessed the biggest annual increase in record sales since 1956.

While "Swinging London" had plenty of transatlantic followers then—with varied reasons to believe—the idea that it represented some kind of triumph of democracy, a "swinging meritocracy" that rendered the once class-bound now class-free, did not appear to stand up to much scrutiny. As Dominic Sandbrook has pointed out, "Far from being open and classless, the swinging scene was essentially the province of a self-satisfied elite . . . a tight, incestuous world [that created] a sense of synthesis between the worlds of art, music and fashion. But it is hard to deny that the swinging elite had simply replaced one form of snobbery with another" (Sandbrook, *White Heat*, 256–59).

For Bernard Levin, reporting on it at the time, the scene represented nothing more than "the froth and scum" (qtd. in Sandbrook, *White Heat*) of a decadent, doomed society—a theme park without substance. This was a view effectively skewered in the Kinks' sardonic "Dedicated Follower of Fashion" (UK no. 4, U.S. no. 36), in which Ray Davies offered up a deceptively arch and caustic lyric that was far from the one-dimensional, upbeat, and self-satisfied celebration, hymning "Swinging London," that it might have seemed at first listen. In fact, "Dedicated Follower of Fashion" is highly critical of the mindless consumerism of a vacuous, hipster "in" crowd, mocking its ridiculous pretentions as it "eagerly pursues all the latest fads and trends" and exists in a "world built around discoteques and parties."

In sharp contrast, "England Swings" (UK no. 13, U.S. no. 8) could not have turned out any better for the English Tourist Board if they had commissioned it themselves, as the American singer Roger Miller urged his listeners to take a vacation in the UK, where they would find "bobbies on bicycles," children with "rosey-red cheeks," and "dapper men with derby hats and canes." As the Kinks had demonstrated, though, homegrown takes on "Swinging London" were apparently less likely to peddle the myth wholesale. If the Kinks had documented the "scene"

from the perspective of outsiders, then the Rolling Stones were arguably well qualified to offer the view from inside. In 1966 both their hit
singles and hit album, *Aftermath*, documented the Stones' engagement
with "Swinging London." As symbols of decadence, the Stones formed
part of, perhaps even led, that "swinging meritocracy," in which it had
been suggested youth, beauty, and wealth could cut across class divides.
On "19th Nervous Breakdown" (U.S. no. 2, February 1966), the Stones
mocked a debutante who had "seen too much in too few years." The
song was rooted in Jagger's own fractious, sometimes violent relationship with fellow "scenester" Chrissie Shrimpton. She would subsequently attempt suicide when Jagger finally extricated himself from the
relationship at the end of the year. The song "19th Nervous Breakdown" depicts a "swinging" demimonde that its narrator views with
some contempt, but its lyric also offers little sympathy for the young
woman on whom life in the fast lane has taken its toll. Looking back in
1968, Jagger noted that songs like "19th Nervous Breakdown" came out
of a particular mind-set—"We felt so freaky and so up-tight and so
'orrible, we just made freaky records, half of which we never released
even. They were so strange" (qtd. in Egan, *Rolling Stones*, 115). Perhaps at least part of the explanation for these "freaky" songs could be
found in the conflicted nature of the band's relationship with "Swinging
London."

In June the sonically and lyrically adventurous "Paint It Black"
reached number one in the States. Featuring the heavy usage of a sitar
and a decidedly unpop lyric about the loss, possibly as a result of death,
of a lover, it gave further indication that the Stones inhabited a dark and
decadent world in which they were unlikely to cross paths with avuncular "bobbies" and rosy-cheeked children. In the fall, "Mother's Little
Helper" became the Stones' third big U.S. hit single of 1966. In highlighting the establishment's hypocritical attitude toward drug taking—
tolerating housewife "pick-me-ups" while coming down hard on youthful recreational drug use—it represented something of a return to the
lyrical territory and lippy stance mapped out in "Satisfaction" and "Get
Off My Cloud."

As London residents and frequent visitors to all its fashionable clubs,
bars, and shops, the Beatles were perhaps as much a part of the "Swinging London" scene as the Stones. However, while their success had of
course contributed much to the creation of the myth, they nevertheless

remained outsiders, whose own good humor and self-deprecation more than anything else prevented full immersion. This did not stop the band from passing judgment, though. On "Paperback Writer," an American number one in June, the Beatles appeared weary of "Swinging London," and so, although the message is delivered in typically sugarcoated and pop-savvy fashion, it is not without satirical edge. In the song, the wannabe novelist has written a "dirty story of a dirty man, and his clinging wife who doesn't understand." In a parody of "Swinging London's" brave new world of classless opportunity, so desperate is he to "make a million" that he is fully prepared to compromise his artistic integrity for celebrity.

As the jokey intertextuality of "Paperback Writer" had demonstrated, if they looked to anyone for inspiration in the early part of 1966, the Beatles continued to look to Bob Dylan. Similarities between the Beatles' "Yellow Submarine" and Dylan's equally carnivalesque "Rainy Day Women, Nos. 12 & 35"—which peaked at number two on Billboard in the spring—highlighted a bond that was galvanized in May of that year, when Dylan toured the UK and visited Lennon at his Surrey home. In July, though, this creative rivalry was effectively put on hold, as Dylan was forced to convalesce following a motorbike accident. It would be eighteen months before he would produce any new music. However, by the summer of 1966, the Beatles had already publicly anointed a new favorite and rival in chief, the Beach Boys' Brian Wilson having dethroned Dylan. The Beach Boys had continued to prosper in the high Invasion era, enjoying major success through 1964 and 1965 with hits like "I Get Around," "Fun Fun Fun," and "California Girls." But this success had come at some great personal cost to the group's principal songwriter Brian Wilson, whose fragile psychological health had withered under the stresses of such responsibility compounded by the heavy demands of touring. It was an irony surely not lost on the Beatles, then, that Wilson's *meisterwerk*, *Pet Sounds*, should have emerged in part as a result of this mental breakdown that enabled him to retreat into the studio. (The Beatles would effectively engineer their own collective "breakdown" in 1966, when their decision to stop performing live enabled them to carve out more studio time.) Although credited to the Beach Boys, *Pet Sounds* was for all intents and purposes a solo LP. While the rest of the band did sing on the album, it was, as Wilson himself admitted and few would disagree, the product of "the single-minded pursuit of a personal vision" (qtd. in Brackett 122). Brian Wilson was as close as it was possible to get at the time to being a pop music auteur. Under the Invasion's influence, America's pop industry had been transformed, granting its most ambitious creative license to operate with relatively few constraints. Wilson was one of the most noticeable beneficiaries of this transformation, taking full advantage of the freedoms it brought. *Pet Sounds* was arguably pop's first concept album. According to Wilson, songs like "I Just Wasn't Made for These Times" "were a telling self-portrait of my troubled psyche" (qtd. in Brackett 120)—parts in a song cycle that documented a love affair from the optimistic "high" of "Wouldn't It Be Nice" to the aching "low" of album closer "Caroline No." Such lyrical ambition was matched by music that warranted equal billing. Wilson took full advantage of the very latest studio technology and the most gifted LA session players to build up densely layered tracks using a wide range of instrumentation, both conventional and nonpop (e.g., the theremin). "God Only Knows" was the product of twenty takes and the input of twenty-three musicians playing simultaneously. It was all a long way from the simplicity of "Barbara-Ann." His fellow Beach Boys dismissed the project as a "collection of sounds more than songs." Mike Love, in particular, was scathing in his criticism, labeling much of *Pet Sounds* "ego music, too avant-garde" and urging Wilson more angrily not to "fuck with the formula" (qtd. in Stanley 220). In the United States, where the album sold quite poorly, it would appear that Love's worst fears were borne out, as Wilson's complex arrangements failed to find favor with Beach Boys' fans apparently locked into the easy satisfactions of the "formula." Tellingly, "Caroline No"—the product of seventeen takes and a key change from C to D—was released as a *solo* 45 and only limped to number twenty-three. At pretty much the same time, another album track, the more familiar-sounding "Sloop John B" was released as a Beach Boys' record, and it reached number three.

Pet Sounds might have sold poorly in the States, but it went on to become one of the UK's best-selling albums of 1966. At year's end, off the back of its popularity, *New Musical Express* readers voted the Beach Boys "Best Group" ahead of the Beatles. British musicians seemed to have loved it more than their American counterparts, too. Paul McCartney declared himself "simply amazed" by Wilson's ambition and invention on an album, ironically, consciously conceived in response to *Rubber Soul*. *Pet Sounds* was released a few weeks after the *Revolver* sessions were completed, and so the direct influence of Wilson on Beatles' music could not be heard on this record. However, over the twelve-month period that followed, from the fall of 1966 to the fall of 1967, it most definitely could and would. In December, the Beach Boys' single "Good Vibrations" made number one on Billboard, which might well suggest that the record-buying majority had finally embraced Wilson's ambition. Recorded in a total of seventeen sessions over six months at a reported cost of anywhere between $50,000 and $75,000—whatever the actual figure more than three times the usual cost of a full LP—this "pocket symphony" raised the bar, setting a new standard of studio-based extravagance that the Beatles could hardly fail to interpret as a challenge.

The Beatles were sensitive to Wilson's challenge because it came at a time when they were at a fork in the road. In the first half of the year, the band had enjoyed continued commercial success, with best-selling singles ("We Can Work It Out," "Paperback Writer") and albums (*Rubber Soul, Yesterday and Today*). However, the summer of 1966 found the Beatles in a "state of acute self-contradiction" (MacDonald 170), principally due to the marked difference between the new musical identity forged in the studio over the past twelve months and the "live" persona that America knew from regular touring, movies, and attendant media appearances. These two "selves"—the maturing, "real" Beatles and the "mop tops" preserved in mass media aspic—could not be reconciled and the strain was beginning to show. New material could not be reproduced within the frame of the conventional pop concert, which—for the Beatles—had also become a deeply unsatisfying scream-fest. On the eve of the band's summer U.S. tour, George Harrison remarked with typical drollery that barely masked genuine dread, "We'll take a couple of weeks to recuperate before we go and get beaten up by the Americans." Harrison's comment came partly out of the frustration that the live gig afforded the band little or no opportunity to showcase developing musicianship. It was also rooted in a controversy that had its origins in something John Lennon had said back in the spring. In March, Lennon was quoted in the *London Evening Standard* claiming that "Christianity will go. It will vanish and shrink. We're more popular than Jesus now." The interview was subsequently reprinted in the *New York Times Magazine* and then the August issue of the

American teen magazine *Datebook*. While these comments were certainly unwise, presumptuous, and injudicious, they were still perhaps understandable in context, coming as they did from a Brit rooted in a culture in which Christianity did seem to be in crisis if not terminal decline. However, the reaction was very different in the States, where Lennon was charged with "blasphemy" by some on the religious Right. So, by August 1966, when the Beatles embarked on their U.S. tour, the band had become hate figures among fundamentalist groups in the Bible Belt, where their records and related merchandise were ritually burned, they were publicly denounced, and a number of radio stations elected not to play their music. "What have the Beatles said or done to so ingratiate themselves with those who eat, drink and think revolution?" asked David Noebel, the author of a series of bilious anti-Beatles tracts that predated the "bigger than Jesus" controversy but predictably gained momentum from it. "The major value of the Beatles to the left in general . . . has been their usefulness in destroying youth's faith in God." In Memphis the city fathers appeared to concur, declaring that "the Beatles are not welcome." At the Beatles' Memphis gig, the Ku Klux Klan held a poorly attended counterdemonstration right outside, while an estimated eight thousand—still well under half the number found inside the auditorium—participated in an anti-Beatles rally across town. At least half of the participants were adults. In Birmingham, a local DJ organized a rally at which protestors threw Beatles' records into a tree-grinding machine, while an estimated thirty radio stations nationwide declared a Beatle ban. Most were in the South, but there were a few in New York and Boston, and, of course, newspapers across the nation ran stories and printed pictures of the burnings, while television news offered extensive coverage of the controversy. Allied to his natural caution and old-school politesse, it was this blanket media coverage that presumably convinced Brian Epstein that, the localized nature of the controversy notwithstanding, a fulsome and very public apology was required. Following up a press release of groveling contrition, Lennon duly appeared before the press in Chicago on the twelfth of August. "I apologise, if that will make you happy. I still don't know quite what I've done. . . . I'm sorry" (qtd. in Wiener 278).

Lennon's barely concealed truculence aside, this represented a climbdown, but it also perhaps marked the end of the Beatles' innocence, changing the nature of their "special relationship" with America forever, as it now entered a new, mature phase. Indeed, rather than chastening them and curing them of any desire or compulsion to engage with controversial topics conventionally deemed outside the remit of pop stars, it appeared to have the opposite effect. For 1966 witnessed the Beatles' involvement in what was rapidly becoming *the* issue, especially for America's young—Vietnam. During that summer, President Johnson had escalated a war to which opposition was clearly growing. The Students for Democratic Society had instigated a teach-in at Berkeley that had drawn an estimated twelve thousand protestors, and antiwar protest was spreading to other university campuses. At the New York press conference on that same summer tour, the very first question had invited the band to share their thoughts on the war. "We don't like war, war is wrong," they repeated as one, and then Lennon went solo, explaining, "We think of it every day. We don't like it. We don't agree with it. We think it's wrong" (qtd. in Wiener 283).

In contrast to earlier press conferences in New York, in which the apparently compliant Beatles were feted as cheeky "mop tops," the band now looked—as the *New York Times* reported—"tired and pale," their collective demeanor exacerbated by a tour of "mishaps, rain-outs, and an undercurrent of fear" that seemed to bear out Harrison's premonitions of dread. To cap it all, Harrison himself even threatened to quit the band at one point—the first of a number of similar threats that would be delivered by all four band members at regular intervals from then on. Yet the controversy had conclusively proved that the Beatles "were becoming identified by admirers and detractors alike with a growing political and cultural movement in the United States. For millions of young people in America . . . the Beatles were pivotal figures in the creation myth of the counterculture" (Gould 344–45, 347).

With such conscious acts of alignment ongoing, 1966 saw the development of a clear divide between those British acts—like the Beatles—who wanted to be part of the burgeoning counterculture and those who were happy to be viewed and perform as pure, pop entertainers. On tour in America, an exchange between Graham Nash, then of the Hollies, and the Hermits' Peter Noone made this abundantly clear, as the former attempted to convince the very skeptical latter of pop's potential power. "We can stop world wars before they ever started," enthused Nash. "We can make this a better place. Using music as a form of communication" (qtd. in *How the Brits Rocked America*).

Released at the end of the summer, *Revolver* demonstrated the Beatles' flexing this cultural power. Although it had reached number one in the UK, "Eleanor Rigby"—a product of those *Revolver* sessions and a standout track on the album—fared less well when issued as a single in America, where it only made number eleven. Its determinedly unschmaltzy orchestral score might have suggested that it was a variant of "Yesterday," but "Eleanor Rigby" is shockingly pessimistic—"No one is saved"—and graphically morbid, as its dead central protagonist, the lonely old spinster, is buried by a priest—another unlikely denizen of the pop song—who matter-of-factly wipes "the dirt from his hands as he walks from the grave." In America, "Eleanor Rigby" formed half of a double A-sided single with "Yellow Submarine." Rather predictably, Capitol Records put most of its promotional muscle behind "Yellow Submarine"—a sensible move at the time of the "bigger than Jesus" controversy and given the religious references that littered "Eleanor Rigby." American Top 40 radio, presumably for the same reasons, preferred to play "Yellow Submarine." Yet even the defiant optimism of one of its sides was unable to send it to the top spot—and it became the first Beatles single to fail to do so since 1963. Clearly, whichever side of the single you played, you were not getting rock 'n' roll. Although "Yellow Submarine" was written as a children's song by Paul McCartney for Ringo Starr to sing, it was sonically rich and inventive in its heavy use of multitracking to feature chains, whistles, hooters, hoses, handbells, and even an old tin bath, while Lennon blew bubbles in a bucket and the Rolling Stones' Brian Jones clinked glasses. It also included an uncredited snippet of brass bands, plus yelled nauticalisms in a somewhat *Goon*-ish style. Not unsurprisingly, given the changed and increasingly charged atmosphere of that summer, "Yellow Submarine" also generated its own controversy, as some fans associated it with yellow capsules of Nembutal or even with the resin-stained hull of a marijuana cigarette. And, of course, it was about a "trip."

Songs from *Revolver* were released to radio stations in twos and threes through July 1966, building expectation and pointing up what was patently a radical new phase in the band's recording career at a pace that—it was presumed—would not prove too alarming to their young fan base. However, although its most progressive track, "Tomorrow Never Knows," had been held back and made its first public appearance just a few days before the LP hit the stores, aural evidence of the Beatles' countercultural engagement was still hard to miss, even on the most apparently "pop" of tracks. *Revolver*, for example, featured pop's most sustained deployment of Indian instruments, musical form, and even religious philosophy thus far—which all came together most notably on the Harrison-penned track "Love You Too." In attempting to incorporate the spiraling raga into Western pop—if not for the first time, then certainly in that most public of arenas, the Beatles' album—this track inspired other musicians to embrace non-Western instrumentation and to even simulate its textures and tonality, and so gave rise to "raga rock." Elsewhere on *Revolver*, McCartney's Motown-y "Got to Get You Into My Life" appeared to document its author's early experiences with psychedelics, as its narrator successfully journeyed from loneliness—"I was alone, I took a ride"—toward that benign state of selfhood the "good trip" was believed to bring—"another road where maybe I could see another kind of mind."

To describe "Rain," a track that emerged from the *Revolver* sessions but that was released as the B-side to "Paperback Writer," as something of a dry run for the greater degree of experimentation found on *Revolver* risks underestimating the significance of a song that gave birth to British psychedelic rock. Delivered by its author Lennon in a tired drawl, "Rain" has a lyric that, in its languid attempt to map out "just a state of mind," preempted the darker narcotic nursery rhyming found on "Strawberry Fields Forever" and, particularly, "I Am the Walrus." It also pilloried the unhip who "run and hide" from life, who "might as well be dead." "Rain" took a Wilsonesque sixteen hours to record, as the Beatles made full use of the studio to employ vari-speeding, multitracking, and backward taping, allied to a drone that further highlighted the growing influence of non-Western musical form. "Rain" might have represented a daring choice for a B-side, but—much like "Got to Get You Into My Life"—it was still dressed in recognizably pop clothing. *Revolver*'s final track, however, made few if any concessions to formula, and so confirmed that the Beatles had unequivocally moved on. "Tomorrow Never Knows" was barely a song, let alone a pop song. With its droney sitar, two-chord harmony, and absence of chorus, release, or refrain, this was a track only made possible in the studio, that could never be reproduced live—"an experiment to make things sound how they shouldn't" (musician Tom Rowlands qtd. in "101 Greatest Beatles Songs," 93). To a backing of swirling and swooping tape loops and thunderous drums, Lennon quoted directly from *The Psychedelic Experience*, the user's bible of LSD's most high-profile advocate, Timothy Leary—"Turn off your mind, relax, and float down stream"—in a song that started out life as "The Void" and, despite its subsequent change of title, still obviously concerned the very nonpop subject matter of ego death.

Musically and lyrically, then, "Tomorrow Never Knows" dismantled the formula, where "Rain" and other songs on *Revolver* had perhaps only tinkered around the edges. Yet, taken as a whole, *Revolver* was still a challenging listen, inviting the many millions of Beatles fans who purchased it to take that "ride" down "another road" with them. In a 1967 interview with the London countercultural newspaper *IT*, Paul McCartney explained that he and the band were "trying to take people with [them]." The sound of "Swinging London" had been superseded by that of "underground London," and *Revolver* would give not only the Beatles but, crucially, other bands on both sides of the Atlantic the confidence to try new things, to light out in new directions, to push further still.

In the six months that lapsed between Donovan's "Sunshine Superman" topping the Billboard singles chart in September 1966 and the Rolling Stones' "Ruby Tuesday" achieving a similar feat in March 1967, there were a total of eleven consecutive "homegrown" number ones. In 1967, British acts were at number one for just nine weeks—with Lulu's movie tie-in "To Sir, with Love" accounting for five of these. This represented easily the lowest return since the Invasion began, and even the Beatles appeared to be struggling to match their (admittedly exceptional) chart performances of the previous three years, occupying the top spot for just three weeks with three different singles—"Penny Lane," "All You Need Is Love," and "Hello Goodbye." In contrast, but not of course without considerable irony, Beatles tribute act the Monkees owned 1967, enjoying a total of ten weeks at number one with "I'm a Believer" and "Daydream Believer." The twenty-two UK-produced singles that made the Billboard Top 10, down eight from 1966, might well suggest that a substantive American "fight-back," a stemming (maybe even turning) of the pop tide, was well under way. However, as with 1966, we need to look elsewhere for the Invasion's continuing influence, impact, and import: to rock's shift in emphasis from the single to the album format, where Brits led the way; to the continued centrality of key artists, especially the Beatles and the Stones, and the emergence of equally influential newcomers like Cream, Jimi Hendrix, and Pink Floyd; and to the new subgenres shaped by the Invasion (like acid rock, progressive rock, and heavy rock), which of course flourish in album form. In 1967 the rock LP came of age as an important document, and here no album contributed more to this than the Beatles' *Sgt. Pepper*, which spent fifteen weeks at number one and sold in the millions.

So, it is possible—for some of the reasons highlighted above—to offer a credible argument for the Invasion's continued significance *after* 1966. However, at the time, it did appear to many observers that pop had been geographically relocated. As the British music journalist Nik Cohn wrote in 1969: "By this time, America was back in control, California was the new pop centre. England just took the signals as they were given and followed as best it could. Simply, London had run out of steam. It had used itself up" (227).

This resiting of influence, though, was unlikely to have occurred without the Invasion. The Beatles, the Rolling Stones, and other Invaders helped birth and nourish the music that emerged from America's West Coast, and in particular in and around San Francisco, during the mid-1960s. It was here that the fusion of rock 'n' roll's energy and excitement with folk's political or polemical sensibility was carried further still, allied as it surely and most evidently was to the profound effect that drugs had on the music and musicians alike. Both Dylan and the Beatles had indulged enthusiastically in speed and pot, and this in turn had undoubtedly affected their music. But a new, widely available, cheap, and—until late 1966—legal drug, LSD, was clearly a key ingredient in the mix "way out west." So much so, in fact, that the terms "psychedelic" or even "acid" rock were alternative names given for the kind of music being played at the time by the likes of the Grateful Dead, Jefferson Airplane, and a host of West Coast bands. Location was a significant factor, too. San Francisco was a historically tolerant and nonconformist city. It also had a vibrant club scene, with dozens of cavernous old Victorian ballrooms—like the Fillmore and Avalon—in which these new bands could make their weird noise, put on accompanying light shows, and invite their audiences to "freak out" in style. It was also the case that Northern California had a plentiful supply of LSD and other "recreational" substances.

In May 1967 Hunter Thompson wrote one of the earliest media pieces on the San Francisco "scene," bringing it to national attention via his article in the *New York Times Magazine* (republished in *The Faber Book of Pop*). He described the Haight-Ashbury district as its epicenter, "a defiant dope fortress" that had taken shape in just six short months: "A run-down Victorian neighbourhood of about forty square blocks between the Fillmore district and Golden Gate Park, the 'Hashbury' is the new capital of what is rapidly becoming a drug culture. Its denizens are not called radicals or beatniks, but 'hippies'" (290).

Thompson reported that the "hippies'" average age was just twenty and that, for the time being at least, most were native Californians—something that made them distinct from the older, more worldly North Beach beatniks. "The word 'hip,'" he reported, "translates roughly as 'wise' or 'tuned in.' A hippy is somebody who 'knows' what's really happening, and who adjusts and grooves with it." As for their values, Thompson told his readers that "hippies despise phoniness; they want to be open, honest, loving, free. They reject the plastic pretence of twentieth century America, preferring to go back to the 'natural life,' like Adam and Eve. . . . They also reject politics, which is 'just another game.' They don't like money, either, or any kind of aggressiveness" (290).

Thompson also reported that drug use was widespread and open—"nearly everyone on the streets between twenty and thirty is a 'head,' a user, either of marijuana, L.S.D. or both," with a "cap of good acid cost[ing] $5" (291, 293). Picking up on a rumor, Thompson observed that more hippies were expected to arrive in Haight-Ashbury that summer "as soon as the school year ends" (296), swelling the population by anything between fifty and two hundred thousand.

The music that soundtracked this burgeoning hippie "scene" was a hybrid reflecting a number of generic influences. The Grateful Dead's Jerry Garcia—who had started out in a band called the Warlocks playing Beatles-inspired sets—referred to it as "rhythm and blues and weirdness." Typically, it incorporated a bit of blues with some jazzy touches, which were particularly evident in its emphasis on improvisation. It could also be folky, and sometimes drew upon Eastern influences. As *Time* magazine pointed out, the San Francisco sound "encompasses everything from bluegrass to Indian ragas, from Bach to jug band music"—and it did so often within the space of the same song.

Acid rock's favored format was perhaps understandably, then, the album. While hit singles tended to evade even those with a national profile, these bands could sell a lot of LPs and sell out a lot of venues. One of the first West Coast groups to achieve national recognition, announce the "scene" to the rest of the world, secure a major-label contract, and enjoy some chart success was Jefferson Airplane. In the spring of 1967 the band even made surprising inroads into the singles charts, when "White Rabbit"—from their second Warner Brothers album *Surrealistic Pillow* (no. 3)—made the Top 10. Like "Tomorrow Never Knows," it was clearly *not* pop or even standard rock. Lead singer and lyricist Grace Slick described it as a combination of Ravel's *Bolero* and Lewis Carroll's *Through the Looking Glass*, noting that she had "been listening to [jazz musician] Miles Davis' *Sketches of Spain* LP" while constructing the song on a piano with eight keys missing! Musically, the track was redolent of Spanish dance, but it also referenced the Middle East with its Arabic guitar figure. Volume, pace, and intensity vary, perhaps to suggest the aural equivalent of a psychedelic trip—an impression reinforced by the climactic exhortation to "feed your head" that would appear to urge its listeners to take drugs as a means to enlightenment. The song, however, operated on a number of narrative levels, which is presumably how and why it managed to get itself played on mainstream, pop radio. Its references to Alice in Wonderland meant that it could pass as a children's parable; but, taken in another way, it offered a generalized critique of authority—the "men on the chessboard" who tell you what to do—that could resonate in these politically changed and charged times. For those who now identified themselves as part of the counterculture, rock music—particularly of the variety peddled by the likes of Jefferson Airplane—was to be a vital means of communication.

West Coast rock was widely understood as "the sound of the American counter culture . . . the central and unique mode of political and cultural expression." As John Storey has pointed out, "it was not possible to be a hippie and not hear West Coast rock as deeply pleasurable *and* profoundly political." But what exactly was being articulated through this music? Could a clear political line be determined? Was it opposition to America's continued involvement in Vietnam? Support for civil rights? Sexual equality? Environmental concerns? Jefferson Airplane's "Somebody To Love"—which had also charted in the Billboard Top 10 in the spring of 1967—opened with the line, "When the truth is found to be lies." Yet it often appeared that what was being expressed through this music was a gut-reactive distrust of authority and stroppy denial of parental and middle-class values that was pretty much identical to rock 'n' roll's "message" of ten years earlier. In 1967 Jefferson Airplane taped commercials for Levis and the band's guitarist, Paul Kantner, recalls, "We didn't give a shit about politics. We felt that we didn't have any responsibilities, except maybe to provide a good example on a personal level, and get along with everyone we met. We wanted freedom to make our own decisions" (qtd. in Doggett).

As Hunter Thompson had noted in his *New York Times Magazine* article, "Unlike the dedicated radicals who emerged from the Free Speech movement, the hippies were more interested in dropping out of society than they were in changing it." This led him to conclude that "political activism is going out of style," and that "the thrust is no longer for 'change' or 'progress' or 'revolution,' but merely to escape, to live on the far perimeter of a world that might have been" (republished in *The Faber Book of Pop*, 298, 301). For this reason, politically music was often rather vague, nebulous, and nonspecific. Looking back—admittedly from the depths of his self-lacerating "hair-shirt" period in the early 1970s—Lennon himself remarked of the 1960s that it was a time when "everyone dressed up but nothing changed." The organizers of January 1967's Golden Gate Park "Human Be-In" had talked of a desire to "communicate something" and of a wish to become a "force in America's social and political framework." But it was unclear exactly how this was to be achieved. "Make love, not war!" was a popular countercultural chant, and "LOVE" was viewed as a social panacea, as the unspecified cure for a wide variety of specified ills. Understandably, it seemed like gross naïveté. Could being childlike—for many, the principal transformative effect of LSD—really achieve lasting social change?

In June 1967, the "underground" went aboveground, presenting a high-profile opportunity to test out the validity of the counterculture's claims and values. Notwithstanding that it took place in the sizeable shadow cast by the Beatles' *Sgt. Pepper* album, which had been released just two weeks earlier, the Monterey International Pop Festival also signaled and helped define pop music's next phase. In so doing, it also appeared to confirm that California—as opposed to London—was now pop's "Mission Control." According to the Byrds' Roger McGuinn,

"Monterey was a great moment . . . a remarkable time, the beginning of the Summer of Love and the whole peace and love generation. The baby boomers were just coming into their twenties and wanted to make a statement. Even the policemen had flowers on their motorcycle antennas" (qtd. in Perrone 16).

Billed as a festival of "Music, Love and Flowers," it took place at the Monterey Fairgrounds, around 150 miles south of San Francisco, between June 16 and June 18. Featuring more than thirty acts, it was the first pop festival to draw more than one hundred thousand people. The Monterey Festival could well be viewed as a calculated attempt to re-create a "Be-In"—the most significant of which had been held in January in Golden Gate Park—as an industry showcase for the benefit of record companies and the national media. There were hundreds of rock journalists and, more importantly perhaps, record company executives in attendance, who sat in designated areas close to the stage and paid $150 for the privilege. These record executives included Columbia's Clive Davis, who would sign Big Brother and the Holding Company on the strength of their performance, Warner's Mo Ostin, and Atlantic's Jerry Wexler.

The festival's organizers had set up a board of directors—or "governors"—that included among their number key Invasion players such as Donovan, Andrew Loog Oldham, Paul McCartney, and the Stones' Mick Jagger, together with Brian Wilson and McGuinn. The organizers themselves comprised the promoter and major business figure Lou Adler, the Mamas and Papas' John Phillips, the producer Alan Pariser, and former Beatles publicist Derek Taylor. They saw the festival as a way to validate rock music as an art form in the way that jazz and folk were regarded, and so ran the event on a nonprofit basis. However, it was envisioned that revenue would come from ticket sales and selling the movie rights. Some believed, then, that the festival was conceived by and for the performers and so reflected their beliefs. "Unlike Woodstock, which was a much more commercial enterprise," explained the attending British journalist Keith Altham, "Monterey was really true to the spirit of peace, love and free music. None of the groups appearing charged a fee" (qtd. in Perrone 16). Regardless of whether the bands received a fee or not, Monterey undoubtedly boosted the profile, and hence sales, of those who participated. It was a bill with a West Coast rock bias—headliners included Jefferson Airplane, Quicksilver Messenger Service, Moby Grape, and the Grateful Dead—and one of the festival's principal beneficiaries was San Francisco band Big Brother and the Holding Company, who secured a major-label contract largely on the strength of lead singer Janis Joplin's mesmeric performance. The Mamas and Papas closed the festival, introducing Scott McKenzie, whose John Phillips–penned single "San Francisco" would help define the "summer of love," spreading the news as it became a global hit.

However, there were others—Invasion acts prominent among them—who benefited from the exposure Monterey granted. The festival, for example, propelled the Who into the rock mainstream, largely as a result of an incendiary performance in which guitars were smashed, smoke bombs let off, and drummer Keith Moon kicked over his kit. The Monterey Festival also represented the first opportunity that London resident Jimi Hendrix had to show his American peers and an international audience what he was capable of as a musician. The Experience's Sunday night set closed with a cover of Invasion act the Troggs' 1966 U.S. number-one single "Wild Thing," as Hendrix poured lighter fluid over his guitar, duly set fire to it, and then, having smashed it on the stage, threw the charred remains into the crowd.

While its status as a genuine countercultural event may well have been debatable, what was less so was the fact that the festival announced the arrival of rock music as "show business," now wholeheartedly embraced by the industry mainstream. In the light of this development, perhaps it did not matter then that key performers missed out. Notable Monterey no-shows included the Beach Boys, who though initially scheduled to headline did not appear, due to a combination of Carl Wilson's feud with U.S. authorities over his refusal to be drafted to fight in Vietnam and Brian Wilson's debilitating depression. Invasion act the Kinks had been invited, too, but could not obtain work visas as a result of the band's ongoing dispute with the American Musicians' Union, while Donovan was denied a visa as a result of a 1966 drug bust. Although the Rolling Stones' Brian Jones had attended the festival, and even introduced some of the acts, Jagger's and Richards's recent convictions for illegal possession meant that, like Donovan, they too would be denied visas. Understandably, though, the most noteworthy absentees were the Beatles, who had declined an invitation to appear, presumably because their music was becoming too complex to play live (and because memories of the previous summer's unhappy

U.S. tour were simply too raw). However, it was at "governor" Paul McCartney's suggestion that both the Who and the Jimi Hendrix Experience were booked. Besides, the Beatles were very much there in spirit if not body, as Monterey took place just two weeks after the release of *Sgt. Pepper* and so "even in absentia, the Beatles were everywhere":

> *Sgt. Pepper* was played constantly, wafting out of the concession booths dotted around the perimeter of the grounds. Festival staffers sported badges with a motto lifted from the *Pepper* album: "A splendid time is guaranteed for all." (Miller 265)

The Beatles had returned to the UK following their final draining U.S. tour in September 1966, took a short vacation, and then reconvened at Abbey Road to begin work on the follow-up to *Revolver* determined to continue to push the creative envelope. "After a bit we got a bit bored with 12 bars all the time, so we tried to get into something else," explained Paul McCartney in an interview with the underground newspaper *International Times* in 1967: "Then came Dylan, the Who and the Beach Boys. . . . We're all trying to do vaguely the same kind of thing. We are all trying to make it into something we know it is. . . . Most people still think it's all just pop [as if] it's below every other kind of music, which of course it isn't" (qtd. in Heylin 113).

And it was clear—as George Harrison confirmed—that this was a highly self-conscious project to which all the band subscribed:

> In the last two years we've been in a good vantage point in as much as people are used to buying our records. . . . We can do things that please us without conforming to the standard pop idea. We are not only involved in pop music but all music. (Qtd. in Heylin 113)

The first fruit of this progressive pop labor was the double A-sided single "Strawberry Fields Forever" and "Penny Lane," which appeared in February 1967. "Strawberry Fields Forever" was the product of over fifty hours of studio time—a similarly lengthy gestation period to Brian Wilson's "Good Vibrations." In fact—much to EMI's horror—by mid-January, the band had racked up a total of 125 hours in the studio and produced only three tracks—"Strawberry Fields Forever," "Penny Lane," and "When I'm 64."

"Strawberry Fields Forever" alluded to a mansion and parkland that had been gifted to the Salvation Army as an orphanage, a place where John Lennon would play as a boy. The track effectively captured its author's narcotically filtered nostalgic reverie. Yet, though evidently autobiographical, it also had a more universal application. According to Lennon, it represented "anywhere you want to go"—or, as Paul McCartney put it, "a secret garden, like in *The Lion, the Witch and the Wardrobe*" (qtd. in Heylin 60–61). It had been painstakingly constructed by splicing a slow version of folky simplicity to a contrasting "baroque" version featuring a standard rock arrangement loaded with sonic tricks—versions that had been presented to George Martin in different keys and at different tempos. So, while the acoustic take was sped up, the "rock" take was slowed down and its pitch dropped. Making heavy use of the mellotron—a recently invented protosynthesizer containing a bank of wind, string, and brass tape loops—"Strawberry Fields Forever" documented a journey to a place "where nothing is real"—and so perhaps demonstrated the positive benefits of an LSD-enhanced neural rearrangement as "it all works out." Positive though its message and meaning might have been, it stalled at number two in the UK, bringing to an end a run of twelve consecutive Beatles' number-one singles. In America where both sides of the single charted in the Billboard Top 10, the deceptively more pop-friendly "Penny Lane" reached number one while "Strawberry Fields Forever" could only peak at number eight.

As the double A-sided single release preceding it had indicated, the *Sgt. Pepper* album began life as a collection of songs loosely connected by autobiographical themes. As Beatles' employee Tony Barrow confirmed: "They had a vague idea of getting back to basics by writing a set of songs about their own past, the Beatles' beginnings and their hometown haunts. The music would be progressive, but the lyrics could be nostalgically retrospective" (qtd. in Heylin 116).

The original concept might have been a song-suite about Liverpool childhoods, then, but record company and manager pressure for a hit single—allied to established UK industry practice dictating that 45s could not feature on an LP released in the same year—led to a rethink when both "Strawberry Fields Forever" and "Penny Lane" were issued in the smaller format. At this point, the whole "Liverpool" album effectively became a nonstarter—as John Lennon subsequently acknowledged in an interview with *Playboy*: "*Sgt. Pepper* is called the first concept album, but it doesn't go anywhere. All my contributions to the album have absolutely nothing to do with this idea of Sgt. Pepper and his band; but it works 'cause we said it worked" (qtd. in Heylin 153).

So, it became—for Lennon at least—a concept album with no definable concept. Yet it was still as much a "concept" as *Pet Sounds*. Maybe even more so. According to the band's road manager and PA Neil Aspinall, *Sgt. Pepper* was "the culmination of our acid days" (qtd. in Whiteley 44). "If we gave L.S.D to all the statesmen and politicians in the world," McCartney told *Life* magazine soon after the album's release, "we might have chance at stopping war," and there were apparently several songs on *Sgt. Pepper* that documented the "trip"—"Lucy in the Sky with Diamonds," "With a Little Help from My Friends," "Fixing a Hole," and "A Day in the Life."

Nearly six months in the making, *Sgt. Pepper* was finally completed on April 21, 1967. Desperate to recoup its unprecedented outlay, EMI launched a full-on marketing and PR campaign of teasers, posters, and proclamations. On May 12 the LP was played in full on UK independent radio. A week later BBC Radio aired it in full minus the final track "A Day in the Life," which the corporation had banned on the grounds that it encouraged a permissive attitude toward drug taking. The album was widely received as an expression of unbridled optimism, consistent with that by now well-established Beatles' sensibility. According to Allen Ginsberg, "There was here an exclamation of joy, the rediscovery of joy and what it was to be alive" (qtd. in Whiteley 40). Yet there was "joy" evidently laced with sadness, in a number of songs that also communicated life's potential loneliness (e.g., "She's Leaving Home," "When I'm 64," or "A Day in the Life"). This apparently paradoxical lyrical content was matched by music that was at once "young" and "old," rock and Tin Pan Alley, LSD and cocoa, progressive and nostalgic, just as likely to employ a brass band as a mellotron. All of which, of course, had been ably demonstrated on the "Strawberry Fields Forever" / "Penny Lane" double A-side.

In America, where it had advance sales of more than a million copies, *Sgt. Pepper* spent fifteen weeks at number one and had sold an impressive two and a half million copies by year's end. The album was heard on record or radio by millions on the very first day of its release, as many American stations simply abandoned their track lists and played only *Sgt. Pepper* for what seemed like hours on end. It was inescapable, "here there and everywhere," and a consensus quickly developed that this record both captured and defined "the moment," that it was real zeitgeisty stuff. "It was the summer of 1967," wrote Ellen Sander,

> the summer that went down as the Summer of Love. . . . *Sgt. Pepper* had just been released. It was the first aroma of summer, it wafted over the horizon like sweet incense, and its permeation was so complete that everyone who heard it lived it, breathed it, and spoke of little else. You could hear it from cars, drifting out of windows where you walked, in your friends' homes, and in your head, always. Its timing, the unequalled beauty of its contents, the pyrotechnical extravagance, the powerful release of inspiration, the awe and hope it projected, made it the opus of the movement. (Qtd. in Gould 418)

In the *London Times*, even the notoriously acerbic critic Kenneth Tynan had let down his normally reserved guard to declare *Sgt. Pepper* to be a "decisive moment in the history of Western civilisation" (qtd. in MacDonald 198). At one level, the record's success ushered in the era of album-oriented rock, radically reshaping how pop music worked economically. Less prosaically, *Sgt. Pepper* went further and deeper. While Paul Williams—who had founded rock's first critical journal *Crawdaddy* in 1966 as a seventeen-year-old—might well have been expected to eulogize wildly, thanks to *Sgt. Pepper* pieces about rock music in the style of jazz criticism began to appear regularly in established organs like *Vogue*, *Playboy*, and even newspapers like the *San Francisco Chronicle*, all of whom would cover rock as "art" from now on. In *Life*, for example, it was claimed that the Beatles were "stepping far ahead of their audience, recording music so complex and so unlike the music that made them successful that they could very likely lose the foundations of their support." *Newsweek* proclaimed the Beatles had "created a masterpiece," producing songs comparable in stature to the art of Sitwell, Pinter, and T. S. Eliot. "A Day in the Life"—in which a forty-piece orchestra had been given a low note to start with and a high note to end on, and been told only that they each had twenty-four bars to make the make the journey during which they should "not try to stay together"—was said to be the equal of the modernist classic "The Wasteland." In the *New York Times*, Richard Goldstein concurred, comparing the track to Wagner. In the *New Yorker*, its fifty-nine-year-old editor William Shawn enthused, "The Beatles have done more to brighten up the world in recent years than almost anything else in the arts," while the *Saturday Review* praised the LP as if it were a work of high culture (all qtd. in Gould 420–21).

The Beatles gave themselves no time to rest on such laurels—and it was perhaps inevitable that anything produced in the immediate wake of *Sgt. Pepper* would suffer in comparison. As Sheila Whiteley has pointed out, the band's very public association with psychedelia had helped highlight the strong countercultural link between drugs and music, and in particular its "emphasis on the freedom to experiment, experience and enjoy" (79). As they had promised in "Being for the Benefit of Mr. Kite," "a splendid time is guaranteed for all"—and a continuing commitment to the delivery of this promise seemed to be behind the band's first post-*Pepper* release, "All You Need Is Love," whose apparently rather trite celebration of love and acid—aided by the permissive manner of its dissemination—almost rendered the "summer of love" a cliché before it was over. "All You Need Is Love" had been premiered on a BBC/European Broadcasting Union joint venture called *Our World*—a three-hour live TV show to commemorate the completion of the first global satellite network, which offered each nation with access to this system the chance to contribute an item of benign propaganda. The Beatles had been invited to represent the UK and wrote the song to order, having promised that it would be lyrically limited to "basic English" so as to ensure maximum reach. Although ultimately diminished by a Soviet bloc boycott and limited coverage in the United States—where only the nascent public TV networks took the broadcast live—so that only a fraction of the hoped-for six hundred million viewers actually saw it, the broadcast still had an enormous global audience. While most of the show comprised rather dry and dull, but worthy, documentary clips—America's contribution, for example, focused on farming in Wisconsin—the Beatles were given a six-minute slot broadcast live from Abbey Road Studios in which they performed "All You Need Is Love," surrounded and backed by many of rock's elite including various members of the Stones, the Hollies, and the Who.

Inevitably, "All You Need Is Love" became the summer's anthem. In the United States, it was the Beatles' second number-one single of the year. Yet this is a song in which any amount of (self)mythologizing is countered by healthy doses of skeptical (self)parody. "All" is not what it might seem at first listen. "Love, love, love," they incant, but there is much tortuous (double) negativity undercutting this ostensibly facile optimism—there is "nothing you can do that can't be done." While many did indeed take it at face value to mean "all things are made possible by love," others, even at the time, heard it—because of its wry, mocking intertextual references to "The Marseillaise," "Greensleeves," "In the Mood," and even the Beatles' own "She Loves You" and "Yesterday"—as a spoof. So, as both *Sgt. Pepper* and "All You Need Is Love" had suggested, the Beatles had not simply abandoned love and joy, but there did appear to be a knowing, distanced, "British" perspective modifying the belief that these could resolve all problems. Although it would be a sweeping generalization, then, to say that British pop in late 1967 was totally dominated by "flower power," there was nevertheless a strong move toward songs combining a heady mix of love and acid, a certain inevitability about songs popularizing the psychedelic experience. However—as the market-leading Beatles had demonstrated—this did not necessarily have to mean that the Brits were slavishly copying the Americans. This was best illustrated by the Beatles' closest rivals, the Rolling Stones. In December 1967 the band belatedly released *Their Satanic Majesties Request*—an album commonly viewed as the disappointing result of an ill-advised dalliance with psychedelia, an aberration apparently confirmed by the poor Billboard showing of its most archetypal track, "She's Like a Rainbow," which had only managed to sneak inside the Top 30. The album had been delayed by a number of summer drug busts that had seen Jagger and Richards both jailed but later released on appeal. These events had directly informed "We Love You," a track that most assuredly does not possess the smiling nonjudgmentalism of the archetypal "flower power" anthem. A product of the summer recording sessions that would eventually deliver the out-of-character *Their Satanic Majesties Request*, "We Love You" is in fact entirely in keeping with the Stones' well-established modus operandi— a snotty statement of defiance only loosely dressed in caftan and bell-bottoms in which Jagger informs the establishment that "we don't care if you hound we" and that it "will never win," and in which the sarcastic phrasing is all—"We love you / Of course we do." Featuring the sound of chains, prison doors slamming, and heavy boot-falls on stone steps, and backed by some thunderous drumming, a heavy drone, and some uncredited Beatles, the track comes to a shuddering, decidedly un-peaceful halt. Furthermore, the promotional film made to accompany "We Love You" openly mocked the judicial system, which had only recently prosecuted Jagger and Richards, by pointedly referencing scenes from Oscar Wilde's trial. Somewhat predictably, the promo was subject to a BBC ban. "I'm not involved in this love and flowers scene," Jagger explained at the time. "But it is something to bring people to-gether for the summer. In the winter, we'll probably latch on to snow" (qtd. in Egan 92). "We Love You," he declared, was "just a bit of fun." It was a sizable hit single in the UK, where it made the Top 10. In the States, where it was backed by the less contentious, literally more flow-ery "Dandelion," it only reached a lowly number fifty, as radio stations tended to favor the safer B-side and so sent it into the Top 20. "We Love You," however, also featured on the U.S.-only LP *Flowers*—a stopgap compilation LP that nevertheless peaked at number three in the fall of 1967.

While most UK psychedelic rock was not as openly cynical as "We Love You," it produced fewer emphatically outward-facing songs marked by their collective embrace than there were coming out of the States at this time. This may suggest that "counterculture" carried dif-ferent meanings and connotations in its different transatlantic contexts. As Tom McGrath noted of the British variant in *International Times*, "This is not a movement of protest but one of celebration. . . . This movement is essentially optimistic. It has a happy view of Man and his potential, based mainly on his creativity" (qtd. in Whiteley 64). The politics of the British counterculture was predominantly of the *cultural* variety, rooted in a desire for personal freedom rather than in any compulsion to smash the system or sometimes even to engage with it on any level at all. In this respect, Procul Harum's inward-looking "A Whit-er Shade of Pale"—a sizeable U.S. hit but, rather tellingly, a six-week UK number one in which the narrator's "eyes were open" but "might just as well been closed"—perhaps represented the apotheosis of Brit-ish psychedelia. It mixed Bach, rhythm and blues, rock, jazz, and pop to accompany a sometimes cryptic, sometimes allusive lyric that suggested both the hallucinogenic and the mystical—as "the room was humming harder / as the ceiling flew away" and the "seasick" narrator did not help matters by "turn[ing] cartwheels across the floor." "My main influence was Bob Dylan," explained cowriter Keith Reid. "I could see how he did it, how he played with words. I was also taken with surrealism, Magritte and Dali." Perhaps somewhat disingenuously given its obvious psychedelic textures and images, Reid also stressed that the song "was influenced by books not drugs" (qtd. in Maconie 80).

Ultimately, the psychedelic identity of "A Whiter Shade of Pale" is as contestable as its status as one of rock music's earliest "progressive" statements. However, with its borrowings from classical music and references to classic literature (e.g., Chaucer's *Miller's Tale*), even if it did not invent the subgenre, the track could at least stake a strong claim to have put "progressive rock" on the map. Prog rock's natural home, of course, would prove to be the long-form format, and it would be another British act that would deliver on this front. According to the band's manager, Peter Jenner, Pink Floyd "were the first band to be signed by EMI with an *album* deal. We didn't have to have the hit singles before we were allowed to make an album" (qtd. in Heylin 138). A lack of contractual obligation, then, made Floyd's distinctive brand of music all the more possible. Yet attempting to define the band's sound at this time perhaps also highlights some degree of concurrency with audio (and visual) developments on America's West Coast. "They'd be playing these weird breaks," Jenner recalls, "so weird I couldn't even work out which instrument the sound was coming from. It was all very bizarre and just what I was looking for—a far-out, electronic, freaky, pop group" (qtd. in Heylin 78–79). Recorded at Abbey Road Studios at the same time as *Sgt. Pepper*, *The Piper at the Gates of Dawn* was not even released in States. However, it laid the foundations for a rock subgenre that would dominate the album charts, particularly in the United States, for much of the next decade. *Piper* featured the fifteen-minute freak-out "Interstellar Overdrive" and also several examples of that patented British psychedelia first heard on "Strawberry Fields Forever," with its rather parochial flavorings and childlike whimsy—songs like "Bike" and characters like Gerald the mouse!

In the late 1960s there were two new Invasion acts of more immediate significance to the development of rock music—Cream and the Jimi Hendrix Experience. Following the band's breakthrough at Monterey, the latter's *Are You Experienced?* was released in America toward the end of the summer, and it would go on to become 1968's best-selling album, propelled by the hit singles "Purple Haze," "Hey Joe," and "Wind Cries Mary." At almost exactly the same time, Cream's *Disraeli*

Gears—which had been recorded at Atlantic Records in New York six months earlier—was released, and it eventually made the Top 10 in early 1968. Cream was the original "power trio"—virtuoso musicians who according to guitarist Eric Clapton "aimed to extend the expressive potential and aesthetic quality of blues-based rock music," filtered through psychedelia, jazz, and even pop (qtd. in Whiteley 7). Not only did Cream demonstrate impressive musical chops, they also had volume in abundance, and by late 1967 the band had become both influential and popular in the States. Although the vast majority of the band's imitators—just as they would with Hendrix—tended not to be quite so deft, subtle, inventive, and technically proficient as their idols, Cream's legacy was most obviously felt (and heard) in the subsequent development and long-lasting commercial success of "hard rock." Listen to "Sunshine of Your Love," a Top 5 hit single in early 1968, to understand in a little over four riff-rich minutes how this came to pass.

Jimi Hendrix admired Eric Clapton and acknowledged Cream as key inspiration for his own blues-based power trio. Prior to his midsixties relocation to London, Hendrix had played in touring soul reviews backing the likes of Solomon Burke and Wilson Pickett. He was also influenced by blues guitarists like Muddy Waters, Willie Dixon, and Little Walter, and had even played with B. B. King. He had also performed with Little Richard, Jackie Wilson, Curtis Knight, and the Isleys. This meant that Hendrix was conversant in jazz, swing, rhythm and blues, gospel, and soul—receiving a deep and broad musical education similar to other Invasion musicians, albeit of course one received firsthand. Reinforcing his Invasion credentials, the former Animals' bassist Chas Chandler had seen Hendrix performing at Café Wha in New York in 1966 and brought him back to London, where they put together a band—with Englishmen Noel Redding on bass and Mitch Mitchell on drums. The Jimi Hendrix Experience played their first gig in Paris and then played regularly in the London clubs through the fall and winter of 1966, building a following and earning maximum respect from fellow musicians who caught the act. Recorded on the same day the Beatles began work on "Strawberry Fields Forever," Hendrix's version of the garage band staple "Hey Joe" was released in the UK in December 1966, where it became the first of four Top 20 hit singles the Experience would enjoy over the next twelve months. Of these, the most noteworthy was "Purple Haze," an explicit celebration of hallucinogenics reputedly named after a brand of acid, which appeared to document the "trip" in all its Technicolor, mind-altering glory: "Purple Haze was in my brain / Lately things they don't seem the same." Just as Cream had done, Hendrix used heavy distortion, phasing, and guitar effects such as the wah-wah to provide apposite sonic bedding for lyrics that left few in any doubt about what the song was describing. When *Are You Experienced?* was released in the United States in late August, it eventually peaked at number five, and would go on to spend over two years on the Billboard chart.

5

"IT'S ALL TOO MUCH"

1968–1969

It is sometimes argued that rock's full-blown emergence in 1967 marked the end of the Invasion. British acts, however, had not only played a major part in defining this new style but would also continue to push developments and of course claim their share in the rewards that it would deliver over the coming years. It is, though, fair to say that, by the end of 1967, the Beatles were pretty much done with acid rock. *Sgt. Pepper*'s follow-up, the band had determined, would be a less baroque affair, and they had found a mix of inspiration and validation for this counterintuitive turn in Bob Dylan's "second coming." In December, Dylan had released *John Wesley Harding*, his first new material in eighteen months. Under the influence of bands like Cream and the Jimi Hendrix Experience, rock had become "hard" or "heavy," with its stress on feedback, guitar effects, drum solos, crescendos, and plenty of trippy interludes and extended flights of improvisation. *John Wesley Harding* was cussedly against the grain—stripped down and loose, lo-fi, and unshowy. Here, there was none of rock's freshly minted pyrotechnics and excess. Just compact songs like the title track or "I Dreamed I Saw St. Augustine," on which Dylan, backed by restrained Nashville session musicians, strummed his semi-acoustic and offered plaintive harmonica breaks while delivering apparently scrutable tales of redemption and penance. This was a sepia-toned world then, not one of vibrant Technicolor—reaching back into America's past for lyrical and musical inspiration, drawing on rural myth and history, country, folk, and blues. *John Wesley Harding*—though it sold very well, climbing to number two on Billboard in early 1968—did not instantly spark a major countermovement. Appropriately enough, though, it did offer the audible expression of a cultural turn that some were ready and willing to follow. In January 1968, for instance, the Byrds released *The Notorious Byrds Brothers*, mixing country, folk, and psychedelia—sometimes, as in "Wasn't Born to Follow," in the same song. By August, the band appeared to have engineered a wholesale switch to country music and abandoned psychedelia altogether. On *Sweetheart of the Rodeo* tracks like the rootsy "Hickory Wind" and a version of Woody Guthrie's "Pretty Boy Floyd" demonstrated an irony-free hymning of the past. Perhaps unsurprisingly given the group's close musical relationship with Bob Dylan, the most high-profile exponents of this turn to roots were his former backing band. When Dylan was forced off the road following his motorbike accident in the summer of '66, the Hawks had been forced to take stock of their own musical career, and had followed Dylan to upstate New York to—literally, as it would transpire—regroup. Jamming in semirural isolation, sometimes with near-neighbor Dylan, the five musicians—four Canadians and an Arkansan—explored America's musical heritage, playing a rich, genre-hopping mix of country blues, work songs and spirituals, mountain music, traditional songs, Irish ballads, rock 'n' roll, and even sea chanteys. This material would eventually emerge in the mid-1970s as the fabled *Basement Tapes*. However, in August 1968, the Band, as they were now known, released *Music from Big Pink*—an album that, whether offering cover version or original, seemed to advance Dylan's project in its similarly stripped-down sound, decidedly unrock song structures, and general sepia vibe. Although the album did eventually reach number thirty on Billboard and even produced a minor hit single in "The Weight," the Band's impact was more immediately registered and duly processed by their musician peers. In the fall of 1968, George Harrison spent several weeks with Dylan and the Band at their Catskills retreat, responding so positively to the mutually supportive creativity engendered there that he returned to England determined to "loosen up" the Beatles. Harrison also reportedly left upstate New York determined to quit the band. In the short term, of course, this did not come to pass. However, *Music from Big Pink* did reportedly hasten the demise of another key Invasion act, when Eric Clapton, upon hearing the album, called time on Cream.

The impact of this American-led turn to roots might well suggest that "normal service" had resumed insofar as the transatlantic trade in cultural influence was concerned (an argument to which sales and chart placings add further ballast). Indigenous rock acts enjoyed considerable album-related success in 1968—the Doors' *Waiting for the Sun* was the nation's best-selling LP for four weeks, Simon and Garfunkel spent a total of sixteen weeks at the top with two albums, while Big Brother and the Holding Company's *Cheap Thrills* had an eight-week run at number one. Other notable successes included Jefferson Airplane's *Crown of Creation*, the Grateful Dead's *Anthem of Sun*, Iron Butterfly's *Heavy* and *In-A-Gadda-Da-Vida*, and Vanilla Fudge's *Renaissance*. Over on the singles chart, Invasion acts occupied the top spot for eleven weeks, up two weeks from 1967. However, this total was composed of just two Beatles' 45s—"Hello Goodbye," which was technically a 1967 release and had bridged the new year spending two weeks at number one in early January, and "Hey Jude." So had the tide finally and unequivocally turned? Indigenous "easy" and country pop accounted for fifteen weeks' worth of Billboard number ones in 1968, with big-selling singles from Herb Alpert and the Paul Mauriat Orchestra, while there were also two psych-flavored bubble-gum pop number ones in John Fred and His Playboys' "Judy in Disguise" and the Lemon Pipers' "Green Tambourine." Here, it was perhaps inevitable that these two should be the first new number-one singles of 1968, as mainstream pop absorbed and then processed the "summer of love." Soul, and in particular Motown, also showed very strongly in 1968, with four different singles racking up an impressive total of eleven weeks at number one—Otis Redding's posthumous "Dock of the Bay," Archie Bell's "Tighten Up," Diana Ross and the Supremes' "Love Child," and Marvin Gaye's "I Heard It Through the Grapevine."

Even though 1967 had apparently witnessed a hardening of the differences between rock and pop, an increasing separation of the album and singles markets, there was still an impressive total of eleven weeks of occupancy at number one for native rock 45s—including the Doors' creepy "Hello, I Love You" and, no doubt boosted by *The Graduate*'s phenomenal box-office performance, Simon and Garfunkel's "Mrs. Robinson." Yet, as other years have demonstrated, the Invasion's continuing and significant influence could arguably be felt, if not always directly heard, in the often seismic, multilevel transformations that popular music was undergoing in the second half of the 1960s. Rock music's scale and scope, its impact and reach, was clearly developing at pace—and for this it had the Invasion to thank in large measure. By 1968, for example, two distinct markets had emerged—different arenas for popular music to be both produced and consumed. In this year, sales of albums surpassed sales of singles for the very first time, marking a commercial watershed for sure but with implications beyond the purely financial. The album had become rock music's natural format; and as it became more than simply a dumping ground for some hit singles and a lot of hastily conceived filler, and as the increasing number of newly formed FM radio stations started playlisting album tracks, songs with more ambition and edge could potentially feature as significant public statements. In 1968, in fact, Invasion acts managed an impressive fifteen weeks at the very summit of Billboard's album chart—the Beatles' *Magical Mystery Tour* and *The Beatles* being joined by Cream's double *Wheels of Fire* and the Jimi Hendrix Experience's *Electric Ladyland*. Confirming that it was now its preferred format, rock music dominated the Billboard album listings, where it spent a total of forty-four weeks at number one, only to be lightly dented by Alpert, Paul Mauriat, and Glen Campbell.

While hindsight would prove them wrong, focusing on the Beatles stateside in the early months of 1968 led some contemporary observers to conclude that the band was if not quite a spent force then certainly a declining one. Here, the final new episode of the Monkees' TV show that went out in late March could only add symbolic grist to the growing sense that the Beatles' American star was dimming. The Beatles' movie *The Magical Mystery Tour* had been poorly received but the soundtrack album had sold very strongly at the start of the year, when it had been America's best seller for two months. However, in the spring of 1968 "Lady Madonna" had the dubious honor of being the first Beatles' single since the "Eleanor Rigby" / "Yellow Submarine" double A-side *not* to reach number one in the States. By the band's own very high standards, it was creatively, critically, and commercially only moderately successful. Based on a barrelhouse piano riff that Paul McCartney had lifted pretty much wholesale from "Bad Penny Blues"—a track by the British musician Humphrey Lyttelton that George Martin had produced in the mid-1950s—it came across as a rather insubstantial, rush job, the end product of pressure to knock out a single. Indeed, this appeared to be openly acknowledged by the Beatles themselves—or at least Lennon, when in "Glass Onion" he sings "Lady Madonna, trying to make ends meet." Yet "Lady Madonna" has its merits. At just two minutes sixteen seconds, for example, did it demonstrate the band's desire to get back to basics? As a modest act of retrieval, did its brazen act of archive raiding show that the Beatles were already following Dylan and the Band's lead? Or, perhaps in the end, it was simply a case that, no different from everyone else, the Beatles struggled to constantly match the impossibly high standards set a few short months earlier by *Sgt. Pepper*.

"Lady Madonna" might have suggested that the Beatles were on a downward curve in the States, but the rest of 1968 would prove that rumors of the band's impending demise were very premature. Released in November, *The Beatles*—commonly known as *The White Album*— had two million advance orders in America and comfortably saw out the year as the nation's best-selling album. "Hey Jude" was the year's best-selling single, occupying the top slot on Billboard for nine weeks in the fall. The Paul McCartney–produced, Apple Corps–distributed single "Those Were the Days," by Welsh singer Mary Hopkin, reached number two—and so, taken together with "Hey Jude," these two recordings accounted for estimated global sales of ten million and made Apple's launch comfortably the most successful label debut of all time.

"Hey Jude" had been earmarked as a single from the first time Paul McCartney played it for the rest of the band. On the face of it, the song could not have been any further away from the modest, "down-home" spirit and scope of *John Wesley Harding* or *Music from Big Pink*. It is an unapologetically grand affair, featuring thirty-six classically trained musicians playing the same four chords repeatedly and an extended fade-out of more than half the song's seven minutes that then repeats the same four-bar, three-chord musical phrase more than eighteen times. Big though it was, it was also abundantly clear that it was not an empty shell of a song. It appeared to do for many exactly what it promised, what it urged them to do for themselves and each other—"take a sad song and make it better." Powered by McCartney's genuinely soulful vocals, "Hey Jude" embraced its listeners, supplying an object lesson in communal redemption and consolation that America desperately needed in the summer of '68. For both parties, then, timing was as crucial as it was back in February 1964. By the middle of 1968, the "summer of love" was a distant memory. As Jeff Nuttall explains it in *Bomb Culture*, "The plain and obvious fact [was] that between the autumn of 1967 . . . and the summer of 1968 . . . young people, under various pretexts, made war on their elders, and their elders, made war on them" (qtd. in Gould 459). Things were getting ugly. Several years of peaceful protest against the Vietnam War had achieved a higher profile for opposition but little else—and the frustrations this engendered led to more open, sometimes violent confrontation. By August 1968, many in America—young and old—had come to the conclusion that the country was falling apart. The Tet Offensive had demonstrated that the war was out of control, there continued to be widespread university occupations and sit-ins, Martin Luther King had been assassinated in April, and then, as if to snuff out any last vestiges of hope, the antiwar presidential candidate Robert Kennedy had been murdered in July.

That rootsy, backward-facing turn notwithstanding, 1968 was a watershed year for rock music that protested the war, tied as it was to these and other key political and military events. Early '68 had witnessed the aforementioned Tet Offensive, a pyrrhic victory for the United States that had precipitated a significant and—as it would turn out to prove—irreversible waning in public support for the conflict. This, in turn, made the climate right for wider acceptance of rock's increasingly vocal antiwar posturing; and, in fact, far from the softening of sound and sentiment that might have been expected as a result of reaching out to the delicate sensibilities of a broader but possibly more conservative audience, a discernible, palpable musical mood swing occurred. Through '68 and beyond, a creeping paranoia and violence had seeped into much of rock music—an apocalyptic edge that was hard to miss and difficult to ignore. As Janis Joplin's biographer Alice Echols points out, from now on one heard "almost as much dread and foreboding as flower-power goofiness" (Echols 108). On June 1 the Rolling Stones released "Jumping Jack Flash," serving notice that their problematic flirtation with "flower-power goofiness" was well and truly over. Here was sour rock for sour times. In the song, Jack is born and raised in an apocalyptic maelstrom and violently tortured and abused— "drowned, washed up and left for dead" with bleeding feet and "spike right through [his] head." Jack is most assuredly *not* Jude. Their lives and prospects are miles apart. There is no consolation, no hope, and no redemption for Jack Flash. The gallows humor of the repeated line "It's a gas" is a bitterly defiant but ultimately joyless and nihilistic cri de coeur.

In these changed and charged times, the seven-minute hymn to hope that was "Hey Jude" could have seemed as out of step as "Hickory Wind." Except of course the Beatles were coming at the "problem" from a different angle. Neither ignoring the conflagration and chaos, nor even offering an amoral diagnosis for that matter. Simply supplying listeners with a means to cope and overcome ("Better! Better! Better!"). Resonating widely, "Hey Jude" would go on to become the Beatles' best-selling American single. Noteworthy particularly in the light of its relative failure in Britain, the Beatles would also enjoy great success with "their" movie *The Yellow Submarine*, which featured eleven of the band's songs—one from *The Magical Mystery Tour*, three from *Sgt. Pepper*, two from *Revolver*, one from *Rubber Soul*, and four previously unreleased tracks. Just as *A Hard Day's Night* had been, this was a transatlantic production. The project was headed by Al Brodax, a forty-year-old New Yorker who had produced the popular weekly Beatles' cartoon series, which had featured the band's music and had gained a spectacular 52 percent audience share when it was launched in 1966. Brodax had proposed a full-length animated movie to fulfill the Beatles' three-movie contract with United Artists. After an initial treatment by Joseph Heller was scrapped following the novelist's withdrawal, Brodax himself suggested using "Yellow Submarine" as the basis for a new script, and brought in playwright Lee Minoff to work up the narrative. In May 1967 this script was finished but eventually featured just two characters—Old Fred and Jeremy Boob/Nowhere Man—who would survive the many rewrites. Brodax hired and fired more writers, until Erich Segal, a Yale professor, came up with something acceptable to the demanding producer, who then gave the London-based company TVC the job of creating *Yellow Submarine* for $1 million. Toward the end of the project, Liverpool poet Roger McGough was brought in to lend the script some authentic Scouse flavor.

Yellow Submarine was a commercial flop in Britain, mainly because it was mispromoted as a children's film. However, in the States—where its release was held back until year's end—it became a massive box-office draw, second only to *The Sound of Music* that holiday season. As the *London Observer*'s movie critic astutely pointed out, there was "more stimulation, sly art references and *pure joy*" in it "than a mile of Op and Pop and all the mod cons" (qtd. in Harris 63, my emphasis). In the States, while *Time* and *Newsweek* panned it—and where even former Beatles "cheerleader" Andrew Sarris did not like it much—reviewers in the *New York Times* and *New Republic* loved it and the *New Yorker*'s Pauline Kael confessed to being "charmed" by the movie. However, it was somewhat ironic given its poor performance in the UK that it should have been that British critic who supplied the most plausible explanation for its astonishing popularity in the United States. Publicity and marketing was undoubtedly spot on here. Merchandising flooded stores just before Christmas, and this of course attracted the youngsters. Yet, as the movie's disappointing box-office receipts in Britain had demonstrated, its success depended on appealing to older teens and young adults. In America, this demographic duly turned up, and—it would appear—found good reason to connect with this extended ode to joy. Once again, context is all. By the end of 1968—as Jonathan Gould has argued—"a great many more young people in America than Britain really did regard the Beatles as the quasi-mythic figures depicted in the film":

> The portrayal of John, Paul, George and Ringo as a quartet of droll, Mod, mock-heroic saviours appearing out of nowhere to free a beleaguered population from the grip of repression and fear—this was precisely the way that many of their fans in America had perceived them all along. (Gould 506)

America's bond with the Beatles, then, had never been stronger, and the strength of this relationship was further demonstrated when the nominal B-side of "Hey Jude" was propelled into the Billboard Top 20. "Revolution," though, seemed to offer a less emollient solution to the trials and tribulations of 1968. Its lyric—which reportedly "alarmed" the always more affable McCartney—had been directly inspired by the May student uprising in Paris. Closer to home, in the UK, university students had been aping their American peers by participating in high-profile occupations of buildings and sit-ins. Lennon's song addressed this fractious landscape but did not appear to be offering the kind of open support for radical action that some had hoped for. Expecting unequivocal backing for their increasingly confrontational behavior, students on both sides of the Atlantic were sorely disappointed in "Revolution," sickened by what they viewed as "Lennon's bland rich-man's assurances that everything was somehow going to be 'alright,' resenting his wish to be counted out of any impending 'destruction'" (MacDonald 226–27). In America, the politicized wing of the counterculture was particularly irked. Here, the track was branded "a betrayal" and "a lamentable petty bourgeois cry of fear"—the Left's anger only fueled by *Time* magazine's applauding of "Revolution" as an "exhilarating" attack on radical activism (qtd. in MacDonald 227). When the right-wing *National Review Bulletin* ran with "the International Communist enterprise may at last have met its match: the Beatles," it seemed to many radicals that the Beatle sellout was complete.

Lennon had agonized over his lyric, constantly flip-flopping over being counted "out" or "in"—and, partly as a result of the furor surrounding the single version, would opt for *both* on the more conciliatory, less urgent album cut, "Revolution 1." However, when the band recorded the single in July 1968, his resolutely apolitical side had won out, as he appeared to commit wholeheartedly to "peace" and so prepare the ground for the various Dada-esque stunts that would invite the derision of both the political Left and Right and give rise to the folky anthem "Give Peace a Chance" through the next year or so. The phrase "it's gonna be alright" had emerged from hours of meditation in India in early 1968, when Lennon arrived at an understanding that God would take care of humans whatever happened politically. So, when quizzed, he declared himself against both the establishment and the New Left, and in the song he admonished both sides—"If you want money for people with minds that hate / All I can tell you is, brother, you'll have to wait." All ideologies, it seemed to point up, were doomed. Even those of the Left, where "carrying pictures of Chairman Mao" will do you no good whatsoever.

The rest of the band, and especially McCartney, urged caution, and balked at Lennon's insistence that it be released as a single. They argued that it was too slow (perhaps to cover their misgivings about its overt, and so inevitably controversial, apolitical message). Ironically, this concern led to the pacier version that eventually emerged on the B-side to "Hey Jude"—a version that was *more* uncompromising musically, with its speed and distortion, and seemed to complement Lennon's strenuous, increasingly desperate efforts to persuade, as those

screamed "alrights" at the very end worked against the assurances normally associated with the word. On 45, "Revolution" was defiantly skeptical, but certainly not cynical or evasive. Just out of step with the ugly
turn the West, and in particular the United States, appeared to have
taken. It was released a few days before the Democratic Convention in
Chicago descended into violence, as the city's police viciously attacked
Vietnam protestors and delegates on the sidewalks in the full media
glare. In stark contrast to its A-side, "Revolution" was quite simply the
rawest and angriest the band had ever been, and would ever be, on 45.
Yet, like "Hey Jude," it addressed the need for positive and peaceful
behavior as a constructive response to increasingly violent, destructive
times. "We all want to change the world," Lennon sang—and this was
arguably as heartfelt as when McCartney urged listeners to "make it
better." However, by the time both songs came on the radio in late
August 1968, images of the Soviet invasion of Czechoslovakia coupled
with those of brutal repression much closer to home on the streets of
Chicago were a graphic reminder for many of what was now at stake.
Some counterculture politicos castigated Lennon for his naïve escap-
ism; others went further still, accusing him of preaching counterrevolu-
tion. In the *New Yorker* Ellen Willis accused the Beatles of having
"taken refuge in self-righteousness and facile optimism" (qtd. in Gould
494).

    In the week of the Democratic Convention, the Rolling Stones re-
leased a new single, "Street Fighting Man." Like "Revolution," it clearly
represented a response to changed and charged times. However, it was
received very differently. According to Greil Marcus, who was demonstrating at Berkeley in the week of the convention, the Beatles "were
ordering us to pack up and go home, but the Stones seemed to be
saying that we were lucky if we had a fight to make and a place to take a
stand" (qtd. in Lynskey 161). Presumably, it was this widely understood
perception of how each song worked that led to bans for "Street Fighting Man"—which only managed to creep into Billboard's Top 50—but
heavy rotation for "Revolution." Nevertheless, disappointed with Lennon's antirevolutionary stance, the Left enthusiastically embraced
"Street Fighting Man"—a track that owed its genesis to an antiwar
demonstration, and so possessed a fine set of countercultural credentials. On March 17, 1968, an estimated twenty-five thousand people had
attended an antiwar rally in central London, during which police on

horseback had rushed protestors, right in front of the U.S. embassy in Grosvenor Square. Some protestors had retaliated by throwing bricks and stones, and a two-hour, most un-British, "battle" ensued. Mick Jagger was there. Sort of. "I didn't march with Vanessa Redgrave," he explained. "Didn't feel like it" (qtd. in Egan, *Rolling Stones*, 108). Although he freely admitted to getting a "buzz" just from being present, he also confessed that he was not "getting into it" but instead "going round it," and Jagger's ambivalence is there for all to hear in "Street Fighting Man." It is belligerent but not in the least bit politically focused. In the song, the narrator expresses frustration, but it is with "sleepy London town." "How do you feel when students riot when you're on stage?" Jagger was asked. "Do you pick up on any energy?" "Yes! Wow! Tingle with it!" he replied, going on to say, "The energy's great. I never went on stage with the idea of keeping everything cool. I never wanted it to be peaceful" (qtd. in Egan, *Rolling Stones*, 106–7). "Street Fighting Man" is about the desirability, the heady rush, of fighting, not political change. It is cynical and nihilistic. "It's difficult to be constructive," Jagger told the *International Times* in May 1968, "because to be constructive in a political manner is just a farce" (qtd. in Egan, *Rolling Stones*, 112). Although it was missed at the time—when "it sounded like revolution, and that was what mattered" (Lynskey 167)—"Street Fighting Man" represented a colossal denial of responsibility, in which the Stones relish indiscriminate violence—"I shout and scream, I kill the king and all his servants." Following the December 1968 release of the album *Beggar's Banquet*, it became difficult to argue that the Stones were anything other than amoral and apolitical thrill seekers, getting their collective "rocks off" on the violence that surrounded them. This would have dire, very real consequences a little further down the line—but for now, as in "Sympathy for the Devil," it was all a game, a "gas." Over the course of six minutes plus, to a skittering, pulsing, percussive shuffle that appropriately led nowhere, "Sympathy for the Devil" took its listener on a tragic(al) history tour. Our guide is the devil, Lucifer himself—a man of "wealth and taste" and exceptional good manners to boot, but, by his own amused admission, also "in need of some restraint." The catalog of murder and assassinations that unfolds in this downright nasty song is simply what it is. There is no moralizing. Only the rather facile, and flat-out wrong, assertion that the

Kennedys were killed by "you and me" and that "every cop is a criminal and all the sinners saints."

Largely the product of their time spent in India back in the first months of the year—when Lennon, McCartney, and Harrison had managed to emerge from their "retreat" with the makings of twenty-six songs—the Beatles' new album was finally released in late November 1968. *The Beatles*—a double LP of thirty tracks running to over ninety minutes—met with mixed reviews. Ellen Sander in the *Saturday Review* declared it to be "woefully inconsistent," "sketchy," "sloppy and diffuse" (qtd. in Gould). Of course, lukewarm critical responses could not prevent it from selling in its millions, and FM radio duly played it all on heavy rotation in the weeks and months after its release. Here though was a record without a unifying concept, comprising songs rarely worked up by all four members of the band, the product—as it would later transpire—of a group of musicians already falling apart. It was all a world away from the gaudy, Technicolor of *Sgt. Pepper* or *The Magical Mystery Tour*. *The Beatles* was certainly varied and variable—"a hodgepodge in a grand way," as Yoko Ono has described it (qtd. in *Mojo* 83)—but it did reflect a conscious desire to strip things down, to return to basics. Richard Hamilton's blank white cover had given visual notice of this intent, but it could be heard within across all four sides, in the lo-fi delicacy of acoustic songs like "Julia," "Cry Baby Cry," and "Blackbird," and even on tracks like the no-nonsense rocker "Back in the U.S.S.R." or the repetitious "Why Don't We Do It in the Road," which barely succeeded in elevating a jam to full song status. Many of the songs on the album were also laced with melancholia, seemingly conflating '68's darker vibes with more personal traumas, as in "While My Guitar Gently Weeps" or "Happiness Is a Warm Gun."

While the market leader's output might well have suggested otherwise, 1968's predominant rock music tendency was for heavier, lengthier, and "uglier"—and, even if the Beatles were not necessarily the masters of sour rock, there were other Invaders who could justifiably lay claim to this title. The Rolling Stones for one, but there were other candidates, too. Cream had played their final gig in November 1968, but not before enjoying a U.S. number one with the double-album *Wheels of Fire*. "White Room" was track one, side one of this bestselling LP, and was also issued as a single, reaching number six on Billboard in the fall. "White Room" spoke of a nightmarish world "where shadows run from themselves" and the "sun never shines," a place of unrelenting sadness for the "lonely" inhabitants of this "black roof country." Although the images might seem random, backed by Clapton's wah-wah, fuzz-heavy guitar work and fixed in time, the song achieved a powerful unity of effect. *Are You Experienced?* had continued to sell heavily in the States right through 1968. In this year, the Jimi Hendrix Experience had also released two new albums—*Axis Bold as Love*, which had peaked at number three in early '68, and the double *Electric Ladyland*, which made number one in November. *Electric Ladyland* featured the band's all-out rock reworking of Bob Dylan's prophetic "All Along the Watchtower," which as a single had kept "White Room" company in the Billboard Top 20 in the fall. The subtleties of Dylan's original were lost, as Hendrix's version ramped up the sense of imminent apocalypse, his guitar, in tandem with heavy phasing, contributing to the creation of a nightmarish landscape in which "there's too much confusion," "no relief," and no possibility of redemption. Songs like "Watchtower" and "White Room" also flagged the dangerous and disturbing flip side of drug use, implying that pharmaceuticals might not offer an escape "someway outta here" after all. While LSD could privilege a valued childlike innocence and spontaneity, it could just as easily open the door to chaos and destruction. "When everything connects, the vision can be one of joy or terror," Nick Bromell explains. "Both possibilities lived side-by-side in the '60s. Bummers and Bliss. Madness and Ecstasy. Evil and Love. . . . *But evil was also in the sensibility of the counterculture because the psychedelic experience of radical pluralism so often includes a rendezvous with the devil. Not just the occasional bummer, but even the normal trip could reveal that malignant power was as much at home in Being as happiness and love and peace. . . . When you break on through to the other side, be prepared to meet something you hadn't quite reckoned on*" (125, my emphasis).

So, much like the rock music of the late 1960s, LSD had its dark side—bad trips, acid panic, psychotic episodes, suicides. If you were mentally fragile, potentially suicidal, or prone to psychosis, acid would not cure you. In fact, it might well bring more bad stuff bubbling to the surface. In the summer of love, the Doors had already demonstrated with songs like "Light My Fire" and "The End" what could happen when you let the id out of the box. "I am interested in anything about revolt, disorder and chaos," lead singer Jim Morrison had explained, "especially activity that seems to have no meaning." It has been argued that it was the Doors who led American rock fans down this dark path, and that in their sulfurous wake others followed. Like Iron Butterfly, whose LP *In-A-Gadda-Da-Vida* sold twenty-five million copies, and Vanilla Fudge, who covered pop hits like "Ticket to Ride" by slowing them down and upping the angsty melodrama. However, it was not the Doors who kick-started all this. Heavy rock was pioneered by a host of British groups, who built on the work of the Rolling Stones, Cream, and the Jimi Hendrix Experience. The year 1968 witnessed the formation of Led Zeppelin (initially billed as the New Yardbirds); the emergence of Deep Purple, a band put together by Chris Curtis of first-wave Invaders the Searchers, whose single "Hush" reached number four on Billboard that summer; the formation of what would eventually become Black Sabbath; and the release of the Jeff Beck Group's protometal LP *Truth*, which sold well enough in the States to reach the Top 20.

In 1969 there were just three Invasion number-one singles. Although this was one more than the previous year, between them this trio racked up a week *less* at the very top of the Billboard chart (their combined total of ten weeks being eclipsed by the eleven the Beatles had enjoyed in '68). Once again, the Beatles had two number ones, spending six weeks at the top with "Get Back" and "Come Together," and they were joined by the Rolling Stones, who managed four weeks with "Honky Tonk Women." There were four other rock number ones of local provenance that between them managed to achieve a total of sixteen weeks at Billboard's peak—Fifth Dimension's "Aquarius / Let the Sunshine In" and "Wedding Bell Blues," Zager and Evans's doomy "In the Year 2525," and Elvis Presley's comeback hit "Suspicious Minds." There were six pop "easy listening" chart toppers—including the Archies' "Sugar Sugar," which was the year's biggest-selling single, Henry Mancini's "Love Theme from Romeo and Juliet," Steam's "Na Na Hey Hey," and Peter, Paul, and Mary's "Leaving on a Jet Plane." Soul supplied four number ones, with Marvin Gaye's "I Heard It through the Grapevine" and Diana Ross and the Supremes' "Someday, We'll Be Together" bookending the chart year, and being joined at the very top by Sly and the Family Stone's "Everyday People" and the Temptations' "I Can't Get Next to You."

While there were noticeably fewer successes for Invasion acts on the Billboard singles chart, extending a downward curve that could be traced back several years, the album market told a different story. Here, the landscape was liberally peppered with British product. Indeed, many of this territory's key landmarks were stamped "Made in the UK." For example, Led Zeppelin's first two LPs—which had made number ten in January and number one in October, respectively—reportedly helped the band generate $5 million in American earnings in their first year. Elsewhere, Cream's post-breakup *Goodbye* peaked at number two, the Who's double-album *Tommy* made the Top 10, while Blind Faith's eponymous LP was a number one on both sides of the Atlantic. Blind Faith was a short-lived but influential supergroup, formed out of the ashes of Cream and Traffic, featuring Eric Clapton, Ginger Baker, and Steve Winwood. The band made just one album and managed just one sellout U.S. tour in the fall of 1969. However, Blind Faith was the archetype for the rootsy blues band of the era. British bands, then, continued to capitalize on the buoyancy of the album market and on the American rock consumer's seemingly unquenchable thirst for live performance. And of course, the more you toured, the more albums you shifted, and vice versa. Perpetual rock motion.

The year 1969 would turn out to be a tale of two gatherings. Both took place in America, but the Invasion would ensure that the most significant of these was undeniably British "made." August's Woodstock Festival had attracted over four hundred thousand rock fans, drawn to upstate New York by the promise of "three days of peace and music" and the opportunity to take in sixty acts, including the Grateful Dead, Sly and the Family Stone, Crosby, Stills, and Nash, the Who, and Jimi Hendrix. By and large, Woodstock delivered on its promise, but it was an anomaly—a deceptively affirmative oasis in the midst of all that unraveling, attended by thousands desperate for some "good news" as all around the mood blackened. This was captured perfectly in Joni Mitchell's downbeat ode to the festival, which seemed to suggest that Woodstock was the very stuff of bittersweet nostalgia from the very moment it occurred, that it had never been real or substantial, mere "stardust." Perhaps Joni simply knew too much to commit to the dream? And perhaps she was not alone: 1969 had witnessed rising campus-based protest, with violence often spilling out onto the streets and so gaining national media coverage. In November, half a million had sung John Lennon's chanty, ramshackle (and most unlikely of Billboard Top 10 singles) "Give Peace a Chance" at the Vietnam Moratorium in

Washington. It has been estimated that four million Americans marched for peace to the rhythms of folk and rock during the war years. Yet declining support for the war in Vietnam was often believed to be the result of pragmatic considerations rather than any major ideological volte-face directly inspired by the peace movement, whose oppositional messages had seeped into the nation's consciousness via rock music. Many Americans, it was pointed out, had simply grown weary of the war and of waiting in vain for an increasingly unlikely victory, while the steady drip-drip cost in lives and spiraling cost in tax dollars made a very strong case for concluding that mass opposition to the war did not grow out of a burgeoning spirit of idealism and liberalism, fueled by counter-cultural rock.

As Woodstock drew to a close, the Rolling Stones' "Honky Tonk Women" had risen to number one on Billboard—a song so sexually frank that it made "Let's Spend the Night Together" and all the controversy it had generated seem a very long time ago indeed. In fact, it had only been just over two years since the Stones had acquiesced to Ed Sullivan's demand that the less risqué words "some time" should replace "the night." However, these were different times, and the single's success appeared to confirm that the Stones' time had come again. On the louche and raunchy "Honky Tonk Women" the Stones were sex tourists. Elsewhere, on the late '69 album *Let It Bleed* on which a version of this song featured, the Stones turned their characteristically amoral gaze to more pressing matters on the portentous "Gimme Shelter," in which "war" is reported to be "just a shot away." Typically, although "love is just a kiss away," this news is delivered in a rather halfhearted fashion, almost as an afterthought, right at the end of a track that has expended most of its nervous energy in the service of documenting the coming apocalypse. Once again there is little here to suggest even the possibility of redemption or hope. It is what it is. *Let it bleed.* As the Rolling Stones had been illustrating over a year now, "revolution" in rock more often than not took the form of free-floating ideas, images, and references to chaos, violence, and disorder; aggressive and apocalyptic, destructive as opposed to constructive, and rarely overtly ideological. Responding to the gathering gloom, rock became a conduit for apocalyptic visions, channeling the counterculture as it had been doing for some time now, but replacing "peace, love, and flowers" with violence, nihilism, and pessimism. Where the Beatles had once led, now it was the Stones' turn.

The Rolling Stones' gig at Altamont Speedway in Northern California—at which they were supported by Santana, Jefferson Airplane, Crosby, Stills, and Nash, and the Grateful Dead—was the last date of the band's U.S. tour, held in the last month of the last year of the 1960s. It's facts like these that continue to make the event ripe for interpretation. A task made all the more easier when it is set beside Woodstock. Here are two events, it has been suggested, that are as diametrically opposed as their summer and winter timings, as their geographical locations. Whereas Woodstock offered a "glimpse of heaven"—however delusional—it was directly counterposed to Altamont. Paradise had been found and then lost in the short space of just four months. In the memorable words of the Grateful Dead's Jerry Garcia, Altamont was a "nice afternoon in hell," which reached its gruesome denouement as the Rolling Stones performed and the Hells Angels—whom the band had naively employed as security for the hastily organized festival—killed a young African American, Meredith Hunter, right in front of the stage. There is then a simplistic but still satisfying, compelling, and enduring symbolism surrounding these tragic events at Altamont that sees it "bringing down the curtain on 60s idealism," with its murderous violence mirroring the "generational, cultural and political rifts endemic to American society" at the time (Gitlin 560).

If the Invasion had helped to bring much of that "idealism" into the world, then here it appeared to be performing the last rites. For the Byrds' Chris Hillman, Altamont represented "the worst scenario you could imagine. I thought that day was the end of the 1960s. . . . It had gone from the wonderful innocence of the Beatles . . . to this" (qtd. in Stanley 266). While the Rolling Stones should not be blamed for the "death of the sixties," they certainly did not help. In "Midnight Rambler," the narrator revels in violence, bloodshed, and (mass) murder. As with "Sympathy for the Devil," there is no pretense to editorialize. Unless, that is, one counts the repeated line "Oh, don't do that," delivered with a sneer and barely suppressed chuckle. On "Midnight Rambler," the Stones were playing with fire, as the narrator—"like a proud Blank Panther"—brings the song to a climax with the grim threat that he'll "stick my knife down your throat, baby, and it hurts." In May 1968, Mick Jagger had told a reporter that "if you haven't got any policemen [at a gig], it's weird, because [the fans] don't know what to do." "But then there's rarely no police," he continued. "That's a mistake the authorities make. They never ought to have any police there at all. If they had no police there, then there wouldn't be any trouble [which only happens] just 'cause they're there" (qtd. in Egan, *Rolling Stones*, 107). Cynical, naïve, or just plain dumb. Whatever lay at the root of those events at Altamont, it was clearly the product of a colossal miscalculation.

Critical response to *Let It Bleed*—which eventually peaked at number three in the States—was noticeably more positive than the generally lukewarm reception that greeted the Beatles' *Abbey Road*. This was arguably the first time in a six-year-long rivalry that the pretenders to the throne had outshone the incumbent kings of rock. Sniffy critics, however, could do absolutely nothing to dent sales of *Abbey Road*, which spent twelve weeks at number one and became the year's best-selling album. Crucially, the Beatles were men out of time, not yesterday's men—an important distinction that stamped pretty much everything the band produced in 1969. If *The Beatles* had demonstrated that fraying personal relationships could be creatively beneficial, could the trick be repeated? As the band limped through an increasingly fractious six months of studio work, many of the songs that emerged from these sessions appeared to take the form of exercises in desperate hope in testing times. "Christ, you know it ain't easy," Lennon sings in the picaresque "The Ballad of John and Yoko" (no. 8). "Get Back," together with its B-side "Don't Let Me Down," was released as a single in May 1969 and spent five weeks at number one. Both sides demonstrated that the Beatles were straining to keep it all together—a message for themselves and their massive audience clearly reinforced when in the fall "Come Together" became the band's second number-one single of the year. In such trying circumstances, a track like "Octopus' Garden" cannot be simply dismissed as an inconsequential sop to Ringo, as it expressed a "yearning for serenity" as both the inside and outside worlds "turned more troubling and uncertain" (Gilmore 40). In the song, elusive "shelter" is found ("We'd be warm below the storm"). But it is, of course, an unapologetic act of wishful thinking, an escapist fantasy in which "no one can tell us what to do" because "we know we can't be found." In "Here Comes the Sun," the "long cold lonely winter" has finally given way to sun and returning smiles. However, it too is a fantasy, its lyric complemented by similarly plaintive and plangent music that yearns to convince but in its fragility ultimately cannot.

As McCartney confirmed, the band were clinging to the joy by their fingertips, but under no illusion even as they did so—"Oh that magic feeling / Nowhere to go" ("You Never Give Me Your Money"). Lennon had already declared his intention to quit the band in September, and within a few months McCartney would announce that the Beatles were no more—a breakup that, for many, would signal the end of the '60s as surely as the Beatles' arrival had marked its beginning.

6

"DOUBLE FANTASY"

1970 and Beyond

Crosby, Stills, and Nash represented the ultimate transatlantic collaboration and arguably a better fit than even the shell-shocked Rolling Stones to replace the Beatles. Graham Nash had been in the Hollies, a Mancunian Invasion band that had formed in 1962 and started out doing Searchers-style cover versions like "Stay." The Hollies were a beat group, and consequently "had absolutely nothing to say about Vietnam, devolution or Hare Krishna" (Stanley 203). Frustrated with this lack of opportunity for artistic growth and engagement, Nash made the decision to leave the Hollies in 1968. If this band could not support his creative ambition, then maybe there were like-minded musicians out there who could? Nash had been introduced to David Crosby by Mama Cass Elliott, when the two had met on the Hollies' first visit to Los Angeles back in 1966—the same year in which the Hollies had enjoyed two U.S. Top 10 hits with "Bus Stop" and "Stop Stop Stop." Despite continued success with songs like "On a Carousel" and "Carrie Anne," Nash grew further apart from the rest of the band through 1967, and things came to a head when his genre-stretching single "King Midas in Reverse" failed to place in the upper reaches of the charts and the rest of the band flat-out rejected the chance to record a new song Nash had written called "Marrakesh Express." When, in 1968, the Hollies determined to record a whole album of Dylan covers, this proved the final straw for Nash—and he quit the band and relocated to California with the initial intention of becoming a songwriter for hire. However, he soon hooked up with his old friend David Crosby, and, joining forces with ex–Buffalo Springfield guitarist Stephen Stills, formed the supergroup that bore each of their surnames.

The band's first album, *Crosby, Stills & Nash*, preceded the demise of the Beatles, peaking at number six on Billboard in the summer of 1969 and spawning two hit singles, "Marrakesh Express"—for which its author, Nash, had now presumably found a welcoming home—and the plaintive workout "Suite: Judy Blue Eyes," which featured the kind of keening multitracked harmonies that would become so synonymous with CSN. If there was a unifying West Coast vibe, then it was also true that the songs on this record represented a variety of music styles and a range of topics that reflected the different personalities of the three men who, it appeared, were each at liberty to express themselves. Here, the band's name was perhaps indicative of this democracy. Like partners in a law firm, each musician was seemingly afforded the same rights and benefits. So, *Crosby, Stills & Nash* had its darker moments, such as on "Long Time Gone," which references the murder of Robert Kennedy and urges the listener to "speak out against the madness" if "you dare." But there was also plenty of joy, often most notable on Nash compositions. The kings were dead, long live the kings!

Less than a week into the new decade, on the evening of January 6, 1970, Paul McCartney was among the crowd at London's Royal Albert Hall to witness the UK debut of the band many were hailing as the "American Beatles." As if to confirm their status as rightful heirs, Crosby, Stills, and Nash were staying at the Dorchester Hotel, where a post–*Hard Day's Night* reception had taken place in the Beatles' honor back in 1964, while the Rolling Stones had loaned the band's managers a city base for the duration of their stay. That night at the Albert Hall, CSN played a version of McCartney's "Blackbird" in front of its author. A bold, confident declaration of intent from musicians whose time had come. In March, their second LP, *Déjà vu*, was released, making number one in America and yielding four hit singles—which included two Nash compositions in the emollient "Teach Your Children" (no. 16) and the ode to domestic bliss "Our House" (no. 30). While the album also featured more abrasive songs like "Almost Cut My Hair" and "Ohio," Nash's contributions arguably reflected his continued commitment to a kind of Beatles-stamped joy. In March, the band also received a Grammy for Best Newcomers, fending off Led Zeppelin in the process. However, tellingly, none of the group attended the award ceremony. Not because they were all together somewhere else, but because they were already falling apart after a working relationship of less than two years.

The early seventies might well have been a post-Beatles world, but it was never empty of the Beatles. Not least because the band had irrevocably changed popular music. Nevertheless, it seemed that America took the band's passing particularly hard. *Abbey Road* was 1970's fourth-best-selling album. It was now, though, less a case of "no direction," more a case of "which direction." A plethora of routes appeared, but no clear signposting. The Beatles had been ever-changing, forward-looking role models, but where to now? Scarred by Altamont, the Rolling Stones entered a period of retreat that would effectively last until the spring of 1971, with the release of *Sticky Fingers*. Pretenders like Crosby, Stills, and Nash would come and go. However, at the very beginning of the decade, they and their music represented one of those paths down which rock headed—one perhaps understandably marked by retreat, retrenchment, and withdrawal. One of 1970's biggest-selling acts was Simon and Garfunkel, whose quasi-hymnal number-one single "Bridge over Troubled Water" captured this sense of comedown, of "weary" lives being lived in a postapocalyptic world in which "Mother Nature was on the run"—as Neil Young concurred in "After the Gold Rush" (1970).

The introspective, solipsistic, and confessional mode of the singer-songwriter enjoyed huge commercial success in the early 1970s. At the same time, in a clearly not unconnected development, some musicians looked to the surety, familiarity, and tradition represented by country music. This continued to be played out in the music of Bob Dylan, the Band, and the Byrds, for example. However, multiplatinum albums like Carole King's *Tapestry* (1971) and James Taylor's *Fire and Rain* (1970) earned the singer-songwriter greater prominence. By turns, nostalgic, wistful, humane, and pseudo-Christian, "the easy-going lull of the songs and Taylor's upright but soothing delivery" meant that what was being heard "wasn't rock 'n' roll, nor was it imbued with even a millisecond of political consciousness" (Browne 23). This was not a path beaten exclusively by American artists, either. Elton John rode into town on the back of this vogue for the singer-songwriter, famously giving some of his earliest American performances at LA's appropriately named Troubadour Club. "My roots are listening to records. All the time," he explained. "I live, eat, sleep, breathe music. Neil Young, the Band, the Springfield, the Dead, the Airplane. *I feel more American than British. Really*" (qtd. in Stanley 290, my emphasis). Elton John's love affair with America, and particularly the mythic west, could be gauged from a cursory scan of the titles of his early '70s albums—*Tumbleweed Connection* (no. 5, 1971), *Madman across the Water* (no. 8, 1971), *Caribou* (no. 1, 1974), and *Rock of the Westies* (no. 1, 1975). Yet this relationship was never skin deep or cynically opportunistic. His lyricist Bernie Taupin was similarly obsessed, and tracks like "Crocodile Rock" (no. 1, 1973) with its references to an idealized American youth neither men obviously lived—all "Chevys," "blue jeans," and "record machines"— merely served to confirm this thorough soaking in Americana. Elton John was more successful in the States in the 1970s than in his native UK. Indeed, in America, the numbers posted were positively Beatles-esque. He has had more than fifty U.S. Top 40 hits; but, between 1970 and 1976, he had six number-one singles, while *Honky Chateau* (1972) started an unbroken run of six number-one LPs. Finding a way to bolt that singer-songwriter tradition to "stadium rock," then, enabled Elton John to become one of the biggest solo rock acts of the seventies.

If the singer-songwriter turn represented one response to American popular music's post-Beatles landscape, perhaps the brush with apocalypse that had coincided with the band's demise prompted some to seek out more s(t)olid ground. Concurrent with those acoustic delicacies, some rock music got even harder and heavier, thanks in no small measure to the drive of British groups like Led Zeppelin, Black Sabbath, and Deep Purple, who led the way for a host of British "stadium rock" acts to clean up in the States through the 1970s. In 1973, Led Zeppelin set a new record ticket gross for a single gig, surpassing the old record established by the Beatles at Shea Stadium; and when the band performed at Knebworth House in rural England in August 1979 it was their first live UK performance in over four years. During this time, Zeppelin had of course extensively toured the States. Though shot through with British-ness, progressive rock also proved very appealing to American fans. In its emphasis on virtuosity and tendency toward pretension, it could be said to have packaged withdrawal in a different form. Solipsism on a grand scale. Yes enjoyed a trio of big-selling albums in the early '70s— *Fragile* (no. 4, 1972), *Close to the Edge* (no. 3, 1972), and *Tales from*

Topographic Oceans (no. 6, 1973)—while Emerson, Lake, and Palmer also placed three LPs in Billboard's Top 10 around the same time—*Tarkus* (1971), *Pictures at an Exhibition* (1971), and *Trilogy* (1972). Jethro Tull's *Thick as a Brick* made number one in 1972. The fact that a band with a flutist as front man could achieve this feat with an album containing just two songs was surely testament to British-made rock's pulling power, both on vinyl and live, during this period. However, perhaps because they managed to combine the best of both worlds, "prog" and "heavy," Pink Floyd's *Dark Side of the Moon* represented the decade's most noteworthy post–Beatles/Invasion American success. Up until the album's release, Floyd had enjoyed solid if unspectacular sales in the States with albums like *Atom Heart Mother* (no. 55, 1970), *Meddle* (no. 70, 1971), and *Obscured by Clouds* (no. 46, 1972). All of these had charted impressively in the UK. *Dark Side of the Moon* reversed this trend, only reaching number two in Britain but making number one in the United States, where a single from it, "Money," even reached the Top 20. *Dark Side of the Moon* was a conceptual feast for your ears, "a treat for your hi-fi." It was also unrelentingly grim, the antithesis of Beatle-stamped joy. But, in the context of the '70s, its "downer vision" resonated with millions of Americans (Stanley 366–67)—"And you run and you run to catch up with the sun that is sinking." It was as zeitgeisty as *Sgt. Pepper* had been just six short years earlier, and it took up a Billboard residency that lasted well into the 1980s and racked up global sales of forty-five million albums in the process. Predictably, its follow-up, the equally "downer" *Wish You Were Here* (1975), also reached number one in the States.

While the continued, often eyebrow-raising, successes of British acts in America suggested that the Invasion was far from over, it sometimes appeared that, through the 1970s, the UK had fallen out of love with the kind of rock music it had played a large part in fashioning. A comparison of the two nations' singles charts in 1973, for example, would seem to indicate that Britain and America were heading down divergent paths. Glam-pop hits dominated the British listings, while Billboard's upper reaches told a very different story—with Stevie Wonder's "Superstition," Marvin Gaye's "Let's Get It On," and a total of seven more soul best sellers, joined by the likes of Grand Funk Railroad's "We're an American Band." Tellingly, Billboard also registered three ex-Beatles at number one in 1973—with Harrison's "Give Me Love,"

Starr's "Photograph," and McCartney's "My Love"—and the Rolling Stones also reached number one with "Angie." None of these made number one in the UK. British fans had apparently moved on, but America—it seemed—was "still pretending the Beatles hadn't split" (Stanley 340). In October, Ringo Starr's solo single "Photograph" had limped into the British Top 10; and, while the album from which it was taken eventually peaked at number two in the States, its UK chart high of number seven perhaps suggested that his star(r) was on the wane. And 1974 further highlighted these contrasting transatlantic fortunes, as Starr's *Goodnight Vienna* reached a respectable number eight in the United States but a very disappointing number thirty in Britain. And things only appeared to get worse for Ringo, at least in his homeland, as the decade progressed. "Snookeroo" had failed to chart in 1975, but it did, however, reach number three on Billboard as the B-side to the "No No Song."

July 29, 1981. Just weeks before my first trip to the States, the "Stars on 45 Medley" had spent a week at the top of the Billboard singles chart. The "Medley" was a Dutch-produced and performed, karaoke-style mash-up of randomly sequenced Beatles' song snippets. In its four minutes, it featured eight Beatles tracks, prefaced somewhat inexplicably by brief snatches of "Venus" and "Sugar Sugar." As if to demonstrate that enduring *American* love affair with the Fab Four, the "Medley" had pointedly *not* made number one in the UK when it was released there a year earlier. Discounting the "Medley," in 1981, there were two British-made American number ones—Sheena Easton's "Morning Train" and John Lennon's "Just Like Starting Over." The latter single had spent a month at the top at the beginning of the year, when it had undoubtedly received a sales boost as a result of Lennon's murder in December 1980. This could of course render any attempt to use 1981 for the purposes of telling the Invasion story rather anomalous. Both countries mourned the Beatle's passing; and, clearly, one way of paying respect was to go out and purchase Lennon product, as both duly did. Yet the measure of the reaction to Lennon's slaying in both countries was telling, too. Americans took it much harder.

Though united in grief, America and Britain still shared no number-one singles in 1981. And with only one LP, Lennon's *Double Fantasy*, in common, the very different looking and sounding singles and albums markets of the two suggested a further hardening of those divergent popular music paths taken since the Beatles' split. In the United States, 1981's best-selling albums included REO Speedwagon's *Hi Infidelity* (fifteen weeks at number one), and a host of other records by adult-oriented rock (AOR) acts like Styx, Pat Benatar, Journey, Australian rockers AC/DC, Foreigner, Stevie Nicks, and Kim Carnes. With the exception of AC/DC, none of these made any impact in the UK at the time. So the gap appeared even wider in '81 than it was in '73. However, the Invasion was still delivering. In addition to Lennon's seven-week run, the Moody Blues' *Long Distance Voyager* and the Stones' *Emotional Rescue* spent a combined total of twelve weeks as America's number-one album. This meant that Brits occupied the top spot for a substantial nineteen of the fifty-two chart weeks. And if America had consistently proved its love for the Beatles throughout the seventies, its admiration for the still-active Rolling Stones was of almost equal strength. During this time, Stones' LPs consistently fared better in the States than in Britain. Between October 1974 and July 1980—with the only exception being *Love You Live*—all four studio albums released placed higher on Billboard, where three made number one. In September 1981, the Rolling Stones opened their latest, lucrative U.S. tour in Philadelphia. In the summer, "Start Me Up" had peaked at number two on Billboard for three weeks. It had just crept inside the UK Top 10.

Four days into my visit, on August 1, 1981, I witnessed the launch of MTV. It would herald the arrival of a second British Invasion of sorts, as a number of UK acts led the way in successfully exploiting the music video platform and consequently would enjoy considerable American success as a result. Bands like Duran Duran, Spandau Ballet, the Human League, and A Flock of Seagulls undoubtedly helped bring the two pop markets a little closer together after more than a decade of musical estrangement. However, in contrast to the first Invasion, their cultural impact was only ever skin deep. Much of the appeal of these bands was rooted in the kind of visual "freshness" that had played some part back in 1964. It was now, though, about the "look" to the exclusion of all else, as the importance of MTV in their success would suggest.

Between 1991 and 1997, SoundScan reported that the Beatles had sold twenty-seven million CDs—a figure no doubt boosted by the *Anthology* project. As Mikal Gilmore notes, in late 1995 "in effect, we got what we were never supposed to get: a Beatles reunion" (Gilmore 34). Five years in the making, *Anthology* comprised a TV documentary, a

three-volume set of double LPs featuring over seven hours of previously unreleased material (studio outtakes, demos, rehearsals, covers, and
live performances), and a book. In November 1995 the documentary
aired on ABC over three nights, granting the Beatles an unprecedent-
ed-for-a-rock-band two hours of prime-time coverage each evening.
The documentary narrated the band's history as collectively authored
biography, chiefly via interviews and archive clips. ABC put its hefty
network muscle behind the broadcasts, billing itself "A-Beatles-C" and
authorizing the use of Beatles' songs to replace the usual opening cred-
its' music on several of that week's sitcoms.

American viewers totaled over fifty million; and these phenomenal
TV ratings were matched by similarly impressive music sales. *Anthology*
sold 450,000 copies in its first day on release. This represented the
highest single-day sales for any LP in U.S. recording history. It was the
first Beatles album to go straight in at number one, selling over 850,000
copies in its first week on release. The double album that comprised the
project's first installment duly topped the Billboard chart and would be
eventually certified eight-times platinum. In all, it would spend twenty-
nine weeks in the Billboard 200. It had stalled at number two in the
UK, perhaps a further indication—if any were required by now—of
that greater American enthusiasm for the Beatles. *Anthology's* U.S.-
generated numbers had played a large part in making 1996 the Beatles'
highest-grossing year to date, earning the band more than $635 million,
selling seven million "new" CDs and a further thirteen million albums
from their back catalog. Of the two "new" songs, "Free as a Bird" and
"Real Love," the former became the Beatles' thirty-fourth single to
make the Billboard Top 10 and also won the Grammy for Best Pop
Performance. As the London-based newspaper the *Observer* reported,
"In 1996 the Beatles have achieved what every group since has failed to
do: become bigger than the Beatles" (qtd. in Gilmore 39). Without the
mutually beneficial, meaningful, and long-standing relationship between the Beatles and America, this would simply not have been possible. For, "in the end, the love you take is equal to the love you make."
And that, of course, is the Invasion story, too.

BIBLIOGRAPHY

Anderson, Terry. "American Popular Music and the War in Vietnam." *Peace and Change* 11 (July 1986): 51–65.

Aquila, Richard. *That Old Time Rock 'n' Roll: A Chronicle of an Era.* Urbana: University of Illinois Press, 2000.

Black, Johnny. "A Tale of Two Cities." In *The Beatles: 10 Years That Shook the World*, edited by Paul Trynka, 22–29. London: Dorling Kindersley, 2004.

Blake, Andrew. "Americanisation and Popular Music in Britain." In *Issues in Americanisation and Culture*, edited by Neil Campbell, Jude Davies, and George McKay, 147–62. Edinburgh: Edinburgh University Press, 2004.

———. *The Land without Music: Music, Culture and Society in Twentieth Century Britain.* Manchester: Manchester University Press, 1997. Although rock music forms a (small) part of Blake's study, he provides an invaluable insight into Britain's relationship with music that allows for a more nuanced appreciation of the Invasion.

Booker, Christopher. *The Neophiliacs: The Revolution in English Life in the Fifties and Sixties.* London: Pimlico, 1992.

Brackett, David. *The Pop, Rock, and Soul Reader.* New York: Oxford University Press, 2005.

Bradley, Dick. *Understanding Rock 'n' Roll: Popular Music in Britain 1955–1964.* Buckingham, UK: Open University Press, 1992.

Breines, Wini, and Alexander Bloom, eds. *Takin' It to the Streets: A Sixties Reader.* New York: Oxford University Press, 2003.

Bromell, Nick. *Tomorrow Never Knows: Rock and Psychedelics in the 1960s.* Chicago: University of Chicago Press, 2000. Effects a winning fusion of the personal and the academic.

Browne, David. *Fire and Rain: The Beatles, Simon and Garfunkel, James Taylor, CSNY, and the Lost Story of 1970.* Cambridge, Mass.: Da Capo, 2011.

Chambers, Iain. *Urban Rhythms: Pop Music and Popular Culture.* London: MacMillan, 1986. Very Brit-centric and focused up to the midsixties. But, like MacDonald, Chambers manages to be both accessible and scholarly at the same time.

Clarke, Donald. *The Rise and Fall of Popular Music.* London: Viking, 1995.

Cohn, Nik. *Awopbopaloobop Alopbambboom: Pop from the Beginning.* London: Minerva, 1969.

Courrier, Kevin. *Artificial Paradise: The Dark Side of the Beatles' Utopian Dream.* Westport, Conn.: Greenwood, 2008.

Darin, Bobby. Interview with *Melody Maker.* April 2, 1960.

Denselow, Robin. *When the Music's Over: The Story of Political Pop.* London: Faber and Faber, 1990.

Dickstein, Morris. *Gates of Eden: American Culture in the Sixties.* Cambridge, Mass.: Harvard University Press, 1997.

Di Martino, Dave. "Hitsville USA." In *Mojo 1000 Days of Beatlemania—The Early Years April 1, 1962 to December 31, 1964,* edited by Chris Hunt, 106–7. London: EMAP Metro, 2003.

Doggett, Peter. *There's a Riot Going On: Revolutionaries, Rock Stars and the Rise and Fall of '60s Counter-Culture.* Edinburgh: Canongate, 2007.

Du Noyer, Paul. "Action!" *Mojo* no. 108, November 2002, 70–82.

Dupin, Christophe. "Free Cinema." Screenonline.org. http://www.screenonline.org.uk/film/id/444789/.

Echols, Alice. *Shaky Ground: The Sixties and Its Aftershocks.* New York: Columbia University Press, 2002.

Egan, Sean, ed. *The Mammoth Book of Bob Dylan.* London: Robinson, 2011.

———. *The Mammoth Book of the Rolling Stones.* London: Robinson, 2013.

Ennis, Philip. *The Seventh Stream: The Emergence of Rock 'n' Roll in American Music.* Hanover, N.H.: University Press of New England, 1992.

Feigal, Bob. "Real Teen Revolt." In *The Faber Book of Pop,* edited by Hanif Kureishi and Jon Savage, 246–48. London: Faber and Faber, 1995.

Frame, Pete. *The Restless Generation: How Rock Music Changed the Face of 1950s Britain.* London: Rogan House, 2007. This memoir supplies a palpable sense of context to help explain why rock 'n' roll hit British youth so hard.

Fricke, David. "Best in Show." In *Mojo 1000 Days of Beatlemania—The Early Years April 1, 1962 to December 31, 1964,* edited by Chris Hunt, 88–89. London: EMAP Metro, 2003.

Gillett, Charlie. *The Sound of the City: The Rise of Rock and Roll.* Rev. ed. London: Souvenir, 1983.

Gilmore, Mikal. "Beatles Then, Beatles Now." In *Night Beat: A Shadow History of Rock & Roll,* 23–42. London: Picador, 1998.

Gitlin, Todd. *The Sixties: Years of Hope, Days of Rage.* Rev. ed. New York: Bantam, 1993.

Gould, Jonathan. *Can't Buy Me Love: The Beatles, Britain and America.* New York: Piatkus, 2007. A forensic labor of love and, consequently, a rich source of information for the Invasion scholar.

Green, Jonathon. *All Dressed Up: The Sixties and the Counterculture.* London: Pimlico, 1999.

Groom, Bob. "Whose 'Rock Island Line'? Originality in the Composition of Blues and British Skiffle." In *Cross the Water Blues: African American Music in Europe,* edited by Neil Wynn, 167–81. Jackson: University of Mississippi Press, 2007.

A Hard Day's Night. Dir. Richard Lester. 1964. DVD, 2 Disc Collector's Edition. Miramax.

Harris, John. "It's All Too Much." *Mojo* no. 224, July 2012, 63–66.

Heylin, Clinton. *The Act You've Known for All These Years.* Edinburgh: Canongate, 2007.

Hicks, Michael. *Sixties Rock: Garage, Psychedelic, and Other Satisfactions.* Urbana: University of Illinois Press, 1999.

Hoggart, Richard. *The Uses of Literacy.* London: Penguin, 1957.

How the Brits Rocked America: Go West. Dir. Ben Whalley. January 27, 2012. BBC4. Made-for-TV doc featuring some great footage and some illuminating talking heads.

Inglis, Ian. "The Beatles Are Coming: Conjecture and Conviction in the Myth of Kennedy, America and the Beatles." *Popular Music and Society* 24, no. 2 (2000): 93–108.

———. "Synergies and Reciprocities: The Dynamics of Musical and Professional Interaction between the Beatles and Bob Dylan." *Popular Music and Society* 20, no. 4 (1996): 53–79.

Kelly, Michael Bryan. *The Beatle Myth: The British Invasion of American Popular Music, 1956–1969.* Jefferson, N.C.: McFarland, 1991. Beatle-centric, as its title suggests. Gets the periodization right, but otherwise rather impressionistic.

Kynaston, David. *Family Britain 1951–57.* London: Bloomsbury, 2009.

Larkin, Philip. *All What Jazz: A Record Diary 1961–68.* London: Faber and Faber, 1970.

Lee, Martin A., and Bruce Shlain. *Acid Dreams: The Complete Social History of LSD, the CIA, the Sixties and Beyond.* London: Pan, 2001.

Leigh, Spencer. "You've Really Got a Hold on Me." *Record Collector* no. 411, February 2013, 72–79.

Lennon, John. Interview with *Melody Maker*. February 9, 1963.

———. Interview with *Melody Maker*. August 3, 1963.

Levy, Shawn. *Ready, Steady, Go! Swinging London and the Invention of Cool.* London: Fourth Estate, 2002.

Light, Alan. "Some Wild Thing." *Mojo* no. 234, May 2013, 53–54.

Loog Oldham, Andrew. *Stoned.* London: Secker & Warburg, 2000.

Lynskey, Dorian. *33 Revolutions per Minute: A History of Protest Songs.* London: Faber and Faber, 2012.

MacDonald, Ian. *Revolution in the Head: The Beatles' Records and the Sixties.* London: Pimlico, 1995. Quite simply, the best book ever written on the Beatles. A blow-by-blow account of the music as it emerged, which is never dry, showy, or daunting for the reader. The introductory essay is equally impressive—to paraphrase Aaron Copland, if you want to know about the Beatles in the '60s, you should read this.

Maconie. Stuart. *The People's Songs: The Story of Modern Britain in 50 Records.* London: Ebury, 2013.

Marcus, Greil. *Like a Rolling Stone: Bob Dylan at the Crossroads.* London: Faber and Faber, 2006.

Marwick, Arthur. *The Sixties: Cultural Revolution in Britain, France, Italy and the United States, c.1958–c.1974.* Oxford: Oxford University Press, 1998.

Melly, George. *Revolt into Style: The Pop Arts in Britain.* London: Penguin, 1972.

Miles, Barry. *The British Invasion: The Music, the Times, the Era.* New York: Sterling, 2002. Breezy and richly, unapologetically subjective—but at least Miles, Zelig-like, was "there." Doesn't look at the music's transformative impact on America, though.

———. *London Calling: A Countercultural History of London since 1945.* London: Atlantic, 2011.

Millard, Andre. *Beatlemania: Technology, Business and Teen Culture in Cold War America.* Baltimore, Md.: Johns Hopkins University Press, 2012. Achieves what it sets out to do. But of course this means that, by its own admission, it steers clear of the music.

Miller, James. *Almost Grown: The Rise of Rock.* London: William Heinemann, 1999.

Morrison, Richard. *Times*, June 2, 2003, 3.

Napier-Bell, Simon. "The First Teenage Dream." *Observer*, May 23, 2004. http://observer.guardian.co.uk/print/0,,4926750-111639,00.html.

Oakley, Ronald. J. *God's Country: America in the Fifties.* New York: Dembner, 1990.

Odell, Michael. "Cliff Richard." *Q Magazine—1958–2008: 50 Years of Great British Music.* 2008, 35–37.

Oliver, Paul. *Black Music in Britain: Essays in Afro-Asian Contribution to Popular Music.* Milton Keynes, UK: Open University Press, 1990.

"101 Greatest Beatles Songs." *Mojo* no. 152, July 2006.

Ono, Yoko. Interview with *Mojo* no. 178, September 2008, 83.

Osgerby, Bill. "'Well, It's Saturday Night an' I Just Got Paid': Youth, Consumerism and Hegemony in Post-War Britain." *Contemporary Record* 6, no. 2 (1992): 287–305.

Palmer, Tony. *All You Need Is Love: The Story of Popular Music.* London: Futura, 1977.

Pells, Richard. *Not Like Us: How Europeans Have Loved, Hated, and Transformed American Culture since World War II.* New York: Basic Books, 1997.

Perrone, Pierre. "The First Woodstock." *Independent*, August 31, 2013, 16.

Pichaske, David. *A Generation in Motion: Popular Music and Culture in the Sixties.* New York: Schirmer, 1979. As kinetic as its topic.

Plant, Robert. "Robert Plant Interview: 'Everyone Feels the Blues from Time to Time.'" By Neil McCormick. *Daily Telegraph*, October 24, 2013, 34.

Riley, Tim. *Tell Me Why: A Beatles Commentary.* Rev. ed. Cambridge, Mass.: Da Capo, 2002.

Rogan, Johnny. *Byrds: Requiem for the Timeless, Volume 1.* Ipswich, UK: Rogan House, 2012.

Sandbrook, Dominic. *Never Had It So Good: A History of Britain from Suez to the Beatles.* London: Abacus, 2005. Sandbrook is a young historian who has managed to carve out a TV career in a relatively short time. Some "real" historians have been a bit sniffy about what they regard as his brazen populism. But Sandbrook tells his stories—on-screen and in print—with persuasive clarity and élan. Invaluable and accessible.

———. *White Heat: A History of Britain in the Swinging Sixties.* London: Little, Brown, 2006.

Sarris, Andrew. "Bravo Beatles!" In *The Pop, Rock, and Soul Reader*, edited by David Bracket, 174–76. New York: Oxford University Press, 2005.

Shuker, Roy. *Key Concepts in Popular Music.* London: Routledge, 1998.

Simmons, Michael. "Hell Hound on My Trail." *Mojo* no. 234, May 2013, 70.

Stanley, Bob. *Yeah Yeah Yeah: The Story of Modern Pop.* London: Faber and Faber, 2013.

Stax, Mike. "Optical Sound: The Technicolor Tales behind the Numerous Nuggets." Liner notes. *Nuggets: Original Artyfacts from the First Psychedelic Era, 1965–1968.* Rhino Records, 1998: 30–90.

Storey, John. "Rockin' Hegemony: West Coast Rock and Amerika's War in Vietnam. In *Tell Me Lies about Vietnam*, edited by Alf Louvre and Jeffrey Walsh, 181–98. Milton Keynes, UK: Open University Press, 1988.

Strong, M. C. *The Wee Rock Discography.* Edinburgh: Canongate, 1996.

Szatmary, David. *Rockin' in Time: A Social History of Rock-and-Roll.* 4th ed. Upper Saddle River, N.J.: Prentice Hall, 2000.

Tacchi, Jo Ann. "Radio Sound as Material Culture in the Home." PhD thesis, University College London, 1997.

Thompson, Gordon. *Please Please Me: Sixties British Pop, Inside Out.* New York: Oxford University Press, 2008.

Thompson, Hunter S. "The 'Hashbury' Is the Capital of the Hippies." In *The Faber Book of Pop*, edited by Hanif Kureishi and Jon Savage, 290–302. London: Faber and Faber, 1995.

Warwick, Neil, Jon Kutner, and Tony Brown, eds. *The Complete Book of the British Charts: Singles and Albums.* London: Omnibus, 2004.

Whitcomb, Ian. "Chas McDevitt and the Skiffle Craze." Picklehead.com, March 1998. http://www.picklehead.com/ian/ian_oldie.html.

Whiteley, Sheila. *The Space between the Notes: Rock and the Counter-Culture.* London: Routledge, 1992.

Wicke, Peter. *Rock Music: Culture, Aesthetics and Sociology.* Cambridge, UK: Cambridge University Press, 1983.

Wiener, Jon. "First Steps toward Radical Politics: The 1966 Tour." In *The Faber Book of Pop*, edited by Hanif Kureishi and Jon Savage, 278–84. London: Faber and Faber, 1995.

Williams, Richard. "1965: Annus Mirabilis." In *Long Distance Call: Writings on Music*, 79–90. London: Aurum, 2000.

Wynn, Neil. "'Why I Sing the Blues': African American Culture in the Transatlantic World." In *Cross the Water Blues: African American Music in Europe*, edited by Neil Wynn, 3–22. Jackson: University of Mississippi Press, 2007.

FOR FURTHER LISTENING

Arranged chronologically for the years of the British Invasion.

"Rock Island Line," Lonnie Donegan (1955), Single, Decca. Donegan's ham-fisted but visceral reworking of this American folk tale kick-started the skiffle craze, and in so doing served as the foundation stone for the Invasion.

"Move It," Cliff Richard (1958), Single, Columbia. This was the earliest example of credible *British-made* rock 'n' roll. For added authenticity, allegedly written on a London double-decker bus.

"Shakin' All Over," Johnny Kidd and the Pirates (1960), Single, HMV. In a British pop landscape then dominated by manufactured teen-idol nonsense, this genuinely exciting track stood out, unselfconsciously loud and proud.

Please Please Me, the Beatles (March 1963), Album, EMI. The Beatles' first album took no more than a day to record but spent thirty weeks at number one in the UK. Featuring the singles "Love Me Do" and the title track, plus a mix of covers and originals like "I Saw Her Standing There," this was ur-beat product, united in its communication of sheer, unbridled joy. Never more evident than on album closer "Twist and Shout."

With the Beatles, the Beatles (November 1963), Album, EMI. Second UK Beatles' LP, released on the day JFK was assassinated. While, in many respects, here was *Please Please Me* part 2, its moody, monochrome band-photo-as-cover was perhaps a clue as to the artistic developments and creative growth already to be found within.

Meet the Beatles, the Beatles (January 1964), Album, Capitol. Number-one U.S. album, packaged tracks from earlier British releases and included the American breakthrough single "I Want to Hold Your Hand."

A Hard Day's Night, the Beatles (July 1964), Album, Capitol. The Beatles' first fully self-authored album included the number-one singles "Can't Buy Me Love" and the title track.

Another Side of Bob Dylan, Bob Dylan (August 1964), Album, Columbia. Still acoustic, but Dylan was signposting his move away from the straitjacket of folk music toward his own version of rock 'n' roll. Loose and humorous, simultaneously progressive and willfully regressive—"so much younger now than [he] was then."

"House of the Rising Sun," the Animals (August 1964), Single, MGM. Raw cover inspired by a Dylan version. A Billboard number one.

"You Really Got Me," the Kinks (September 1964), Single, Reprise. The Kinks' first American hit. Primal beat fare, all power chords and fuzz. Highly influential as a template for heavy rock, and much copied by garage bands (and by the Kinks themselves on their next single, "All Day and All Night").

Beatles '65, the Beatles (January 1965), Album, Capitol. It contained eight tracks from the UK album *Beatles for Sale*, including the Billboard number one "Eight Days a Week." It also featured the late '64 number-one single "I Feel Fine." Lennon-authored tracks like "I'm a Loser" and "No Reply" betrayed the influence of Bob Dylan, and gave further indication that the band's creative evolution was picking up pace with every release.

Bringing It All Back Home, Bob Dylan (March 1965), Album, Columbia. Dylan's ramshackle semi-electric album featured the hit single "Subterranean Homesick Blues."

"Mr. Tambourine Man," the Byrds (May 1965), Single, Columbia. And lo, folk rock was born! A U.S. number one in the summer of '65.

Highway 61 Revisited, Bob Dylan (August 1965), Album, Columbia. The epic "Desolation Row" came in at a genre-busting eleven minutes plus. But it was the comparatively brief at a mere six minutes long "Like a Rolling Stone"— released in all its unedited glory as a single— that effectively bottled all that Dylan "meant" in '65.

Out of Our Heads, the Rolling Stones (August 1965), Album, London. U.S. version featured the snotty, fuzz-fest number-one single "Satisfaction."

Help!, the Beatles (September 1965), Album, Capitol. Rather compromised American iteration still included the avant-garde-masquerading-as-pop single "A Ticket to Ride" and the upbeat suicide note title track. It also featured the folky "You've Got to Hide Your Love Away."

Rubber Soul, the Beatles (December 1965), Album, Capitol. U.S. version included the genre-stretching triad "Norwegian Wood," "I'm Looking Through You," and "In My Life."

December's Children (and Everybody's), the Rolling Stones (December 1965), Album, London. A U.S.-only release that included the fall number-one single and "Satisfaction" companion piece "Get Off My Cloud."

"Eight Miles High," the Byrds (April 1966), Single, Capitol. Given just how edgy and experimental this record is, it is perhaps surprising that it still made the U.S. Top 20. An angular travelogue, documenting the Byrds' first trip to the UK, it was in fact the controversy it generated over its supposed celebration of drug usage that finally stopped it in its tracks.

"Dedicated Follower of Fashion," the Kinks (May 1966), Single, Reprise. On which Ray Davies skewers the empty pretensions of "Swinging London."

"Paperback Writer b/w Rain" (May 1966), Single, Capitol. The A-side offered the Beatles' take on "Swinging London," while the B-side, all tape loops and druggy vibes, served notice of the direction in which the band was now headed.

Pet Sounds, the Beach Boys (May 1966), Album, Capitol. Brian Wilson's ambitious pop symphonic song cycle was particularly well received by critics, musician peers, and fans alike in the UK, where it sold well enough to reach number two on the British album chart. The album met with a much cooler reception in the States, where it just managed to make the Top 10.

Aftermath, the Rolling Stones (July 1966), Album, London. U.S. version—which peaked at number two—featured the nihilistic number one "Paint It Black" and the hypocrisy-busting "Mother's Little Helper," plus nasty, misogynistic tracks like "Under My Thumb" and "Stupid Girl."

Revolver, the Beatles (August 1966), Album, Capitol. Audibly drug influenced and featuring the most experimental, nonpop track the Beatles would ever record—"Tomorrow Never Knows."

"Good Vibrations," the Beach Boys (October 1966), Single, Capitol. Vindication at last, it would seem, for Wilson, as this epic (and very expensive) single made number one in December '66.

"Strawberry Fields Forever b/w Penny Lane," the Beatles (February 1967), Single, Capitol. The first two tracks to emerge from the *Sgt. Pepper* sessions were released as a double A-side single. While the ostensibly more experimental "Strawberry Fields" peaked at number eight, the apparently more conventional "Penny Lane" made number one.

Sgt. Pepper's Lonely Hearts Club Band, the Beatles (June 1967), Album, Capitol. Zeitgeisty stuff. Fifteen weeks at number one in the States.

"All You Need Is Love," the Beatles (August 1967), Single, Capitol. It capped the *Pepper* project and became the definitive statement on the summer of love. "All" was not what it seemed, however.

Are You Experienced?, the Jimi Hendrix Experience (August 1967), Album, Reprise. The American version, released in the wake of Hendrix's memorable Monterey performance, included the singles "Hey Joe," "Wind Cries Mary," and "Purple Haze."

Piper at the Gates of Dawn, Pink Floyd (August 1967), Album, Tower. The first Floyd album did not chart in America, but with tracks like the ten-minute acid wig-out "Interstellar Overdrive" and the quirky antipop of "Bike," it pointed to a progressive future.

"We Love You b/w Dandelion," the Rolling Stones (August 1967), Single, London. The typically sardonic A-side told the story of the Jagger and Richards drug bust that initially saw both men jailed. This subject matter clearly proved too rich for American radio palettes, and the B-side was duly preferred and consequently outperformed "We Love You" on Billboard.

Disraeli Gears, Cream (November 1967), Album, Atco/Atlantic. The power trio recorded this album in New York in the spring. Included "Strange Brew," the Billboard Top 10 hit "Sunshine of Your Love," and the antidraft track "Take It Back."

John Wesley Harding, Bob Dylan (December 1967), Album, Columbia. Dylan's lo-fi, against-the-grain "comeback" still reached number two in early '68.

Their Satanic Majesties Request, the Rolling Stones (December 1967), Album, London. Delayed by the drug bust noted above, the Stones' "psychedelic" LP appeared to be ill starred and ill conceived. Tellingly, "She's a Rainbow" was a minor U.S. hit.

"Jumping Jack Flash," the Rolling Stones (May 1968), Single, London. The Stones' flirtation with psychedelia was now officially over.

"Hey Jude b/w Revolution," the Beatles (August 1968), Single, Apple. The communal, soulful, and redemptive A-side was backed by Lennon's unfashionably apolitical *cri de paix*.

"Street Fighting Man," the Rolling Stones (August 1968), Single, London. Altogether more palatable to the Left than "Revolution," Jagger's combative "Street Fighting Man" was in fact a much more evasive and ultimately much less honest act of intervention than Lennon's widely reviled effort.

The Beatles, the Beatles (November 1968), Album, Apple. This ninety-minute-plus double LP was rarely, if ever, the product of a band working as one—and it showed.

Beggar's Banquet, the Rolling Stones (December 1968), Album, London. "Sympathy for the Devil" kicked off an album that seemed to effectively document the "bad moon rising" in the long winter of '68.

Led Zeppelin, Led Zeppelin (February 1969), Album, Atlantic. Opening salvo from a British band, which would go on to dominate the American rock scene right through the next decade. Reached the Top 10.

Crosby, Stills & Nash, CSN (June 1969), Album, Atlantic. The transatlantic supergroup's first album featured Graham Nash's "Marrakesh Express."

Abbey Road, the Beatles (September 1969), Album, Apple. The sound of a band desperately trying to "Come Together" and stay together. Side two's masterful medley turned song fragments into one last statement of Beatle joy.

Let It Bleed, the Rolling Stones (December 1969), Album, London. "Gimme Shelter" and "Midnight Rambler" communicated a sense of all-encompassing violence that the Stones seemed inclined to revel in rather than look to avoid, let alone counter with anything constructive.

Déjà vu, Crosby, Stills, Nash, and Young (March 1970), Album, Atlantic. Multiplatinum second album, featuring Nash's emollient "Teach Your Children" and his ode to domestic bliss, "Our House."

John Lennon / Plastic Ono Band, John Lennon & Plastic Ono Band (December 1970), Album, Apple. The sound of Lennon purging himself of the sixties— heard specifically on tracks like "God" and the raw exposure of "Mother."

Tumbleweed Connection, Elton John (January 1971), Album, Uni. A "love letter" to America(na). "Burn Down the Mission," two songs about guns, and one called "Country Comfort"!

Dark Side of the Moon, Pink Floyd (March 1973), Album, Capitol. A doomy, downer, stoner, "proggy" behemoth for dark times. As zeitgeisty as *Sgt. Pepper*, it took up residency on Billboard for over ten years.

Band on the Run, Paul McCartney & Wings (November 1973), Album. Apple. One of the biggest-selling records from one of the decade's biggest-selling acts. Bombastic Bond theme "Live and Let Die" made number two in the summer of '73, while the title track was a Billboard number one in the spring of '74.

It's Only Rock 'n' Roll, the Rolling Stones (October 1974), Album, Rolling Stones. An unironic commitment to the only cause that now mattered.

Double Fantasy, John Lennon (November 1980), Album, Geffen. A disappointing comeback LP. Understandably, cool appreciation of it got rather lost in the wake of Lennon's murder in December 1980. A transatlantic number one, though.

"Stars on 45 Medley," Stars on 45 (June 1981), Single, CBS. A Dutch-made, karaoke-style medley featuring eight Beatles' song snippets. A global phenomenon, it made number one in America in the summer of 1981 and number two in the UK a year earlier.

"Start Me Up," the Rolling Stones (August 1981), Single, Rolling Stones. This last great Stones' single—with a riff to rival "Satisfaction"— featured on the Billboard-topping album *Tattoo You*.

Anthology, the Beatles (1995–1996), Album(s), Apple. A career-spanning three-album retrospective of versions, outtakes, live recordings, and two "new" Jeff Lynne–produced songs, "Free as a Bird" and "Real Love." Phenomenal sales and massive media interest, particularly in the States, suggested it was what the world was waiting for.

INDEX

ABOUT THE AUTHOR

Simon Philo is head of American Studies at the University of Derby. He has published extensively on transatlantic popular culture. In over twenty years at Derby, he has been instrumental in working popular music studies into the heart of the curriculum. In addition to teaching the intermediate class American Popular Music, he delivers sessions on music and protest, soul and civil rights, the British Invasion, punk, and Brit-pop. He drums poorly and plays the guitar with even greater incompetence. He lives in the Peak District with his wife, his daughter, two guinea pigs, and a growing collection of '60s box sets that are key to his academic research.